Critical Criminological Perspectives

Series Editors
Reece Walters
Faculty of Law
Deakin University
Burwood, VIC, Australia

Deborah H. Drake
Department of Social Policy & Criminology
The Open University
Milton Keynes, UK

The Palgrave Critical Criminological Perspectives book series aims to showcase the importance of critical criminological thinking when examining problems of crime, social harm and criminal and social justice. Critical perspectives have been instrumental in creating new research agendas and areas of criminological interest. By challenging state defined concepts of crime and rejecting positive analyses of criminality, critical criminological approaches continually push the boundaries and scope of criminology, creating new areas of focus and developing new ways of thinking about, and responding to, issues of social concern at local, national and global levels. Recent years have witnessed a flourishing of critical criminological narratives and this series seeks to capture the original and innovative ways that these discourses are engaging with contemporary issues of crime and justice. For further information on the series and to submit a proposal for consideration, please get in touch with the Editor: Josephine Taylor, Josephine.Taylor@palgrave.com.

More information about this series at
http://www.palgrave.com/gp/series/14932

David Polizzi

Toward a Phenomenology of Terrorism

Beyond Who is Killing Whom

David Polizzi
School of Criminology & Security Studies
Indiana State University
Terre Haute, IN, USA

ISSN 2731-0604 ISSN 2731-0612 (electronic)
Critical Criminological Perspectives
ISBN 978-3-030-76404-3 ISBN 978-3-030-76405-0 (eBook)
https://doi.org/10.1007/978-3-030-76405-0

© The Editor(s) (if applicable) and The Author(s), under exclusive licence to Springer Nature Switzerland AG 2021

This work is subject to copyright. All rights are solely and exclusively licensed by the Publisher, whether the whole or part of the material is concerned, specifically the rights of translation, reprinting, reuse of illustrations, recitation, broadcasting, reproduction on microfilms or in any other physical way, and transmission or information storage and retrieval, electronic adaptation, computer software, or by similar or dissimilar methodology now known or hereafter developed.

The use of general descriptive names, registered names, trademarks, service marks, etc. in this publication does not imply, even in the absence of a specific statement, that such names are exempt from the relevant protective laws and regulations and therefore free for general use.

The publisher, the authors and the editors are safe to assume that the advice and information in this book are believed to be true and accurate at the date of publication. Neither the publisher nor the authors or the editors give a warranty, expressed or implied, with respect to the material contained herein or for any errors or omissions that may have been made. The publisher remains neutral with regard to jurisdictional claims in published maps and institutional affiliations.

This Palgrave Macmillan imprint is published by the registered company Springer Nature Switzerland AG.
The registered company address is: Gewerbestrasse 11, 6330 Cham, Switzerland

Contents

1	What Comes Before	1
2	What's in a Name: Constructing Terrorism	25
3	The Phenomenology of the Nomos	55
4	Toward a Phenomenology of Jihad: Salifist Jihadi Perspectives	83
5	Al-Qaeda and the Rise of Global Jihad	121
6	The Islamic State and the Return of the Caliphate	145
7	The Taliban and Hezbollah: Political Parties or Terror Organizations	173
8	White Supremacy and the Digital World: The Social Construction of White Identity	193

| 9 | The Reemergence of the Far-Right | 223 |
| 10 | Beyond Who Is Killing Whom | 245 |

| Index | | 257 |

1

What Comes Before

The Nomos, the Who, and the Whom

As the title suggests, any attempt to configure a phenomenology of terrorism, must go beyond simply an identification of who is killing whom. Such a "score keeping" approach to a topic as complex as terrorism is not very helpful and provides little understanding concerning the phenomenology of this process. If as Roger Griffin (2012) contends, the phenomenon of terrorism is really an attempt to embrace the human search for meaning, then it becomes incumbent upon us to focus more upon the meaning of terrorism, rather than the acts of the same. This observation is not to imply that the consequences of terrorism are not significant or the loss of life unimportant; rather, it simply alerts us to the fact that the phenomenology of terrorism is never simply configured by the actions taken in its name. As Richard Quinney (2000) has observed concerning the study of crime:

> What is important in the study of crime is everything that happens before crime occurs. The question of what precedes crime is far more significant to our understanding of the act of crime itself. Crime is the reflection of something larger and deeper. (p. 21)

The phenomenology of terrorism is no different.

In her text, *Regarding the Pain of Others*, Sontag (2004) employs the phrase "who is killing whom," to configure the way in which photographs of political violence are constructed by the viewer. She argues that "To those who are sure that right is on one side, oppression and injustice on the other, and that the fighting must go on, what matters is precisely who is killed by whom" (Sontag, 2004, p. 10). From this perspective, a specific relationality emerges between viewer and depicted content, which allows for the possibility of self-recognition to occur. Using the examples offered by Sontag (2004), if the image is of a Palestinian child killed in Gaza by an Israeli tank round or a Jewish child killed in a Jerusalem pizzeria by a Palestinian suicide-bomber, how one configures moral certainty and oppressive injustice will in turn construct the meaning of those images from that point of view (p. 10). As Sontag (2004) observes, "To the militant, identity is everything" (p. 10).

Identity may indeed be everything, but it cannot be "anything" without a clear understanding of the phenomenology of social experience that makes this recognition possible. Taken from this perspective, identity formation emerges as an artifact of social experience that both constructs individual identity and provides it with its specific individual and social meanings. The very ability to identify a victim as Palestinian or Jewish immediately evokes this social relationality between individual perspective and the specific meanings this social context evokes. As a result of this phenomenological process, the ability to recognize victimization often becomes predicated upon the degree to which the viewer can recognize his or her own vulnerability in these violent acts.

The images of these murdered children take on a much different significance if they were not situated within the context of the Israeli/Palestinian struggle. In fact, the very meaning of these images becomes both proof of this unrelenting tragic conflict, as well as supportive evidence for its continuation and validation (Moghaddam, 2018). If the point of view of the spectator is focused on the ongoing oppression of Palestinians in Israel, then the death of this Palestinian child simply reflects the reality of that oppression; if on the other hand, the spectator is focused on the right of Israel to exist, then, the murdered Jewish child becomes proof of the continued desire to kill Jews.[1] What is strikingly absent from either of these perspectives is the possibility of an "anonymous" death.

The possibility of an anonymous death, a death whose social meaning is not contingent upon the specific ethnicity of the identified victim, requires a perspective from the viewer that is not itself already constructed from a specific point of view. Such an identity would have very limited utility for the militant. Identity becomes "everything" when it can be totalized from a very specific point of view and manipulated by the same. As Heidegger (2012) observes in his construct of the they-self, it is the they which determines what will be validated and what will not and it is through this process of validation that self-recognition becomes possible.

If terrorism or fanatical violence, as Griffin (2012) observes, is fundamentally related to this desperate search for human meaning, then the construct of one's social identity, be that political, religious, or some configuration of the two, becomes an essential component of this phenomenological process. Taken from this perspective, it is important to recognize that these various examples of political or religious violence are often perpetrated by individuals or groups, who rationalize these attacks as a type of self-defensive action.

It will be recalled that the Society of Muslim Brothers was founded by Hasan al-Banna in Egypt in 1929 in response to the perceived existential threat posed by the increasing presence of Western interests in that country, which were believed to greatly threaten the Islamic identity of that culture (Gerges, 2018; Kepel, 1993, 2005, 2008; Khatab, 2006; Mitchell, 1993).[2] More recently, Dylann Roof, on June 17 2015, murdered nine African-American parishioners at the historic Emanuel African Methodist

---

[1] This observation is not to argue that only two possible positions can exist within this context; in fact, a variety of positions exist on both sides of this debate that certainly differ from these more extreme points of view. However, it is equally true that images such as the ones described by Sontag can be employed to further the divide between these groups and make it much more difficult to arrive at a peaceful solution. Authentic change is likely only possible, when alternative meanings of these images are capable of breaking the hold of this oppressive phenomenology.

[2] The inclusion of the Society of Muslim Brothers is intended here as an example of various iterations of the Salifist Jihadi perspective that this society later influenced and who will be discussed later in this text. Though Mawlana Sayyid Abu-A'la Mawdudi's Jama'at-i Islami party has also had an influencing role in contemporary Salifist Jihadi thought, its role has been arguably less significant (Nasr, 1996). Both of these groups will be discussed in this text.

Episcopal Church located in Charleston, SC, in the hope that his actions would be the catalyst for a "race war" in the U.S. (Morris, 2017; Simi et al., 2017). Robert Bowers on October 27, 2018 entered The Tree of Life Synagogue in Pittsburgh, PA, killed eleven worshipers, and wounded six others. Bowers claimed that his act was in response to the perceived actions of the Hebrew Immigrant Aid Society (HIAS), who Bowers believed was helping Central American immigrants come to America to kill white people (Katz, 2018).

For each of the examples briefly mentioned above, a specific existential threat was perceived, and a line of defense constructed by which to address the "immediate" danger. For the Society of Muslim Brothers, the expanding influence of British interests in Egypt represented such a threat to their understanding of the construction of the Islamic identity of Egypt that the failure to act immediately to confront this incursion would mean the cultural death of that country (Gerges, 2018; Kepel, 1993; Mitchell, 1993).[3] Though other groups seeking to create an independent Egypt viewed this threat differently, the Brotherhood believed that action was necessary before the Islamic character of Egypt was lost. For Roof and Bowers, the perceived threats they sought to confront were those "inflicted" by the reality of the expanding diversity of American society and the implications this had for "White America." Roof "defended" his acts of violence as his attempt to avenge what he believed to be the daily murders of white folk by black perpetrators. Bowers argued similarly that his actions were based on his need to kill Jews, who were encouraging Mexican and Central Americans to immigrate to the U.S. to kill Americans.

What each of these examples reveals is the way in which personal identity is configured by a specific structure of social meaning that not only provides individual experience with its grounding in social reality, but also provides direction concerning how this social world will be defined.

---

[3] The increasing influence of European interests in Egypt spans over five decades. By the 1920s that threat become more pronounced. However, as this influence grow, so too did the push for Egyptian independence, which in turn saw the creation of religious and secular groups seeking to end what was viewed as the colonialization of Egypt (Gerges, 2018; Mitchell, 1993). This process of competing political and religious groups within Egypt culminated with the Free Officers revolution which occurred in 1952. It is also important to note that the foundations of the contemporary Salifist Jihadi movement have its beginnings in the history of the Society of Muslim Brothers in Egypt (Mitchell, 1993).

Once established, the social world only becomes recognizable through the lens this structure provides to individual lived-experience. If the foundations of this structure remain intact, personal identity retains its social moorings and one's place in the world remains familiar and secure. However, if unaccepted change in society moves in directions where individual or group identity is called into question or if these former taken for granted meanings are in some way perceived to be in danger, violence becomes possible.

To situate the context of the phenomenology of terrorism, we will begin with the construct of the nomos offered by Peter Berger in his text *The Sacred Canopy: Elements of a Sociological Theory of Religion*. For Berger, Nomic ordering becomes essential to the process of identity development within a given social structure. We will, then, briefly explore the influencing aspects of this Nomic ordering as it relates to the phenomenology of fanatical violence discussed by Roger Griffin (2012) in his important text, *Terrorist's Creed: Fanatical Violence and the Human need for Meaning*. We will conclude this introductory description by situating the constructs of the nomos within the Heideggerian context of being-in-the-world and the they-self.

The Phenomenology of the Nomos and Personal Identity

Berger defines the concept of the nomos as a structure of social meaning that is "imposed upon the discrete experiences and meanings of individuals in a given society. To say that society is a world-building enterprise is to say that it is ordering or nomizing activity" (Berger, 1967, p. 19). However, Berger (1967) also warns that it would be incorrect to conclude that this process of nomic ordering is inclusive to all aspects of human experience and its individual meaning. As a result, certain examples of discrete experience will not be located under this common nomic structure. Given this likelihood, there is no guarantee that this nomizing process will allow for "wider areas of meaning" to be incorporated into the existing nomic structure; rather, the response to this attempted expansion of social meaning may simply be rejected, resulting in the continuing exclusion of those examples of subjective experience, which are not consistent with this meaning-generating process (Berger, 1967).

The distinction, which Berger makes concerning the common nomos and those social meanings that are marginalized by it, provides an important insight into how this social relationality is lived. Of particular importance to this discussion is the way in which one's relationship to this common nomos is transformed during moments of social change. As the existing nomic structure expands to accommodate those formally marginalized examples of social experience, not all will likely be accepting of such changes. For some, this expansion of social validation may reflect a necessary and long sought desire for cultural change, while for others, it will likely be experienced as a direct threat, calling into question the very foundations of their own sense of identity and connection to this changing social world.

As various degrees of change enter and transform the existing nomic structure, personal identity must be able to tolerate the implications of this transformative process, if it is going to be able to find comfort and safety under this new canopy of meaning. In the U.S., direct threats to the existing "American" nomos, which gives their identity its core meaning and value, have been perceived by such examples as same-sex marriage, the election of the first African-American president, or the legal rights of individuals attempting to enter the U.S.[4] As these formally marginalized identities are recognized and validated by this expanding nomic ordering, others may perceive this process as an anomic disruption that must be confronted.

What seems to be most central to the relationship between an expanding nomic structure and the continued integrity of personal identity is the degree to which one's sense of self remains recognizable within this

---

[4] This observation is not intended to serve as an apologist for those attitudes and beliefs that have been responsible for the denial of civil rights to any number of marginalized groups within American culture; rather, its simple intent is to recognize that as these changes occurred, these nomic meanings did not magically disappear. It is also important to recognize that as this nomic structure slowly expanded, it triggered a type of "nomic splintering," which continues to give life to many of the beliefs that we thought had been relegated to the dustbin of our social history. What the "age of Trump" clearly reveals is how these formally marginalized and outdated understandings of social existence that reappeared with a ferocity that is both disturbing and unexpected.

new context of social meaning. Once the existing nomic structure has been internalized by the individual, it becomes the "psychological mechanism" by which the meaning of subjective experience is structured (Berger, 1967). As such, individual identity is now capable of recognizing and making sense of its own experience (Berger, 1967). However, it is during these moments of nomic expansion that the recognition of one's biography may no longer resonate within this new context of social meaning.

As the expanding nomos moves farther and farther away from familiar manifestations of normative certainty, the individual must reevaluate their own relationship to this new ordering process. What were formerly bedrock configurations for social identity and subjective experience now are called into question, threatening the entire structure of meaning on which they were based. Berger (1967) observes the most immediate consequence of such a process is the experience of separation from a specific network of social meaning, which now threatens the individual with the possibility of a "meaningless" existence. As the context and meaning for social experience changes, so too does the relationship for personal identity with this newly configured nomic structure.

Social separation and the experience of meaninglessness, which it may evoke, often emerges as an artifact of social change or nomic ordering that is no longer compatible with the individual's established sense of personal identity. When confronted with such a disruption of social meaning, personal identity will either need to employ some strategy of adaptation concerning these evolving nomic demands or risk the threat of a meaningless and unrecognizable existence. However, just as no structure of nomic ordering can account for all aspects of discrete subjective experience, neither can this expanded nomic structure eliminate all connection to those previously embraced social meanings it now threatens to replace.

If the expansion and transformation of this process of nomic ordering were able to include the "guaranteed" elimination of all of those social meanings no longer compatible to it, self-recognition may become impossible for those individuals unwilling or unable to embrace such change. However, such a result is rarely, if ever, achieved. As such, it becomes much more likely that any expansion of nomic ordering will also include a degree of "nomic splitting," which allows for certain aspects of the former nomic structure to retain its ordering power, albeit at a diminished level of social validity. Such examples of nomic splitting, though present, become particularly significant and visible during difficult periods of religious or social transformation (Berger, 1967).

As was witnessed in the U.S. during the 1950s and 1960s with the rising social influence of the Civil Rights Movement, the nomic ordering of American culture became more and more fragmented. Though it could be argued that this expansion of nomic ordering was more or less accepted by the majority of American society, albeit in less than perfect ways, a variety of groups emerged in response to this transformational process, for significantly different reasons. For example, during this same span of twenty years, The Nation of Islam, created by the Honorable Elijah Muhammad, emerged as a powerfully influential alternative perspective, which sought to challenge the logic of the Civil Rights Movement and its integrationist strategy (Clegg, 1997; Dyson, 1996; Lincoln, 1961; Marable, 2011; Polizzi, 2019; Turner, 2003).

Though a variety of theoretical and strategic differences existed between the leaders of the Civil Rights Movement and The Nation of Islam, perhaps the most glaring disagreement between them was the fundamental clash over the possible success of the integration of African-Americans into white society (Cone, 1991). From the perspective of the Nation, integration could never work because white America would never accept blacks as equals (Malcolm, 1973). As a result, the Nation pursued a strategy of separation that would have striking similarities with various anti-black white supremacist groups that also were fundamentally opposed to integration. From this white supremacist perspective, integration was little more than "race mixing," which threatened to destroy the genetic integrity of the white race and often resulted in various horrific examples of racially motivated anti-back violence (Morris, 2017). Add to these powerful tensions, the ongoing conflict in the Viet Nam War, the ultimate resignation of then President Richard Nixon due to the Watergate Scandal, and the reemerging battle of the sexes.

In the aftermath of such profound social transformation, a clear configuration of the American identity would be difficult to easily identify, as would any agreement concerning the specific structure of nomic ordering, which gave this identity its specific social meaning and validity. Over the next forty-five years any number of unfolding moments of nomic crisis would once again rattle and reconfigure the landscape of American social identity: the Iran-Contra Scandal under President Ronald Reagan, The War on Drugs, the 1993 attack on the World Trade Center in New York, the 1994 Crime Bill, Ruby Ridge, David Koresh and the Branch Davidians, the bombing of the Alfred P. Murrah Federal Building in Oklahoma City by former U.S. Army Sergeant Timothy McVeigh, the impeachment of President Bill Clinton, the suicide-bomb attack on the *USS Cole* by al-Qaeda, the 9/11 attacks, the various wars in Afghanistan, Iraq, and Syria, the War on Terror and its use of extraordinary rendition and political torture, the detention facility at Guantanamo Bay, Cuba, the election of Barak Obama, the first African-American president, the rise of the Tea Party Movement, Russian efforts via cyber-attacks to destroy trust in the American electoral system, the election of Donald Trump, and the landslide of criminal investigations which ensued, resulting in his impeachment, same-sex marriage, legal immigration, and the erosion of various U.S. political and legal institutions. Though this list is hardly exhaustive of other significant events, which challenged certain aspects of the American process of nomic ordering, the above examples do represent specific pockets of individual and group meaning that helped to deepen the divide within the meaning-generating process of this phenomenology.

For each of those individuals whose biography was threatened by the onset and transformational possibilities of the above events, the search for meaning can be viewed as one of the core motivating factors by which a new type of self-recognition can occur. Whether this evolving version of social identity is able to find some degree of compatibility with this newly emerging social reality, or choses instead, to remain steadfast and faithful to those once "well regarded" social meanings that now no longer hold the same social currency they once did, some type of nomic assistance will be required to ward off feelings of separation and the experience of a meaningless existence.

Fanatical Violence and the Phenomenology of Nomic Assault

> Anomy is unbearable to the point where the individual may seek death in preference to it. Conversely, existence within a nomic world may be sought at the cost of all sorts of sacrifice and suffering—and even at the cost of life itself, if the individual believes that this ultimate sacrifice has nomic significance. (Berger, 1967, p. 22)

Berger's observation provides powerful clarity to the phenomenology, which emerges from the relationship between the endangered nomic structure and threatened individual identity; in the face of this unbearable anomy, the shattering anxiety, which this experience evokes, must be resolved. Death may indeed be an option, if no other resolution to this existential crisis is available or preferable. However, as Berger eludes, the embrace of other existing nomic structures can represent the possibility of safe haven, capable of restoring those aspects of nomic ordering that have been lost in the ensuing storm of nomic contradiction and marginalization. For Griffin, such a phenomenology is central to the embrace of fanatical violence and the nomic ordering which it seeks to achieve.

In his text, *Terrorist's Creed: Fanatical Violence and the Human Need for Meaning*, Griffin (2012) explores the phenomena of fanatical violence from the perspective, which views the act of terrorism as "a particular objective *cultural* threat or existential dilemma, or combination of the two" (p. 7). Griffin then borrows the construct of the nomos from Berger's the *Sacred Canopy* and applies it to the contexts of political and religious terror. For Griffin, terrorism takes on an existential formulation and meaning, which becomes a response to the perceived assault on an existing nomic structure or as a response, which recognizes the collapse of the same.

By linking the phenomenology of terrorism, with the process of nomic ordering, a fuller context for the meaning of social existence and the behaviors it evokes can be more easily identified and explored. Taken from this perspective, the phenomenology of terrorism unfolds as a type of nomic crises that emerges as a specific manifestation of and response to this experience of existential threat. The actual configuration of this threat will be specific to its social context and nomic structure, but not necessarily confined by it.[5]

Take for example the current reemergence of anti-black attitudes in the U.S. since the election of President Barak Obama. Though the presence of anti-black racism has never truly been eradicated from the American body politic or exclusively contained within the recesses of the American psyche since the inception of this country, specific violent acts directed toward African-American citizens have increased over the last few years. Add to this troubling development, the increase in violent acts against Jewish citizens both in the U.S. and Europe, the increasing villainization of Islam and those who practice that religion, and the increasing vitriolic rhetorical assault directed at immigrants fleeing the economic and political violence of El Salvador, Honduras, and Guatemala by Donald Trump and others of his ilk, one gets a clearer sense of what is being proposed here.

As social change continues to erode certain aspects of nomic ordering, for some, these changes will reflect a fundamental existential threat to the psychological foundations of group and individual identity. As newer manifestations of social experience and personal identity become included and legitimated by this expanding nomic order, so too does the level of alienation for those who are no longer able to situate their own biographies within this newly evolving social structure. As a result, personalities of resistance start to emerge and coalesce around nomic structures no longer validated or with those threatened by "total extinction." If this process of nomic expansion continues unabated, the response to this meaning-generating process often turns to violence.

---

[5] Take for example the experience of the Islamic Brotherhood in Egypt. Though this group emerged from the specific socio-political context of early twentieth-century Egypt and developed from that historical starting point, its nomic influence has reached far beyond its initial country of origin. The nomic reach of this group continues to have a powerful influence on a variety of violent Salifist Jihadi groups worldwide. In very similar ways, the nomic ordering of the alt-right and various iterations of neo-Nazi groups, though societally specific in origin, also have nomic connections with groups that exist outside of the traditional boundaries of these countries.

Nomic Assault and Personalities of Resistance

In his text, *Terrorist Creed: Fanatical Violence and the Human Search for Meaning*, Griffin (2012) provides two descriptive categories by which to situate the developmental process of the phenomenology of terrorism: Zealots and Modernists. For the purposes of this introduction—a more thorough discussion of these constructs will be provided in Chap. 3 of this text and will be employed in subsequent chapters—Zealots are those who feel threatened by the perceived loss of a specific configuration of nomic ordering and seek to protect and reestablish the cultural power of that structure of social meaning (Griffin, 2012). The Zealot is viewed by Griffin as a member of a specific religious group or domination, who feels currently threatened by the process of nomic expansion, which threatens to marginalize or completely destroy one's relationship to this life defining structure for social experience and identity. Central to this phenomenology is the desire to restore those aspects of this threatened nomic structure to its former power and significance. Examples of this type of nomic process can be witnessed in the rise of the Islamic Brotherhood in Egypt during the 1930s and beyond (Bergesen, 2008; Kepel, 1993, 2020; Mitchell, 1993; Qutb, 2008; Vannetzel, 2021); the rise of the Taliban in Afghanistan (Anas & Hussein, 2019; Johnson, 2017); the rise of al-Qaeda (bin Laden, 2008; Kepel, 2008); and the rise of the Islamic State (Gerges, 2016; Wood, 2017), along with a variety of Islamic groups found in various countries in the Middle East, North Africa, and elsewhere (Adraoui, 2013; de Koning, 2013; Hasan, 2013; Hwang, 2019; Kepel, 2017, 2020; Maruf & Joseph, 2018; Nasr, 1996; Salomon, 2013; Wagemakers, 2012; Walker, 2016). Regardless the specific iteration of these personalities of resistance, what remains generally consistent across these groups, is the perceived assault on a specific nomic configuration of Islam and Islamic identity that must be confronted.

For Griffin (2012), the Modernist example of nomic ordering, is focused on the future. It views the current foundations and structures of nomic ordering to be weak or in the process of complete collapse. Regardless the specific details of this nomic decline, it is viewed as no longer capable of providing the life defining structure it once did.

Examples of this secular version of social life are easily witnessed with the emergence of various revolutionary movements that ultimately resulted in the creation of new social structures and meanings for individual existence, which these failing institutions could no long provide: such examples as the American & French Revolutions, the revolution of the Proletariat in Czarist Russia, the Mexican and Cuban revolutions, and the Viet Nam War come immediately to mind.

Taken from this perspective, the process of nomic ordering offered by Griffin has a number of theoretical similarities to the Heidegger's constructs of being-in-the-world and the they-self. As such, being-in-the-world-as-Zealot reflects a specific engagement with the social world that is defined and structured by this Salifist Jihadi configuration of the they-self. Though Griffin clearly does not intend to evoke Heidegger when describing the identity-producing structure of this nomic ordering process, it is nonetheless a methodologically useful approach by which to situate, nomic ordering, identity creation, and the phenomenology of terrorism.

Being-in-the-World and the Nomizing Influence of the They-Self

The process of nomic ordering described above has a number of similarities that can be recognized in the relationship between being-in-the-world and the they-self. As a meaning-generating process, the they-self orders human existence from a specific nomizing "point of view," which in turn provides being-in-the-world a structure of meaning by which to pursue its projects. Heidegger (2012) observes:

> In its being, the they is essentially concerned with averageness. Thus, the they maintains itself factically in the averageness of what belongs to it, what it does and does not consider valid, and what it grants or denies success. This averageness, which prescribes what can and may be ventured, watches over every exception which thrusts itself to the fore. Every priority is noiselessly squashed. (p. 123)

Heidegger's construct of the they-self configures a similar type of relationality that is recognizably present in both the constructs of the nomos and the process of identity formation, which it evokes. For Heidegger, the they-self structures the meaning of being-in-the-world through its consideration of what is valid and what is not; what will be granted success and what will not. From this perspective, human existence finds itself (Richardson, 2012) within the meaning-generating process established by the they-self and reveals to being-in-the-world, a group of others that are much like them. "The relation of being to others then becomes a projection of one's own being toward oneself 'into the other.' The other is a duplicate of the self" (Heidegger, 2012, p. 121). This process takes on a particular significance when applied to the phenomenology of terrorism.

When one encounters the various narrative presentations of individuals involved in this type of fanatical violence, this relationship between being-in-the-world and a very specific manifestation of the they-self is almost always present. Whether this meaning-generating process is situated within the context of Salifist jihadi terrorism, White Supremacy and racism, anti-Semitism, or other types of similarly situated violent encounters with specifically targeted victims, some very specific manifestations of the they-self are also implicated. In each of these examples, as well as numerous others, the they-self structures a field of social relationality that values certain types of being-in-the-word while devaluing others. When Dylann Roof decides that "I must kill" (Polizzi, 2020), he does so from the motivation provided by the racist-they-self that objectifies the presence of black-being-in-the-world as that of a danger or threat. When Richard Bowers decides impulsively that "I must kill," he does so from the perspective of the they-self of anti-Semitism, which seeks to deny the very existence of Jewish life.

However, it is also important to recognize that the configuration of the they-self is probably never a singular process of meaning construction. Given that each manifestation of the they-self is taken-up within the context of social relationality, there is undoubtedly various overlapping iterations of social meaning that either join with or compete against any singular version of this ordering process. It will be recalled that Malcolm X/Malik Shabazz (1973) describes in *The Autobiography of Malcolm X* such a competing clash of manifestations of the they.

For Malcolm, this clash of competing manifestations of the they-self is recognized by the various ways in which black-being-in-the world is and will be defined in that text (Polizzi, 2019). Though Malcolm must confront the they-self of anti-black racism, he does have access to more positive configurations of blackness offered by his parents, who were members of Marcus Gravey's Back to Africa Movement (Cone, 1991; Lincoln, 1961; Rashad, 2013; Turner, 2003). In fact, Malcolm's later attraction to the teachings of the Prophet Elijah Mohammad was in part made possible by the familiarity that this perspective shared with some of the ideas taught to him by his parents when he was a young boy (Cone, 1991; DeCaro, 1996). As an adult, Malcolm is able to employ this competing version of the they-self to resist the objectifying gaze of this type of racism. Add to this process the introduction of his conversion to Sunni Islam, his ability to resist the they-self of racism is further strengthened, as he attempts to make sense of these overlapping possibilities for existence (Polizzi, 2019).

Another point of accessibility to these competing versions of the they-self has become powerfully visible through the emerging significance of social media. Though certainly not exclusive to the topic of terrorism, social media has become an important factor in the introduction of and radicalization by various configurations of the they-self found on blog sites and other digital venues. These sites attract a variety of like-minded individuals seeking to join a community of "believers," who will incorporate the nomic ordering these sites provide and then impose this newly fabricated identity on the world (Sageman, 2008). As a result, these individuals are now able to share their beliefs with similarly inclined others without fear of being marginalized or rejected, as they pledge their fidelity to this version of the they-self.

The dominant influence of social media in the digital age provides an important quality of access that was previously unavailable to these different iterations of the they-self: the possibility for anonymity. What we will see in the examples of Dylann Roof, Richard Bowers, and those attracted by the actions of ISIS/IS is how their involvement with social media sites not only provides the structure by which the radicalization process can take place, but how it also affords the opportunity for one to speak their mind without concern of upsetting the normative sensibilities of others around them. It is not insignificant that almost no evidence exists that either Roof or Bowers openly shared their ideas with those in their daily life. It therefore seems appropriate in certain instances to view the digital process of identity formation as witnessed within the phenomenology of online radicalization as a presencing of formerly repressed or suppressed attitudes and beliefs that can now be viewed more or less in real time.

The They-Self and the Digital World

The reality of the digital age has evoked a number of challenges to both governmental agencies and law enforcement practice as this relates to the phenomenology of terrorism. Perhaps one of the more significant aspects of these challenges is the degree of accessibility the digital world provides to those individuals, who find themselves attracted to extremist content. Though it is certainly not novel for various political or religious groups to take advantage of the opportunities offered by a new evolving technology,[6] the introduction of the internet and the opportunities it provides represent an algebraic difference when compared to these technological advances of the past (Sageman, 2008). The ability of individuals to come into contact with multiple examples of extremist imagery and theoretical propaganda and to be able do so in a more or less secure environment help to provide a space for these individuals to once again "make sense" of their personal biographies.

What seems to be most phenomenologically significant to this process of "sense making" is the transformational relationality that emerges within this new experience of nomic ordering. When one is confronted by this material, it becomes rather obvious that a different structure of nomic ordering is in place and with it, a different set of valued attitudes and beliefs that personal identity is required to embrace. Prior to this

---

[6] This can be witnessed by the role played by the printing press during the Protestant Reformation, the role played by still photography in its depictions of the horrific battlefield scenes from the American Civil War, the use of television and film during World II and the subsequent use of mimeograph machines, copy machines, VHS, and cassette tapes to disseminate audio or video messaging by specific political groups, all of which were employed to reach out to their supporters.

unprecedented access, individuals holding similar beliefs were more likely to feel isolated and perhaps unwilling to discuss these ideas with others in their immediate network of social relationships. However, with the more or less assured anonymity of private chat rooms, such fears can literally be left at the door. Once inside, it becomes very clear that a different type of political correctness is required.

As a result, it becomes essential that we recognize the internet not merely as a vehicle, or sophisticated machine, but as a process of transforming networks (Latour, 2013) or assemblages (Bryant, 2014) of digital interactions, which not only extends the parameters of human existence, but takes part in the creation and transformation of the human self as well. The process of nomic ordering, which takes place within the phenomenology of digital radicalization, as a result, is really no different than other processes of radicalization, which occurs in face-to-face interactions. The interactions this process invites has no need for actual individuals, only the ideas and images these figures represent. Constructs such as leaderless jihad and lone wolf terrorist, really lose a great deal of their currency in the contemporary context. Access to the digital world of extremist ideas simply reflects an indirect and safer interaction to the same attitudes and beliefs, except that this digital experience provides a more powerful visceral experience of the same.

About This Book

Perhaps it is important to begin by observing what this book is not. Though the discussion, which follows, will incorporate brief descriptions of historical material, its intent is not history per se, a strategy that falls outside of the scope of the current discussion. Rather, it will employ the use of brief historical backdrops by which to better contextualize the phenomenology, which this history helps to construct.

In Chap. 2, "What's in a Name: Constructing Terrorism," the topic of terrorism will be introduced. The term will be taken up from a variety of theoretical perspectives. What becomes most interesting, as well as problematic, is the inability of the multiple disciplines focused on this topic to craft a definition that everyone can accept. It will be argued that one of the main barriers to such a resolution is located in the inability to significantly account for behaviors, which are in various ways rationalized as being necessary, but yet employ questionable strategies by which to achieve an identified goal.

Given that the phenomenology of terrorism reflects a configuration of the who is killing whom relationality, it will be helpful to explore this dynamic from a variety of political and religious points of view. Taken from this perspective, the phenomenology of terrorism reflects a process of meaning construction that is concerned with different processes of nomic ordering and identity formation as this relates to the construction of the social world. How one constructs the meaning of terrorism will, in turn, also provide some meaningful insight into how they construct human existence and social experience as well.

Chapter 3, "The Phenomenology of the Nomos," will focus on the construct of the nomos as it is explored by Roger Griffin in his text *Terrorist's Creed: Fanatical Violence and the Human Need for Meaning*. The basic structural aspects of this construct will be identified and its influence on identity creation explored, as this specifically relates to the phenomenology of secular and political fanatical violence. A thorough discussion will be offered concerning the constructs of the Zealot, Modernist, and Griffin's hybrid configuration of current manifestations of al-Qaeda. Griffin's hybrid configuration of al-Qaeda, which he theorizes as representing aspects of both Zealot and Modernist construct, will be thoroughly explored. I will conclude this chapter with a discussion of the phenomenology of nomic ordering, from the phenomenological perspectives of Martin Heidegger and Giorgio Agamben. Heidegger's constructs of the they-self and being-in-the-world and Agamben's configuration of the apparatus and living being will be employed to provide a richer theoretical context to the construction of the phenomenology of terrorism.

Chapter 4, "Toward a Phenomenology of Jihad: The Salafist Jihadi Perspectives," will explore a variety of theological perspectives, which can be generally viewed as the foundational influences for the Islamist movement. The discussion will begin with a brief exploration of the various meanings of jihad from a variety of perspectives. We will then take up the Salafist Jihadi perspective beginning with the work of Islamic scholar ibn

Taymiyya, who is often viewed as one of the earliest proponents of what has come to be known as offensive jihad and then transition to a variety of contemporary theological and theoretical approaches that have been influenced by his work. The discussion will then move to an exploration of the work of Pakistani theoretician Mawlana Mawdudi and his understanding of Islamic revivalism, as this relates to the version of the Muslim self his construct of revisionism seeks to evoke. A similar focus will be applied to the work of Egyptian lay-theologian Sayyid Qutb and Muhammad abd-al Same Faraj, who was directly involved in the murder of Anwar Sadat and strongly influenced by Qutb's work. The chapter will conclude with a discussion of the Palestinian cleric Abdullah Azzam, considered the father of modern-day jihad.

With each of these Salafist Jihadi or Islamist theorists, a transformative nomic structure is offered which seeks to "liberate" Muslim belief from various aspects of failed religious practice and to revive Islam to a state of former glory. However, as is the case with any nomic structure, individual identity can only be transformed, if this structure of nomic ordering is evidenced in one's daily lived-experience.

Chapter 5 will explore the rise of al-Qaeda and the nomic ordering this group represents. The phenomenology of al-Qaeda will be traced through a variety of texts outlining both its specific process of nomic ordering, as well as the type of subject this structure of meaning seeks to construct. As an example of global terrorism, al-Qaeda initially emerged as the vehicle by which their specific brand of Islam would be imposed on the world of non-believers. Included here will be a discussion of Osama bin Laden and his specific construction of the Islamic nomos of Salifist Jihadi fundamentalism. A phenomenology of jihad as constructed by this process will be analyzed.

In Chap. 6, the development of the Islamic State will be explored from its initial creation as al-Qaeda in Iraq to the various iterations, which followed; a specific emphasis will be given to the various texts related to this developmental process and the structure of nomic ordering they reveal. The Islamic State will be explored relative to its emergence as a competing iteration of the Salifist Jihadi nomos that sought to replace al-Qaeda as the leading voice within this nomic narrative. Included here will be an analysis of this group as it developed through its various iterations and how it consolidated its significance once the caliphate was established. The chapter will conclude with IS in the aftermath of its defeat in Iraq and Syria. A phenomenology of jihad will be explored from this perspective.

In Chap. 7, "The Taliban and Hezbollah: Political Parties or Terror Organizations," the discussion will explore the way in which these two organizations defy easy categorization. Though both of these groups have been designated as terrorist organizations by the West, their activity and behavior within their specific context of influence reflect a far more complex structural reality. These actions become further complicated by their relationship to state actors, where they function as a proxy insurgency force aligned with these larger state and regional interests. This configuration evokes a complex phenomenology given both of these groups have emerged from the aftermath of long-fought domestic conflicts, which have become simultaneously intertwined within larger regional venues. As a result of these overlapping areas of interest, various nomic structures have been employed by which to define this political or terrorist activity. Each of these organizations or parties enjoy considerable support within their respective countries. How this success is measured and legitimated is often configured by specific political or religious interests, which are also reflected in the competing nomic structures these groups represent.

Chapter 8 will explore the emerging significance of white supremacy and the digital world. Over the past decade, a number of societies have witnessed the return of violent racism, anti-Semitism, and the hatred toward immigrants; however, what has become a troubling feature of this process is the apparent normalizing of some of these groups and ideas. Though it would be incorrect to argue that anti-black racism, anti-Semitism, sexism, or the current vitriol directed toward immigrant populations were ever completely removed from the body politic of many of these societies, neither can it be denied that their "return" has been made possible by the unexpected level of support some of these ideas received.

What this phenomenology reveals is the reemergence of systems of nomic ordering that were presumed either defeated or marginalized. Such a process has been aided by the vast opportunity offered by the digital age to not only disseminate various manifestos of hate, but to use this material to fabricate identities of intolerance. Though not as tightly configured as the Islamic iteration of this process, or as openly supported, the process of digital radicalization of the far-right continues to be a difficult problem that must be addressed. The following topics will be discussed: Phenomenology of radicalized white supremacy, the case of Dylann Roof; the case of Richard Bowers, and the case of Brenton Tarrant.

In Chap. 9 an analysis is offered concerning the reemergence and normalization of these far-right perspectives. Of particular interest is the way in which the insurrectionist assault on the U.S. Capitol Building on January 6, 2021 reflects this process of normalization. Past iterations of these white supremacist ideologies, though never absent from American politics, have not been so dangerously connected to the political process, as they currently are. Again, this is not to argue that these attitudes and beliefs were ever completely absent from the social consciousness of the American Body Politic; only that the emerging phenomenology, which they reveal reflects a degree of nomic threat for a large number of American citizens that it may be difficult to reconcile. Chapter 10 will conclude this discussion by adding some further reflection concerning the phenomenology of who is killing whom and the possibilities which lay beyond this point. Included in this chapter will be a discussion of Agamben's text *The Coming Community*.

Chapter 10 will explore how the who is being killed by whom dynamic offered by Sontag takes on a central role in unraveling the phenomenology of terrorism. The main target of this process is the construct of individual identity and its ability to be manipulated by various processes of nomic ordering that seeks to keep in place the duality recognized by Sontag. The chapter will conclude with a brief discussion of the Whatever discussed by Agamben in his text *The Coming Community*.

References

Adraoui, M.-A. (2013). Salafism in France: Ideology, practices, and contradictions. In R. Meijer (Ed.), *Global Salafism: Islam's new religious movement* (pp. 364–383). Oxford University Press.

Agamben, G. (1993). *The coming community*. University of Minnesota Press.

Agamben, G. (2009). *What is an apparatus? And other essays* (D. Kishik & S. Pedatella, Trans.). Stanford University Press.

Anas, A., & Hussein, T. (2019). *To the Mountains: My life in Jihad, from Algeria to Afghanistan*. Hurst & Company.

Berger, P. (1967). *The sacred canopy: Elements of a sociological theory of religion*. Anchor Books.

Bergesen, A. J. (2008). Sayyid Qutb in historical context. In A. J. Bergesen (Ed.), *The Sayyid Qutb reader: Selected writings on politics, religion, and society* (pp. 3–13). Routledge.

bin Laden, O. (2008). The companions' den. In G. Kepel & J.-P. Milelli (Eds.), P. Ghazaleh, (Trans.), *Al Qaeda in its own words* (pp. 41–46). The Belknap Press of Harvard University Press.

Bryant, L. R. (2014). *Onto-cartography: An ontology of machines and media*. Edinburgh University Press.

Clegg, C. A. (1997). *An original man: The life and times of Elijah Muhammad*. St. Martins Press.

Cone, J. (1991). *Martin & Malcolm & America: A dream or a nightmare*. Orbis Press.

de Koning, M. J. M. (2013). Changing worldviews and friendship: An exploration of the life stories of two female Salafis in the Netherlands. In R. Meijer (Ed.), *Global Salafism: Islam's new religious movement* (pp. 404–423). Oxford University Press.

DeCaro, L., Jr. (1996). *On the side of my people: A religious life of Malcolm X*. New York University Press.

Dyson, M. E. (1996). *Making Malcolm: The myth & meaning of Malcolm X*. Oxford University Press.

Gerges, F. A. (2016). *ISIS: A history*. Princeton University Press.

Gerges, F. A. (2018). *Making the Arab world: Nasser, Qutb, and the clash that shaped the Middle East*. Princeton University Press.

Griffin, R. (2012). *Terrorist's creed: Fanatical violence and the human need for meaning*. London & New York: Palgrave Macmillan.

Hasan, N. (2013). Ambivalent doctrines and conflicts in the Salafi Movement in Indonesia. In R. Meijer (Ed.), *Global Salafism: Islam's new religious movement* (pp. 169–188). Oxford University Press.

Heidegger, M. (2012). *Being and time* (J. Stambaugh, Trans.). SUNY Press.

Hwang, J. C. (2019). Dakwah before jihad: Understanding the behaviour of Jemaah Islamiyah. *Contemporary Southeast Asia, 41*, 14–34.

Johnson, T. H. (2017). *Taliban narratives: The use and power of stories in the Afghanistan conflict*. Oxford University Press.

Katz, R. (2018, October 29). Inside the online cesspool of Anti-Semitism that housed Robert Bowers. *Politico*. Retrieved from www.politico.com/magazine/story/2018/10/29/inside-the-online-cesspool-of-anti-semitism-that-housed-robert-bowers-221949

Kepel, G. (1993). *Muslim extremism in Egypt: The prophet and pharaoh*. University of California Press.

Kepel, G. (2005). *The roots of radical Islam*. Saqi.

Kepel, G. (2008). *Beyond terror and martyrdom: The future of the Middle East*. The Belknap Press of Harvard University Press.

Kepel, G. (2017). *Terror in France: The rise of jihad in the West*. Oxford University Press.

Kepel, G. (2020). *Away from chaos: The Middle East and the challenge of the West*. Columbia University Press.

Khatab, S. (2006). *The political thought of Sayyid Qutb*. Routledge.

Latour, B. (2013). *An inquiry into modes of existence: An anthropology of the moderns* (C. Porter, Trans.). Harvard University Press.

Lincoln, C. E. (1961). *The Black Muslims in America*. Africa World Press.

Malcolm, X. (1973). *The autobiography of Malcolm X: As told to Alex Haley*. Ballantine Books.

Marable, M. (2011). *Malcolm X: A life of reinvention*. Viking.

Maruf, H., & Joseph, D. (2018). *Inside al-Shabaab: The secret history of al-Qaeda's most powerful ally*. Indiana University Press.

Mitchell, R. A. (1993). *The society of the Muslim Brothers*. Oxford University Press.

Moghaddam, F. M. (2018). *Mutual radicalization: How groups and nations drive each other to extremes*. American Psychological Association.

Morris, T. (2017). *Dark ideas: How Neo-Nazi and violent jihadi ideologues shaped modern terrorism*. Lexington Books.

Nasr, S. V. R. (1996). *Mawdudi & the making of Islamic revivalism*. Oxford University Press.

Polizzi, D. (2019). *A phenomenological hermeneutic of antiblack racism in the autobiography of Malcolm X*. Lexington Books.

Polizzi, D. (2020). Righteous slaughter and the phenomenology of the assailed self. In D. Polizzi (Ed.), *Jack Katz: Seduction, the street and emotion* (pp. 57–72). Emerald Publishing.

Quinney, R. (2000). Socialist humanism and the problem of crime: Thinking about Erich Fromm in the development of critical/peacemaking criminology. In K. Anderson & R. Quinney (Eds.), *Erich Fromm and critical criminology* (pp. 21–30).

Qutb, S. (2008). In A. J. Bergesen (Ed.), *The Sayyid Qutb reader: Selected writings on politics, religion, and society* (pp. 35–42). Routledge.
Rashad, S. (2013). *Black Muslims in the U.S.* Palgrave Macmillan.
Richardson, J. (2012). *Heidegger.* Routledge.
Sageman, M. (2008). *Leaderless jihad: Terror networks in the twenty-first century.* University of Pennsylvania Press.
Salomon, N. (2013). The Salafi critique of Islamism: Doctrine, difference and the problem of Islamic political action in contemporary Sudan. In R. Meijer (Ed.), *Global Salafism: Islam's new religious movement* (pp. 143–168). Oxford University Press.
Simi, P., Blee, K., DeMichele, M., & Windisch, S. (2017). Addicted to hate: Identity residual among former white supremacists. *American Sociological Review, 82*, 1167–1187.
Sontag, S. (2004). *Regarding the pain of others.* Picador.
Turner, R. B. (2003). *Islam in the African-American experience.* Indiana University Press.
Vannetzel, M. (2021). *The Muslim Brothers in society: Everyday politics, social action, and Islamism in Mubarak's Egypt* (D. Tresilian, Trans.). The American University in Cairo Press.
Wagemakers, J. (2012). *A Quietist Jihadi: The ideology and influence of Abu Muhammad al- Maqdisi.* Cambridge University Press.
Walker, A. (2016). *'Eat the heart of the infidel':* The harrowing of Nigeria and the rise of Boko Haram. Hurst & Company.
Wood, G. (2017). *The way of the stranger: Encounters with the Islamic State.* Random House.

2

What's in a Name: Constructing Terrorism

Defining the Construct of Terrorism

Former U.S. Supreme Court Justice Potter Stewart wrote in his concurring opinion in the *Jacobellis v. Ohio*, 378 U.S. 184 (1964) pornography case, what would become known as one of the more recognized lines in the history of that institution (Berger, 2018). He observed that though he could not say what actually constituted a pornographic film, he would know it if he saw it (*Jacobellis v. Ohio*, 1964). Such an opening for a book on terrorism may seem odd but does have some metaphorical relevance to the current topic under study. How do we understand the phenomenon of terrorism and would we recognize it if we saw it? The most immediate response to this question is likely, "Of course." But is this answer actually correct?

As anyone familiar with the ever-increasing literature on terrorism will immediately attest, the most difficult question yet to be conclusively resolved centers around the ability of this same literature to configure a specific agreed-upon definition for this construct (Berger, 2018; Griffin, 2012; Hoffman, 2006; Laqueur, 1999; Laqueur & Wall, 2018; Post, 2007; Schanzer, 2017; Stampnitzky, 2017). Now this is not to contend that no real answer to this question has been offered; rather, it simply recognizes that numerous attempts have indeed been made, but no definitive agreement has actually been reached between those who have attempted to answer this question.

To the above point, Stampnitzky (2017) makes the following observation concerning the challenges of arriving at an agreed-upon definition for terrorism:

> But of course, terrorism *can* be defined; the true problem is not a surfeit, but rather a *surplus*, of definitions. Yet neither experts, nor politicians, nor the lay public has been able to come to an agreement as to which of the many definitions circulating is correct, and the so-called problem of definition has been a central and enduring aspect of both public and expert debate on terrorism. (p. 11)

Stampnitzky (2017) continues by observing that prior to the 1970s, acts of violence which today would be explained as acts of terrorism were often viewed within the context of political insurgency. Perhaps more importantly, these politically motivated acts of violence contained within them an observable "rationale," which appeared to be consistent with the types of social change these groups sought to evoke. However, with the onset of terrorist-related violence, an explanatory shift occurred, concerning how these acts would be constructed. What had been previously viewed as an artifact of political ideology, now became an artifact of the immoral nature of the terrorist identity (Stampnitzky, 2017).

What seems most apparent within the shifting phenomenology, which Stampnitzky describes, is inability to relocate or reconfigure an understanding of terrorism that could still resonate with its former political construction and meaning. Most significantly absent from a number of these newer versions of extremist violence was the former political rational, which helped to make these acts more or less comprehensible. As scholars and policy makers continued to flounder in their ability to provide a clear definitional framework for terrorism, a variety of competing explanations were offered that actually helped to not only confuse the process further, but ironically, helped to clarity, why it was likely that such a definition would be rather different to achieve: No definition for terrorism would ever be possible if it was not first depoliticized (Stampnitzky, 2017).

Laqueur and Wall (2018) in their text, *The Future of Terrorism: ISIS, al-Qaeda, and the Alt-Right*, make a similar observation concerning the challenges related to an agreed-upon definition for terrorism:

> The fact is that terrorism is a phenomenon rife with inconsistencies, conspiracies, mixed ideologies, and the ability to generate immense fear, which is exploited by both politicians and terrorists alike. This has made giving an objective accounting of the subject nigh impossible largely because in the public sphere, there is no common ground in terms of a definition, modality, or strategic purpose. (pp. 1–2)

Laqueur and Wall (2018) observe that the failure to find an acceptable definition for the phenomenon of terrorism has left the public confused and uncertain concerning "what distinguishes terrorism from other forms of political violence waged by nonstate actors." (p. 2). They continue by recognizing that the phenomenon of terrorism has a powerful ability to upend the political order and usher in changes that can greatly transform the current political environment of a given society (Ahmed, 2015, 2018; Kepel, 2017; Pisoiu & Prucha, 2014). Laqueur and Wall (2018) place particular emphasis on how the Western response to these acts of violence has evoked a variety of "solutions" to this problem that actually appear to contradict some the core democratic values of these countries. The use by the U.S., of extraordinary rendition, waterboarding of detainees, and the lack of due process at Guantanamo Bay, Cuba, is perhaps one of the more egregious examples of this type of political contradiction. Taken from this perspective, the authors recognize the most basic question that must be resolved is: how is it possible to construct a response to terrorism, without a clear understanding of that phenomenon?

The introduction of this study began with Sontag's observation concerning "who is being killed by whom," as this relates to the depiction of the consequences of political violence. Her observation was in relation to Virginia Wolf's book-length essay, *Three Guineas*, and its exploration of the roots of war, but her critique of the author's conclusion is pertinent here. In that text, Wolf (1938/1966) concludes that when individuals are confronted with the gruesome details of war, the rational conclusion will be that war must be abolished. The evidence, which Wolf presents to prove her case, are the horrific images of the mangled bodies of the victims of the Spanish Civil War. Once the individual is confronted by these images, there can be no other conclusion other than all war must be abolished. In response to this Sontag (2003) observes:

> Who believes today that war can be abolished? No one, not even pacifists. We only hope (so for in vain) to stop genocide and to bring to justice those who commit gross violations of the laws of war (for there are laws of war, to which combatants should be held) and to be able to stop specific wars by imposing negotiated alternatives to armed conflict. (p. 5)

In her critique of Wolf's conclusion, Sontag argues that the images of war employed by the author really do not accomplish the goal she intends, that is, to depict war as such; rather, what she provides is "a particular way of waging war, a way at that time routinely described as 'barbaric,' in which civilians are targeted" (Sontag, 2003. p. 9). Sontag (2003) adds that Wolf's read of the images she employs from the Spanish Civil War can only provide "a general abhorrence of war," (p. 9) a conclusion that ignores or dismisses the political context from which these images emerge. Such omissions have similarly plagued the attempt to define terrorism.

As we have seen, Stampnitzky (2017), Laqueur and Wall (2018) and Sontag (2003), all in their own way, insightfully identify perhaps the most important factor involved in defining the phenomenon of terrorism: the inability to account successfully for the political dimensions of the process. To some degree, this challenge is reflected in Quinney's (2000) observation: "The question of what precedes crime is far more significant to our understanding of the act of crime itself" (p. 21). Not only is this no different for the phenomenon of terrorism, it may in fact be perhaps one of the main "causes" concerning why it remains "nigh impossible" for an agreed-upon definition to be constructed. Could the act of terrorism be better understood, if the focus was shifted to that which came before?

Competing Conclusions and Entangled Biases

As was stated above, the problems concerning the inability to define the phenomenon of terrorism are certainly not due to any lack of effort. Numerous definitional approaches are currently available yet none of them seem sufficient in their ability to finally answer the question; this process is further complicated by the rise of powerful non-state actors, groups that have shown the ability to control large areas of territory within the confines of a given country, often described as a failed state: Groups such as Hezbollah (Daher, 2019; Daher, 2016; Farha, 2019), the Taliban (Anas & Hussein, 2019), IS (Gerges, 2016), Al-Shabaab (Maruf & Joseph, 2018), and the various warlords currently craving up Libya (Lacher, 2020) to simply name a few represent this relatively new phenomenon (Kepel, 2020). Though the rise and perhaps even renewed legitimacy for extremist right-wing groups has also been witnessed with concern, this result was achieved via the electoral process and the willingness of voters in both Europe and the U.S. to provide these formally marginalized voices more legitimacy due to these electoral victories and not "necessarily" attributable to the conditions of a failed state.

However, even this description is insufficient, given that it fails to recognize the electoral victories of Hezbollah in Lebanon and the Muslim Brotherhood in Egypt and the popular support enjoyed by the Taliban in certain areas of Afghanistan (Kepel, 2020). Add to this the various consequences of the Arab Spring and this question gets more complicated still (Kepel, 2020). Though the political must be directly accounted for, if any legitimate possibly remains concerning the goal of defining the phenomenon, it is certainly a possibility that will be extremely difficult to achieve. Perhaps the most useful place to start is with the distinction offered by a variety of competing authors concerning the definition of terrorism.

Bruce Hoffman (2006), in his text *Inside Terrorism*, makes the following observation concerning the inherent difficulties related to the construction of a definition for terrorism.

> Not surprisingly, as the meaning and usage of the word changed over time to accommodate the political vernacular and discourse of each successive era, terrorism has proved increasingly elusive in the face of the attempts to construct one consistent definition. (p. 20)

Hoffman continues by lamenting the "good ole days" of terrorism, exemplified by a variety of groups from the late nineteenth and early twentieth centuries, who openly proclaimed their strategy as terrorism. He observes that more recently, terror groups or organizations have failed to identify themselves as such, and instead have embraced names more positively recognizable with liberation movements or freedom fighters (Hoffman, 2006). He concludes by observing, "What all of these examples suggest is that terrorists clearly do not see themselves as others do" (Hoffman, 2006, p. 22). However, is it actually true that we know how others view them?

Hoffman continues by attempting to use a comparative type of analysis to establish his point. He argues that an individual from a particular political persuasion would have no difficulty in self-identifying their specific ideological orientation; similarly, the individual, who robs banks, would have no difficulty in identifying as a bank robber (Hoffman, 2006). The construction of the individual as terrorist follows this same logic. However, does it? The process of self-identification that is embraced by the political adherent and the bank robber is not the same process that Hoffman applies to the Hezbollah terrorist/ fighter, which he offers in his discussion.

In the exchange, which Hoffman provides between captured American journalist Terry Anderson and his Hezbollah guard, a disagreement ensues concerning whether or not this individual is a terrorist:

> The guard had objected to a newspaper article that referred to Hezbollah as terrorists. "We are not terrorists," he indignantly stated, "we are fighters." Anderson replied, "Hajj, you are a terrorist, look it up in the dictionary. You are a terrorist, you may not like the word and if do not like the word, do not do it." (Hoffman, 2006, p. 23)

Though this example may seem superficial to the current conversation, it does capture, at least in a very general sense, the difficulties related to this process and its complexity.

The statement "We are not terrorists, we are fighters" cannot be dismissed or refuted simply because another individual refuses the "legitimacy" of the claim. Though the act of imprisoning a journalist, in this case for seven years, certainly is a violation of accepted international norms concerning the press, as Quinney observes, the act is much less significant than what comes before. From each of the perspectives provided above, a distinct process of social construction emerges, which simply cannot be dismissed by the imposition of an uncontestable privileged point of view. It is also not surprising that such uncontested privilege is what has made such a definition so elusive.

J. Berger (2018), in his text, *Extremism*, attempts to answer a similar question: What is extremism? He begins with the following observation:

> If you believe that only "the other guy" can produce extremists and that your own identity group cannot, you may be an extremist yourself. History provides ample evidence that extremism is part of the human condition and not the exclusive province of any single race, religion, or nation. (Berger, 2018, p. 4)

If as Berger (2018) contends, "extremism is part of the human condition," (p. 4) and additionally, that all acts of violence are not necessarily related to extremism, what then are the conditions which marries extremism with violence resulting in terrorism?

By identifying extremism (terrorism) as an aspect of the human condition, Berger must first situate this characteristic within the phenomenology of individual identity and group relations. Given that extremism can be viewed as a predicate of human experience, violent extremism reveals a fracturing within the "structure" of human relationality and the various meanings these interactions help to construct. As was discussed in Chap. 1 of this text, nomic ordering helps to situate and structure the meaning of individual identity as this relates to the social world one inhabits. The more closely one follows these accepted social meanings, the more likely they will provide varying degrees of protection which this canopy provides. However, if an individual or group fails to exhibit appropriate fidelity to these social meanings, they may find themselves cast out or punished for violating those prohibitions that were expected to heed. Berger situates this phenomenological process within the context of social identity theory.

Central to the study of social identity theory is the configuration of ingroup and outgroup identities. As Berger observes, to be a member of any group implies a degree of shared belief. However, regardless the various benefits such a phenomenology provides, it is also necessary to recognize that identification and membership within a specific configuration of a group also helps to identity those who do not belong (Berger, 2018). Furthermore, the specific identification and membership within a more general group structure will likely reveal various categories of ingroup identities that are not compatible; as a result, a variety of categories or characteristics are employed, usually by those most capable of wielding some degree of social currency relative to the process of ingroup identity construction. It is also possible, as a result of these ingroup processes of identity formation that one's general membership within a more loosely configured structure of social belongingness is fractured by these ingroup divisions, resulting in one's "practical explosion" of this process.

In his text, *Mutual Radicalization: How Groups and Nations Drive each Other to Extremes*, Moghaddam (2018) applies this ingroup/outgroup phenomenology to the process of what he calls mutual radicalization and violent extremism. Moghaddam observes that "mutual radicalization highlights a destructive process that can become self-perpetuating, self-contained, and independent from ideology other characteristics of the group" (p. 6). He then makes the distinction between motivation, reason, and the lack of rationality, which seems to perpetuate this type of radicalization and the violence which follows and then offers what he identifies as the psychological factors concerning the process—or phenomenology—of mutual radicalization.

Moghaddam turns to cognitive psychology by which to situate his discussion. He specifically focuses on the strand of cognitive psychology that is most concerned with cognition and its relation to "often nonconscious motivations and emotions" (Moghaddam, 2018, p. 25). He has particular interest in the construct of "cogitative dissonance" originally offered by Festinger, a construct that would later prove to be influential relative to the theory of motivated reasoning. Moghaddam (2018) describes motivated reasoning as "the tendency for people to be directed by prior motivations and associated emotions when they think through issues and problem-solve" (p. 25). Moghaddam applies the theory of motivated reasoning to his model of mutual radicalization.

He begins by observing that the process of mutual radicalization will consistently move through three distinct stages, with each stage consisting of four different steps, which may or may not be witnessed in every case examined by this model. The stage of Group Mobilization begins the process whereby ingroup and outgroup identifies become configured by a process which employs existing stereotypes by which to construct the "meaning" of each group. "Categorization results in a tendency to exaggerate differences between groups and minimize differences within groups: 'they, those others,' are all the same and different from us" (Moghaddam, 2018, p. 31). The tendency to exaggerate differences often emerges when some degree of social competition or struggle begins to emerge; as this process of social competition develops and intensifies, the distinction between ingroup/outgroup identification and orientation deepens as well.

Though Moghaddam conceptualizes this process as irrational, for its inability to recognize mutual benefits, which both groups share, he seems to overlook how meaning all too often circumvents and manipulates "rationality," or the process of "rational decision-making." However, this observation is not to imply that such a process is by definition irrational. It is not. To argue that rationality may only be configured by a specific set of pre-determined a priori established possibilities simply resorts to a specific type of philosophical reductionism that must objectify the construct of rationality in very limited ways to reach its desired conclusion (MacIntyre, 1988). The individual who continues to use heroin, for example, because he or she has no real desire to stop using that drug is not really being irrational because of their continued use; if only treating such addictions was that easy. A similar dynamic is likely present in the Group Mobilization process identified by Moghaddam.

Taken from a phenomenological perspective, the construct of motivated reasoning is simply an example of the social construction of reality. As such, experience and the shared meaning of social existence are what drives this process of "motivated reason." Meaning construction is usually contextual and always taken up from a very specific point view. The "reason" or "rationality" which emerges from this type of meaning-generating process will reflect the place from which the social world becomes accessible and that place is rarely apolitical. The "rational" embrace of shared benefit is unlikely even to be recognized in certain examples of ingroup/outgroup conflict, given the degree of unresolved social animosities. Moghaddam's lament concerning the inability to recognize the realization of shared benefit is not unreasonable, but it is unrealistic. Apolitical solutions to political conflict cannot be resolved without the resolution of those conditions that drive the phenomenology of this type of social radicalization.

The second stage of mutual radicalization is identified by Moghaddam as Extreme Ingroup Cohesion. In this stage, a greater focus is placed on group cohesion, which results in a more aggressive stance toward creating and strengthening group obedience and conformity (Moghaddam, 2018). Central to this process is the way in which the ideology of the group is employed to configure ingroup/outgroup identity in more ethnically specific ways. As conflict between groups continues to escalate, the need for more aggressive strategies of compliance are required to remove voices of moderation and better to insure greater control of group dynamics.

For Salifist Jihadi groups like IS and al-Qaeda, the need to strengthen group obedience and conformity is probably more necessary than it is for alt-right groups, given the strong cultural legitimacy and visibility that Islam enjoys in a variety of cultures worldwide.[1] It could also be argued that the Group Mobilization stage for these groups to some degree has already occurred and as a result is focused on consolidating group identity and obedience from the perspective of its very conservative interpretation of the Holy Qur'an. However, given that this interpretation of the Holy Qur'an is not widely shared by the faith community or *ummah* the process of group conformity becomes much more difficult to achieve, particularly when these specific "constructions" related to the interpretation of this sacred text are challenged from a variety of sources.

A similar challenge exists for alt-right and neo-Nazi groups insofar as neo-Nazi ideology is not well supported in Europe, the U.S., or elsewhere; however, this lack of widespread public support, has not prevented the reemergence of various right-wing political groups and authoritarian

---

[1] Though this idea will be explored more thorough in subsequent chapters, it is perhaps helpful to briefly discuss this point here.

attitudes from re-appearing in Europe, the U.S., and elsewhere. It is also important to note that for these groups, Group Mobilization and Extreme Ingroup Cohesion has been greatly aided by the opportunities provided by the internet and various social media outlets. Group Mobilization can take place online and Extreme Ingroup Cohesion can be developed through the availability of posted ideologically based materials of various kinds; these materials are then discussed in online chat sites and blogs, which helps to clarify further the intensity of these beliefs, while continuing to identify outgroup enemies.

In each of the examples briefly discussed above, the process of Extreme Group Cohesion helps to configure outgroup adversaries, while using a variety of rationales to justify the continuation of violent acts against these identified enemies. Though these violent responses continue to evoke some degree of physical response by the identified adversary, these responses are used as further evidence for the dispositional evil of their opponent and as the rationale by which to continue the fight.

The last stage of the radicalization process is identified by Moghaddam as Antagonistic Identity Transformation:

> Collective identity transformation becomes an even more dominant theme during Stage 3, which begins with each group showing more extreme reactions to the perceived outgroup threat. An echo chamber develops within each group, so that group members constantly hear about serious threats not necessarily from outside, but from echoes of what they themselves have been shouting to others. (Moghaddam, 2018, p. 34)

As these perceived threats continue, so too does the growing animosity between these groups; however, as Moghaddam powerfully observes, the echo chamber effect does not need to reflect what is actually true. Once these socially constructed "subject" positions have been established, this echoed discourse simply reinforces what already is believed to be the truth. In fact, it is preciously these socially constructed certainties, which gives the echo chamber its legitimacy. A concomitant result of this meaning-generating process is the way in which it marginalizes and vilifies those more "moderate" voices within these groups, who seek a different resolution of the current conflict.

Moghaddam's model for mutual radicalization captures the powerful phenomenology, which develops between social groups and evolves over time based on the perception of ongoing existing threats. He applies his model to a variety of social contexts, both domestic and international, by which his construct of mutual radicalization is applied. With these examples, he identifies how these processes have developed based upon the social context from which it emerged. Whether this exploration is focused on the Israeli-Palestine conflict, the U.S./Iranian relationship since 1953, the current dynamics related to the current administration of Donald Trump, or many of the other examples provided, it remains fundamentally predicated upon a co-constituted process of social meaning, which this phenomenology reveals. Taken from this perspective, the process of mutual radicalization becomes a specific example of how unresolved social strains become utilized by competing groups to drive subsequent conflict.

In his article, A General Strain Theory (GST of Terrorism, Agnew (2010) explores the phenomenon of terrorism. Agnew (2010) observes that "Terrorism is most likely to result from the experience of 'collective strains' or strains experienced by the members of an identifiable group or collectivity, most often a race/ethnic, religious, class, political, and/or territorial group" (p. 136). However, the experience of collective strain does not necessarily result in a collective response by those forced to endure the same. Though the collective group is likely to experience this type of strain in more or less the same way, the specific socially constructed meaning of this event will emerge from very specific points of view within this group dynamic. As was witnessed with Moghaddam's construct of Group Mobilization, the collective experience of strain or social threat will help to strengthen group cohesion but will not necessarily result in a definitive or unchallenged construction of this experience. As the frequency, intensity and regularity of these social strains develop, so too does the shared social meaning of the experience.

Agnew (2010) defines strains as a set of conditions or experiences that individuals generally dislike (p. 135). These experiences are perceived as so painful or humiliating that a response is necessary to alleviate the negative feelings they evoke. These strains may be objective, subjective, vicarious, or anticipatory in nature, but all are made meaningful from the specific subjective perspective of the individual confronted by this experience. Though Agnew includes the construct of "objective strain" for specific theoretical and methodological purposes, it is superfluous to the phenomenology it describes.

Whether the experience of strain is subjective, vicarious, or anticipatory, it must be in relation to some perceived event or situation that really is not separable from this process of perception. The need for these perceptual distinctions seems to address a methodological concern that never sufficiently addresses the underlying phenomenological structure of these experiences. Regardless the specific construct of strain under consideration, all become meaningful based upon the perspective(s) provided by the individual(s). How the specific meaning of these experiences is constructed will have a major psychological influence on how these strains are resolved.

Though a phenomenological approach to the experience of strain may remove it somewhat from its original theoretical frame of reference, it still can be successfully employed in the study of the terrorism. In fact, it could be argued that the general constructs of subjective, vicarious, or anticipatory strains, when taken up phenomenologically and applied to the phenomenon of terrorism, help to identify the experiential contours of this event. Taken from this perspective, subjective, anticipatory, and vicarious strains, rather than being viewed as separate isolated experiences, reflect the complexity of the phenomenology of terrorism, which eludes any simplistic conclusion.

If we stay within the perspective of the social construction of strain as this relates to the phenomenon of terrorism, Agnew's descriptive constructs of this experience provide some important insights into this topic. In most, if not all examples of violent terrorism, some configuration of the experience of subjective, anticipatory, or vicarious strain(s) is offered by which to justify the group's specific response to the same. How these events and experiences are ultimately constructed become specifically meaningful relative to the context from which they emerge. Whether the specific response employed is provided by a terrorist organization or a formal state actor,[2] it is likely delivered from one of the general constructs of strain discussed above.

---

[2] It is essential that the actions of a given state are included here, or else, we fall into the well-worn trap of privileging certain perspectives over those that tend to contradict certain established

However, the specific manifestation of strain, be it anticipatory, subjective, or vicarious, when situated within the phenomenology of terrorism, is often configured as an individual response to a collective threat that can no longer be tolerated. Taken from this perspective, the experience of strain becomes configured as a collective threat that effects the whole community and not just a specific individual. My experience of this example of social strain becomes translated into the experience of the entire community and as a result requires me to act, even if the specific threat has not been specifically directed at me. Such a psychological dynamic is easily witnessed in any number of terrorist-related "manifestos" and provides helpful insights into recognizing the contexts from which various types of terror-related emerge.

Morris and Crank (2011), in their article, "Toward a Phenomenology of Terrorism: Implications for Research and Policy," explore how counter-terrorism approaches to this problem, often ignore, or minimize the most important aspect of this issue: the perspective of those involved in terrorist activities. The authors make the following observation:

> The phenomenology of counter-terrorism rebuilds the identity of the terrorist into a meaningful whole – an "other" who carries a fully developed way of thinking about the world and their purpose in it. It seeks to understand their local customs, traditions, and values. This approach emphasizes the importance of understanding the social world and everyday activities by those we define as terrorist. In a word, it legitimizes the need of "perception" to fully understand and counter terrorists/insurgent groups. (Morris & Crank, 2011, p. 225)

The significance which Morris & Crank place on the importance of understanding the socially constructed meanings of a given society or specific group within that society should not be underestimated or ignored. How the individual constructs and takes up their world is fundamentally related to the process of social or nomic ordering that provides that identity its very reason to be. Two-dimensional caricatures of

---

political interests of a given country or group. This observation is not intended to retreat into an untenable relativism; rather, it is simply to remain cognizant of the fact that this type of violent behavior cannot be taken up in isolation.

2 What's in a Name: Constructing Terrorism

images of "evil doers" may provide a degree of psychological cover for those perplexed about the dynamic of contemporary terrorism but will do little in facilitating a greater understanding of the problem or its solution.

Throughout the above discussion, the inability to construct an effective definition for terrorism has been explored and that inability must be fundamentally situated within the unwillingness to view the perpetrators of these violent acts as all too human as well. Though a phenomenological approach to terrorism may complicate further an already complex phenomenon, it also provides an important philosophical foundation by which to better answer the question. As Crank & Morris observe, no truly legitimate response to terrorism can be possible, if it ignores the process by which such actions have become meaningful and necessary for those willing in some cases to give up their lives for that cause.

Given the continual failures in successfully constructing a definition for terrorism, another one will not be offered here, at least not in any categorical way. However, perhaps a definition of terrorism is not what is really needed. Defining terrorism becomes the goal, becomes the conclusion that we need, a type of scholarly certainty to what appears incomprehensible. What phenomenology offers is not a definition, but a process of unfolding meaning, which emerges from a variety of social perspectives that at times result in the horrific events of this type of violence.

However, our ability to successfully construct the terrorist identity and understand this way of thinking is not in itself a sufficient strategy by which to understand this process; if we begin with the construct of "terrorist," or the construct of "terrorist identity," our concluding observations will likely reflect pre-existing attitudes or beliefs that reveal more about our process of social construction than it does about the individual or group under study. Terrorist activities or behaviors are more likely to emerge at the end of this hermeneutic process and not at its beginning. When we begin with the construct of "terrorist" identity, we effectively erase all that has come before, and construct a paradigm of strategic practice, which actually allows us to do so.

Agamben (2009), in his text, *The Signature of all Things: On Method*, explores the construct of paradigm offered by Kuhn (1962) in his seminal text, *The Structure of Scientific Revolutions*. Agamben (2009) observes that

Kuhn "used the concept of paradigm in two different senses" (p. 11). Kuhn's first use of paradigm is concerned with the intellectual practices and methods of a given community of practitioners and thinkers, which all members more or less accept (Agamben, 2009). The second use of the construct reflects the identification of a "single case that by its repeatability acquires the capacity to model tacitly the behavior and research practices of scientists" (Agamben 2009, p. 11). It is with this second use of paradigm where the construct of "terrorist identity" becomes problematic.

It could be argued that this notion of "repeatability" has become one of the core barriers to not only a successful resolution to the definitional difficulties related to terrorism but also may help to hinder a more thorough understanding of those underlying differences that exist between these various groups and the individual identities this process helps to create. To begin with, the premise of a "terrorist" identity by definition implies a fixed sense of self, rather than a process of identity development that culminates in this specific manifestation of self-understanding. Though the authors are correct in observing the need to situate individual identity within social context, the resultant emerging "self" still remains "fluidly constructed" by a variety of competing points of view which is central to this phenomenological process.

Further Impediments to Defining Terrorism

Perhaps one of the core difficulties in defining terrorism is less with its conceptual challenges as it is with how these conceptual constructs are applied to specific groups. As has been discussed above, any legitimate definition of terrorism must be depoliticized; however, the problem becomes, how can this be legitimately accomplished when applied to groups, who are defined as terrorist organizations? For example, is the Kurdistan Workers' Party (PKK) and their Syrian counterpart the Peoples Protection Units (YPG) terrorist organizations or a collection of forces seeking Kurdish independence? Though from the perspectives of the Turkish and Syrian governments, these groups would certainly be viewed as terrorist organizations; however, during the rise of ISIS and the Islamic

State, the PKK and the YPG played significant roles in stopping the advance of IS in both Iraq and Syria (Kepel, 2020).

Perhaps if one was to use Kuhn's (1962) notion of repeatability as it applies to the attempted construction of terrorism, it would be the Kurdish example: these constructs are simply not reducible to singular conclusions. In fact, what the current contemporary environment may be witnessing is the transformation of traditional terror groups into insurgent forces often linked or collaborated with traditional state actors. Taken from this perspective, it is not at all surprising that both Syria and Turkey, generally considered adversaries in the region, both provided support to IS in its fight against the Kurdish forces in Syria, particularly in those areas adjacent to the Turkish southern border:

> Although the definition of a terrorist remains highly controversial and subjective, the systematic sponsoring of "freedom fighters" employing terrorist tactics to achieve ideopolitical goals has developed into an effort to disrupt public law and order in its immediate neighborhood and overseas. (Krieg & Rickli, 2019)

As Krieg and Rickli (2019) as well as others have observed (Ghattas, 2020; Kepel, 2020), numerous state actors have employed and supported non-state organizations as proxy forces in the pursuit of national and regional agendas. However, the relationship between these surrogate forces and their state-sponsored benefactors takes on various forms and strategic importance, the use of such arrangements allows for the extension of state(s) interests without the need to employ their own military resources in these operations. As a result, a complex and often contradictory set of dynamics emerge, which makes it difficult to distinguish between state actors, insurgency, or terrorism. Are these military operations acts of terrorism, or terror-related strategies utilized by non-state actors in the employee of regional benefactors interested in waging a type of undeclared war related to shared regional and international interests?[3]

---

[3] This distinction is not easy to untangle or easy to resolve. The relationship between various non-state actors and state supporters does seem to reflect some of the similarities, which existed during the Cold War, except the current relationships seem to be constructed more loosely. Whereas with the Cold War, these relationships were more clearly defined and acknowledged, within the current

Similar difficulties have been witnessed around the constructs of "political Islam" and lone wolf terrorism.

Lone Wolf Terrorism

In the post-9/11 age, the construct of the lone wolf terrorist has gained a great deal of popularity and notoriety. The lone wolf terrorist is described as an unaffiliated individual with extremist political or religious views, who performs acts of violence, without the support of another individual or group (Hamm & Spaaij, 2017). Such an individual is believed to plan, target, and perform the attack without any supervisory oversight from any organized group, even when this same individual claims to be acting in some way on the group's behalf or in fidelity with their stated beliefs and goals (Hamm & Spaaij, 2017). The main distinction here seems to be focused upon whether or not the lone wolf actor has had any direct interaction or instruction from an existing political or religious terror organization. However, this distinction seems less relevant in the digital age.

If the internet and its numerous social media outlets have provided anything to the contemporary context of terror-based radicalization, it is that the direct interaction with individual group members is no longer necessary. In fact, it could be easily argued that social media platforms have made it increasingly easier for individuals to access these sites without fear of immediate apprehension by government or policing organizations. It has also easily overcome issues related to distance, linguistic accessibility, and the ability to proliferate its message to millions of viewers in a very short period of time. Furthermore, the interaction with a "real" member of the group is superfluous insofar as one can easily access extensive audio, video, and textual content outlining the group's mission and set of beliefs that clearly provides a far more powerful visceral impact; an impact that would likely not be present in the same way within a more traditional face-to-face interaction.

---

environment, ideological compatibility appears to be less important than is political expediency and specific group interests of the moment.

Taken from this perspective, the online content provided by these groups, in all of its various manifestations, is really all that is necessary for individuals to be radicalized by this process. The strategic significance of this availability and accessibility, which these online sites provide, was powerfully witnessed and manipulated by the Islamic State. IS was able to utilize the fact of its rapid military successes in Northern Iraq and later in Syria to great advantage by establishing the "legitimacy" of its emerging "brand" and its ability to provide potential supporters, particularly those living in Australia, Canada, Western Europe, and the U.S.—"proof" of its power and evolving success (Atwan, 2015; Clarke, 2019; Ostovar, 2017; Pokalova, 2020; Winkler & Pieslak, 2020). It also allowed supporters not able to join the caliphate to perform acts of violence in the group's name without ever needing to make the potentially difficult journey to the region.

One of the main distinctions that is often made between more traditional members of a terror organization and the lone wolf terrorist is the degree of autonomy enjoyed by the latter. The lone wolf terrorist can determine both the target and mode of attack and can do so without concern of being overruled by the supervising authority of the group. Additionally, this attack can be performed in the name of al-Qaeda or IS or for any other group to which the individual identifies without any actual contact or official affiliation with the same. In fact, groups like IS and to a lesser degree al-Qaeda have encouraged such individuals to carry out attacks in their name.

Though it is certainly true that some individuals will not fall under the more general structure briefly outlined above, it is equally true that all of these individuals experience some degree of allegiance to these groups without ever being physically present in their ranks. As a result, the phenomenology of this experience is structured by one's encounter with the surrogate presencing of the group and its system of beliefs or nomic ordering, which the net provides. Taken from this perspective, the internet is no longer simply a vehicle for this process; rather it becomes a type of "virtual patron," which helps to create and solidify this relationship. This type of surrogate relationship has a degree of similarity with more traditional examples of this construct.

In discussing the various types or examples of surrogacy, Krieg and Rickli (2019) make the following observation:

> The variation in the form of surrogacy arises from the degree by which synergy between the strategic or operational command of the patron and the executive forces of the surrogate is direct, indirect, or coincidental. The higher the degree of cooperation between patron and surrogate, the more the former has control over surrogate operations. Conversely, the more the surrogate retains control over his own operations, the less direct-surrogate relations are. In some cases neither direct or nor indirect links between the patron and the surrogate exist, making the form of surrogacy entirely coincidental. (p. 23)

The dynamic described by the authors as it relates to patron/surrogate relationships can also be applied to the concept of digitally radicalized individual.

By conceptualizing the process of digital radicalization as a set of relational encounters that are either direct, indirect, or coincidental, a greater degree of clarity to this type of phenomenological experience can be witnessed. For those individuals who seek a more cooperative relationship with their "digital patron," a more direct type of surrogate encounter is recognized. These individuals likely reside far from the areas of control of their patron, but direct cooperation still exits, and various types of specific resources are likely provided by the patron for these operations to be launched. This group is likely to include individuals who were at one time directly involved in the patron's area of interest, but now reside in their home countries, where they continue to act cooperatively with this group.

Indirect cooperation with a patron probably best describes a certain configuration of the "lone wolf terrorist," who perceives some degree of connection and fidelity to the patron group and its leadership, but has not formally joined that organization; this allows these individuals to retain control over the specifics of their operation while still experiencing a degree of fidelity to a "larger cause." This type of indirect relationship with the patron is often witnessed with terror groups of the far-right. For these groups, various digital social media sites tend to become the structuring hub for this type of nomic ordering. Serving as the "virtual patron," this nomic process provides a configuring of group values and beliefs, while also identifying those who have been deemed as legitimate targets for liquidation. Similarly, both al-Qaeda and IS have used this indirect surrogate approach to encourage individuals to pursue jihad by whatever means that they have available to them.

The coincidental surrogate is the type of relationship that is lacking any direct lines of communication and may unintentionally aid one's adversary (Krieg & Rickli, 2019). The authors provided this example of their concept:

> In the Syrian Civil War, Hezbollah coincidentally advances the interests of its archenemy Israel by guaranteeing the survival of the Assad regime against Salafi jihadists, who for Israel are arguably the worse of two evils. (Krieg & Rickli, 2019, p. 27)

Taken from this example, the coincidental surrogate emerges as the actor who receives some degree of benefit from a pre-exiting client-patron relationship in which they are not directly involved. When we apply this construct to the individual a similar type of pattern can be witnessed.

If the main descriptive characteristic of the coincidental surrogate is as described above, then a number of appropriate examples come to mind. The government raids on the Randy Weaver property at Ruby Ridge, ID in 1992 and the military-like assault on David Koresh and his Branch Davidian compound located in Waco, TX in 1993, had the unintended result of fueling the far-right anti-government movement in the U.S., which resulted in the bombing of the Alfred P. Murrah Federal Building in Oklahoma City, OK in 1995 by former U.S. Army Sargent Timothy McVeigh, who was later executed for that crime. More recently, Dylann Roof entered the historic Emanuel African Methodist Episcopal Church located in Charlestown SC, killing nine and wounding one in 2015. When asked why he committed such a crime, he simply stated that it was due to the killing of Trayvon Martin by George Zimmerman. However, his reasoning was based on the fact that black individuals are killing and raping whites daily and something needed to be done to protect white folks and straight a race war (Polizzi, 2012, 2020).

Given the unpredictability of the coincidental surrogate, particularly when these characteristics are situated within the perspective of a single individual, they become more difficult to stop. When viewed from the perspective offered by Krieg and Rickli (2019), the current contemporary environment of the Middle East and Near East does help to make possible the type of coincidental surrogate they identify; however, it is much more likely to have powerful effects on individuals, who can easily access online various text-based and audio-visual materials along with the numerous social media outlets and discussion boards and be transformed by them. Unlike more traditional patron/surrogate relationships, which place immediate importance on a specific situation or immediate objective and tend to tolerate a certain degree of unintended benefit to an adversary, such a dynamic is likely rarely present for the coincidental individual surrogate.

Whether one is describing a direct, indirect, or coincidental example of surrogacy, all of these are greatly enhanced by the accessibility, which the internet provides. The direct and indirect examples of this process are likely the most lasting; however, for the coincidental surrogate, a developmental process is probably more present. For the coincidental lone actor, any number of possible configurations are possible. Does this individual remain on the fringes like the more traditionally configured lone wolf actor, does he or she become more indirectly involved through a developing attraction to a specific type of online-driven operations, or do they ultimately decide to join a more established group?

What becomes the most definitive characteristic of the lone wolf actor is the rather obvious fact that he or she works alone; however, this fact is really not very helpful in providing insight into this type of perpetrator. As has been discussed above, too much is often made of the fact that the lone wolf acts without any specific guidance, instruction, or supervision from an established group structure. Though it is certainly possible for a lone wolf to act in accordance with the more traditional understanding of this type of radicalization, it is equally true, particularly in the post-9/11 age, for this same individual to act in the name of a given group without ever having formally met with group members or without ever having their specific operation formally approved before execution of the attack.

The influence of the internet and the vast network of social media networks, which it provides, has radically transformed the process by which radicalization can occur, to the extent that an individual contact is no longer even necessary to achieve that result.

Terrorism and the Construct of Political Islam

Much like the construct of lone wolf terrorism, the term Political Islam, when applied to contemporary Salifist jihadi groups, seems to be in contradiction to the way they self-identify. In its most general sense, Political Islam has been defined as a process by which Islam structures both the political and social life of a given Muslim society (Fuller, 2003). Others have argued that Islamism is "a form of instrumentalization of Islam by individuals, groups and organizations that pursue political objectives" (Denoeux as quoted in Ayoob, 2004, p. 1). However, what seems most central to these configurations of the construct of Political Islam is the desire to impose a decidedly Western Enlightenment understanding on the relationship between the political and the religious in these Muslim societies; a relationship, which has not only been rejected by many these extremist groups such as Islamic Jihad and al-Gamaa al-Islamiah of Egypt, al-Qaeda, and the Islamic State, but has been one of the rationales for their call to arms (Auf, 2016; Ayoob, 2004; Calvert, 2010; Cook, 2015; Kepel, 1993, 2020; Qutb, 2002).

However, it is also important to note that this general call to arms in the defense of this specific manifestation of the Islamic nomos is hardly a contemporary artifact of the post-9/11 environment, and should be seen as an ongoing and evolving phenomenon that has its roots in the late nineteenth and early twentieth centuries, which saw the increase in the European colonial presence in the Middle East prior to World War I and saw that presence expand in the aftermath of the collapse of the Ottoman Empire. John Esposito has observed:

> The nineteenth and twentieth centuries proved to be a period of major transformation in the history of Islam: a time of humiliation and subjugation, independence and revolution, revival and reform. Islamic history had

witnessed the emergence of Islam, its rapid and dynamic expansion, the spawning of vast Islamic civilization, but European colonialism seemed to bring that all to crashing halt. (Esposito, 1999, p. 644)

One response to the conditions both material and psychological identified by Esposito was exemplified by the emergence of Hasan al-Banna and his founding of the Society of the Muslim Brothers in Egypt in 1928.

The creation of the Society of Muslim Brothers was very much a response to the deteriorating effects imposed by the growing influence of Western economic and political interests, which al-Banna perceived was destroying the Islamic identity of Egyptian culture, and needed to be immediately confronted (Mitchell, 1993; Kepel, 1993; Sageman, 2008). al-Banna's recognition of the problem facing Egyptian society was addressed in an essay while still a student at Dar al-Ulum[4] (Mitchell, 1993). In that essay, he was asked to explain his hopes for the future. In that essay he observed

> "that my people, because of the political stages through which they have passed, the social influences which have passed through them, and under the impact of western civilization…materialist philosophy, and *franji* [foreign] traditions, have departed from the goals of their faith." As a result, the heritage of youth has been a "corrupted" faith; "doubt and perplexity" have overwhelmed them and "rather than faith there is apostasy." (Mitchell, 1993, p. 6)

Given the intensity and clarity of thought provided by al-Banna, it seems difficult to construct his position as anything but fundamentally religious. If any distinction needs to be made, it was al-Banna's recognition that Western economic and political influences represented the main threat to the Islamic nomos of Egyptian culture. The solution, therefore, by which to address this existential threat was not to be found in secular or political options; rather, it was to be found in Islam according to al-Banna's specific interpretation of the religion. From this initial position, al-Banna formed the Muslim Brothers and activity sought to confront

---

[4] While at Dar al-Ulum, al-Banna focused on Islamic studies and was also trained as a secondary school teacher (Mitchell, 1993).

the dangers, he believed, were killing the Islamic identity of Egypt and its people (Gerges, 2018; Kepel, 2020; Mitchell, 1993). al-Banna continued to expand both the legitimacy and presence of the Brothers within numerous aspects of Egyptian religious and social life, all of which being predicated upon his call for the culture to renew its faith and fidelity to the Qur'an (Mitchell, 1993). His attempts to revitalize the Islamic identity of Egyptian culture continued until his assassination, likely performed by government agents, in February of 1949, which is believed to have been in retaliation for the assassination of Prime Minister Nuqrashi Pasha, which occurred in 1948 (Mitchell, 1993).

In the aftermath of the murder of al-Banna, the Society of Muslim Brothers was disbanded and was forced underground until it reemerged in 1952 after the successful coup by the Free Officers, who brought to an end the rule of King Farouk (Mitchell, 1993). Gerges (2018) observes that members of the Ikhwan and officers in the pre-1952 Egyptian military shared a similar interest in ending the monarchy. Kepel (2020) has observed that the Brothers initially viewed Nasser as the secular arm of this movement, but soon became disappointed when Nasser failed to "install a political regime based on sharia, the Islamic law inspired by the Holy Scriptures" (Kepel, 2020, p. 12). The perceived betrayal by Nasser quickly resulted in a rapidly deteriorating relationship between the Ikhwan and the government. As political violence increased, Nasser's government brutally repressed Muslim Brotherhood members with incarceration, torture, and execution; the Brotherhood was now deemed as an illegal group, and membership could be punished by the gallows. Perhaps, the most well-known target of this repression was Sayyid Qutb who was executed in 1967.

The purpose of using the Society of Muslim Brothers as an example by which to critique the construct of Political Islam in this discussion is twofold. First, the emergence of the Muslim Brotherhood in Egypt is directly related to the perceived threat of Western political and economic interests as this related to the existential threat posed to a specific manifestation of the Islamic nomos. It is significant that in the face of this threat, al-Banna's call for Islamic renewal had a powerful resonance within Egyptian culture and its reverberations exist to this day. Secondly, the example of the Muslim Brotherhood has been used by groups outside of

Egypt to propel their own version of Islamic renewal. Even in those examples where the Brotherhood is held up as a model that should be repeated, these disagreements remain theological and not political (Anas & Hussein, 2019).

Whether the focus is on the Pakistani religious scholar Mawlana al-Mawdudi (Nasr, 1996), who was a contemporary of al-Banna, and an important influence on the work of Sayyid Qutb, or the important contemporary Islamic scholar Sheikh Abdullah Azzam, considered the father of Jihad and one of the first Arab fighters to join the Afghan jihad (Anas & Hussein, 2019; Hegghammer, 2020), Mullah Omar (Anas & Hussein, 2019), the founder of The Taliban in Afghanistan or the Grand Ayatollah Ruhollah Khomeini, what remains shared by each, albeit from different theological perspectives, is the need for a type of Islamic renewal: a renewal that is not only religious in nature and practice, but a renewal, which seeks to redefine the relationship between religious and political authority. From these perspectives, the political is reduced to a function of religious authority as ordained by sharia law (Cook, 2015). For theoreticians such as Sayyid Qutb (2002) the existing political order is viewed as creating competition between the laws of man and the laws of God.

References

Agamben, G. (2009). *The signature of things: On method* (L. D'lsanto & K. Attell, Trans.). Zone Books.

Agnew, R. (2010). A general strain theory of terrorism. *Theoretical Criminology, 14*, 131–153.

Ahmed, S. (2015). The 'emotionalization of the "war on terror"': Counterterrorism, fear, risk, insecurity and helplessness. *Criminology & Criminal Justice, 15*, 545–560.

Ahmed, S. (2018). From threat to walking corpse: Spatial disruption and the phenomenology of "living under drones". *Theory & Event, 21*, 382–410.

Anas, A., & Hussein, T. (2019). *To the Mountains: My life in Jihad, from Algeria to Afghanistan*. London, England: Hurst & Company.

Atwan, A. B. (2015). *Islamic State: The digital caliphate*. University of California Press.

Auf, Y. (2016). *Islam and Sharia Law: Constitutional and political context in Egypt* (Policy brief). Atlantic Council.
Ayoob, M. (2004). Political Islam: Image and reality. *World Policy Journal*, (Fall), 1–14.
Berger, J. M. (2018). *Extremism*. The MIT Press.
Calvert, J. (2010). *Sayyid Qutb and the origins of radical Islamism*. Columbia University Press.
Clarke, C. P. (2019). *After the caliphate*. Polity.
Cook, D. (2015). *Understanding Jihad*. University of California Press.
Daher, A. (2019). *Hezbollah: Mobilisation and power*. Oxford University Press.
Daher, J. (2016). *Hezbollah: The political economy of Lebanon's Party of God*. Pluto Books.
Esposito, J. (1999). Contemporary Islam: Reformation or revolution? In J. Esposito (Ed.), *The Oxford history of Islam* (pp. 643–690). Oxford University Press.
Farha, M. (2019). *Lebanon: The rise and fall of a secular state under siege*. Cambridge University Press.
Fuller, G. (2003). *The future of political Islam*. Palgrave Macmillan.
Gerges, F. A. (2016). *ISIS: A history*. Princeton University Press.
Gerges, F. A. (2018). *Making the Arab world: Nasser, Qutb, and the clash that shaped the Middle East*. Princeton University Press.
Ghattas, K. (2020). *Black wave: Saudi Arabia, Iran, and the forty-year rivalry that unraveled culture, religion, and the collective memory of the Middle East*. Henry Holt & Company.
Griffin, R. (2012). *Terrorist' creed: Fanatical violence and the human need for meaning*. Palgrave Macmillan.
Hamm, M., & Spaaij, R. (2017). *The age of lone wolf terrorism*. Columbia University Press.
Hegghammer, T. (2020). *The caravan: Abdallah Azzam and the rise of global jihad*. Cambridge University Press.
Hoffman, B. (2006). *Inside terrorism*. Columbia University Press.
Jacobellis v. Ohio, 378 U.S. 184 (1964).
Kepel, G. (1993). *Muslim extremism in Egypt: The prophet and pharaoh*. University of California Press.
Kepel, G. (2017). *Terror in France: The rise of jihad in the West*. Oxford University Press.
Kepel, G. (2020). *Away from chaos: The Middle East and the challenge of the West*. Columbia University Press.

Krieg, A., & Rickli, J.-M. (2019). *Surrogate warfare: The transformation of war in the twenty-first century.* Georgetown University Press.

Kuhn, T. (1962). *The structure of scientific revolutions.* Chicago University Press.

Lacher, W. (2020). *Libya's fragmentation: Structure and process in violent conflict.* I.B. Tauris.

Laqueur, W. (1999). *The new terrorism: Fanaticism and the arms of mass destruction.* Oxford University Press.

Laqueur, W., & Wall, C. (2018). *The future of terrorism: ISIS, Al-Qaeda, and the Alt-Right.* Thomas Dunne Books.

MacIntyre, A. (1988). *Whose justice? Which rationality?* University of Notre Dame.

Maruf, H., & Joseph, D. (2018). *Inside al-Shabaab: The secret history of al-Qaeda's most powerful ally.* Indiana University Press.

Mitchell, R. A. (1993). *The society of the Muslim Brothers.* Oxford University Press.

Moghaddam, F. M. (2018). *Mutual radicalization: How groups and nations drive each other to extremes.* American Psychological Association.

Morris, T., & Crank, J. (2011). Toward a phenomenology of terrorism: Implications for research and policy. *Crime, Law, Social Change, 56,* 219–242.

Nasr, R. A. (1996). *Mawdudi & the making of Islamic revivalism.* Oxford University Press.

Ostovar, A. (2017). The visual culture of jihad. In T. Hegghammer (Ed.), *Jihadi culture: The art and social practices of militant Islamists* (pp. 82–107). Cambridge University Press.

Pisoiu, D., & Prucha, N. (2014). When terrorists talk back. In D. Pisoiu (Ed.), *Arguing counter- terrorism: New perspective* (pp. 121–140). Routledge.

Pokalova, E. (2020). Online terrorist propaganda: Strategic messaging employed by al-Qaeda and ISIS. In J. Vaca (Ed.), *Online terrorist propaganda, recruitment, and radicalization* (pp. 267–290). CRC Press.

Polizzi, D. (2012). Social presence, visibility and the eye of the beholder: A phenomenology of social embodiment. In G. Yancy & J. Jones (Eds.), *Pursuing Trayvon Martin: Historical contexts and contemporary manifestations of racial dynamics* (pp. 173–183). Lexington Books.

Polizzi, D. (2020). Righteous slaughter and the phenomenology of the assailed self. In D. Polizzi (Ed.), *Jack Katz: Seduction, the street and emotion* (pp. 57–72). Emerald Publishing.

Post, J. M. (2007). *The mind of the terrorist: The psychology of terrorism from the IRA to al- Qaeda.* Palgrave Macmillan.

Quinney, R. (2000). Socialist humanism and the problem of crime: Thinking about Erich Fromm in the development of critical/peacemaking criminology. In K. Anderson & R. Quinney (Eds.), *Erich Fromm and critical criminology* (pp. 21–30).

Qutb, S. (2002). *Milestones*. Islamic Book Service.
Sageman, M. (2008). *Leaderless jihad: Terror networks in the twenty-first century*. University of Pennsylvania Press.
Schanzer, D. H. (2017). Terrorism as tactic. In M. Stohl, R. Burchill, & S. Englund (Eds.), *Constructing terrorism: An interdisciplinary approach to research and policy* (pp. 38–52). University of California Press.
Sontag, S. (2003). *Regarding the pain of others*. Picador.
Stampnitzky, L. (2017). Can terrorism by defined? In M. Stohl, R. Burchill, & S. Englund (Eds.), *Constructing terrorism: An interdisciplinary approach to research and policy* (pp. 11–20). University of California Press.
Winkler, C. K., & Pieslak, J. (2020). Daesh's multimodal strategies of online propaganda. In J. Vaca (Ed.), *Online terrorist propaganda, recruitment, and radicalization* (pp. 291–304). CRC Press.
Wolfe, V. (1938). *Three guineas*. Hogarth Press.

3

The Phenomenology of the Nomos

Nomos and Identity

As was described in Chap. 1 of this discussion, the nomos reflects a structure of social existence that is "imposed upon the discrete experiences and meanings of individuals in a given society" (Berger, 1967, p. 19). The nomic structure orders social experience, and expectation, providing culture its unique set of social characteristics, while at the same time providing the foundational ground for various manifestations of individual identity. However, as Berger (1967) observed, though this process of nomic ordering provides a comprehensive set of social meanings for various examples of discrete individual experience, it is not exhaustive in its scope. Certain examples of human experience will be situated outside of the protective canopy of this meaning-generating process and will either be marginalized, completely prohibited, or at some point be incorporated into this existing structure of nomic ordering.[1] How these examples of

---

[1] It is important to recognize that though certain lines of social experience and meaning fall outside of an existing structure of nomic ordering, this does not imply that an alternative process of nomic ordering is not taking place. As the existing process of nomic ordering evolves, certain aspects of that structure may continue to remain important for certain groups of individuals whose identity remains tied to these formally "normalized" social meanings.

social incongruency are resolved becomes very important to the phenomenology of the nomos and the potentiality of terrorism.

Though all cultures offer a structure of social meaning, which provides individual identity its sense of self and social purpose, this phenomenology is not exclusively configured by singular processes of nomic ordering. Within a given society, any number of possible nomic variants may be recognizable and embraced by the citizenry of that culture. It is possibly also true that the degree to which these variants are allowed to exist side-by-side without incident will help to reveal the degree of social stability enjoyed by that culture. If Berger (1967) is correct in observing that the process of nomic ordering is never able to situate every aspect of human experience under its canopy of social meaning, then the strategies by which these under-represented examples of individual experience are constructed and lived become highly significant relative to ongoing social stability.

When the structure of the nomos is framed within the context of the phenomenology, which it constructs, it helps to better reveal the ways in which individual meaning becomes co-constituted within that process. Such a strategy becomes relevant for the current discussion given that one's engagement with the nomos will not always reflect a consistent configuration of the same. Though a general process of nomic ordering will always be present in a given society, the specific configuration of that structure will unlikely be constructed in the same way by those claiming a fidelity to the same structure of meaning. Take for example the notion of the American nomos in the age of Trump.

How do we understand the process of nomic ordering that allows the U.S. Constitution and the battle flag of the confederacy to be held by some at the same level of symbolic regard? How do we understand the U.S. Declaration of Independence written by Thomas Jefferson (2019), which proclaims that "We hold these truths to be self-evident that all men are created equal, that they are endowed by their Creator with certain unalienable Rights, that among those are Life, Liberty, and the pursuit of Happiness" (p. 55), when these words, though certainly aspirational, were never intended to be valid for everyone in American society?

What is of course shared, by both of these examples, is the process by which social meaning becomes self-evident. However, what becomes "self-evident" to one group of individuals, is not necessarily shared by a different group, even when embracing the same nomic narrative. What are commonly identified as culture wars are actually conflicts over the ontological meanings, which construct the various possibilities for human existence and experience. How the process of nomic ordering "moves" from one set of social meanings to another, will likely determine the varying degrees of social unrest within a given culture. As the process of nomic ordering changes—be it in a more inclusive or exclusive way—the possibility for a nomic "fracture" becomes more and more likely.

The Nomic Ordering of the They-Self and Being-in-the-World

The structure of nomic ordering and the process of identity formation, which it evokes, shares a variety of phenomenological similarities with Heidegger's constructs of the they-self and being-in-the-world. As a process of nomic ordering, the they-self seeks to structure the meaning of being-in-the-world via the demands, which it imposes on human experience. Heidegger observes

> The compound expression "being-in-the-world" indicates, in the very way we have coined it, that it stands for a unified phenomenon. This primary datum must be seen as a whole. But while being-in-the-world cannot be broken up into components that may be pieced together, this does not prevent it from having a multiplicity of constitutive structural factors. (Heidegger, 2010, p. 53)

Heidegger's description of being-in-the-world as a "unified phenomenon" reveals the inseparable ontological character of human being and world but does not impose or define the ontic potentiality of that being. Though human existence always finds itself in a shared world along-side-others, the potentiality of this ontically recognized "there" is never completely foreclosed or pre-determined. As a result, the constitutive factors of being-in-the-world will always reflect a degree of ontic singularity, insofar as any given manifestation of the emerging "there" will be structured from the vantage point of one's individual engagement with their social world.

If being-in-the-world is a description of a unified ontological phenomenon, the "there" of that existence reflects the point from which being-in-the-world finds itself and takes up its projects. However, as this observation implies, though human existence always finds itself within a world, the meaning of that world reflects and reveals a multiplicity of ontic possibilities that can validate, prevent, or deny the ability to be like others are allowed to be. As a unified phenomenon, the meaning for being-in-the-world becomes structured by this process of nomic ordering, which co-constitutes the "there" of individual existence. How the individual finds himself or herself in this "there" will greatly influence the degree to which human experience will recognize itself in this structure of individual and social meaning.

What seems most central to the developmental phenomenology of insurgent or "terrorist" identities is the degree to which the current structure of nomic ordering allows for a sufficient experience of individual and social recognition, or as Berger has stated, allows one "to make sense of one's own biography" (Berger, 1967, p. 21). In the absence of such recognition, certain aspects of this fractured nomic structure may be embraced and become reconfigured as the core meaning-generating process for those feeling socially alienated from this perceived erosion of social experience and identity. Though this process does not ultimately guarantee the construction of a nomic structure, which creates "terrorist/insurgent identities," it certainly can.

One possible result of this splintering of the nomic structure is the emergence of alternative group identities, which find degrees of recognition in the process of nomic ordering they embrace. Berger (1967) observes, "Every nomos is established, over and over again, against the threat of its destruction by the anomic forces endemic to the human condition" (p. 53). However, as this process evolves, the threats, which it must confront, are often related to lingering aspects of social meaning that continue to inflict a degree of anomic force on certain groups within a given culture. As the process moves forward it would be naïve to conclude that all groups within a given society recognize the presence of these anomic threats in the same way. In fact, for some, this evolving process of nomic ordering itself becomes the configuration of the existential threat that must be defeated.

It is important to observe that how one "makes sense" of personal experience and history will often reveal multiple areas of contradiction or incongruence within the existing nomic structure. As the process of nomic ordering expands its canopy of social meaning and identity formation, it will also concomitantly evoke a possibility of alienation for those who remain connected to these now marginalized aspects of the nomic order. As individual identity finds it more difficult to make sense of its own biography within this transforming nomic structure, it will likely attempt to continue to embrace those aspects of nomic ordering that best reflect the meaning of their own existence. Certain aspects of the larger nomic structure may be retained, while very specific social meanings which are often in direct contradiction to those now embraced by the culture will now be configured as a competing nomic structure. Such a meaning-generating process has many similarities to Heidegger's construct of the they-self and its significance to being-in-the-world.

It will be recalled from the brief introduction of this concept in chapter one that Heidegger (2010) describes the they-self as that which structures the meaning of human being as a being-with. It determines what will be valued and granted success and what will not. As a result, being-in-the-world-with-others becomes constructed and recognized by this structure of being-with, which the they-self provides. From this perspective, the they-self or the process of nomic ordering which it evokes constructs the various possibilities for human experience based on the canopy of meaning which it provides; the possibility for belonging, success, or validity becomes predicated upon the degree to which being-in-the-world remains faithful to these social meanings.

Such a process of social fragmentation seems evitable given that what appears as progress for one group may be viewed by others in the same society as an example of cultural or moral decline. This splintering of the nomic structure evokes the layered quality of the they-self, and provides for being-in-the-world that point of entry from which the world is confronted and lived. As one's social identity seems to become more and more unrecognizable in an evolving context of social meaning, another manifestation of the they-self will be necessary by which to define and affirm belonging, success, and validity once again. It is not surprising therefore that some of the most extreme and violent political or religious groups often perceive themselves as living in a state of existential threat and embrace a manifestation of the they-self that not only validates their fear, but justifies the behavior they pursue by which to confront this threat.

The Apparatus of the Machine of Terrorism

Agamben (2009) observes that all of human existence finds itself within the struggle between living being and the apparatus and it is from the in-between of that struggle, which the "subject" emerges:

> [W]e have then two great classes: living beings (or substances) and apparatuses. And, between these two, as a third class, subjects. I call a subject that which results from the relation and, so to speak, from the relentless fight between living beings and apparatuses. (Agamben, 2009, p. 14)

In his attempt to expand upon what he identifies as the class of Foucauldian apparatuses, he observes that "I shall call an apparatus literally anything that has in some way the capacity to capture, orient, determine, intercept, model, control or secure the gestures, behaviors, opinions, or discourses of living beings" (Agamben, 2009, p. 14).

As is witnessed in the photographs discussed by Sontag, these images do indeed have the capacity to capture the gestures, behaviors, and opinions of living beings. The who is killing whom "qualifier" that Sontag emphasizes is the artifact of this process of subjectification, which is manufactured by this struggle with this photographic apparatus. The emerging subject, therefore, becomes configured by the structure of meaning which the apparatus seeks to impose. From this perspective, it becomes essential that what is recognized is a specific type of ethic death and not simply the tragic death of a child. In fact, once so engaged, it is likely no longer possible for many to simply view these images as a "simple" act of murder. The very recognition of victim and perpetrator immediately evokes what Agamben describes as the desubjectification of the subject.

"A desubjectifying moment is certainly implicit in every process of subjectification. As we have seen, the penitential self is constituted only through its own negation" (Agamben, 2009, pp. 20–21). However, what we see in the process of "who is killing whom" is the negation of the unworthy self,[2] the self who refuses to act, the reconstructed self of vengeance and violence; here there is nothing to repent except perhaps the unwillingness to have acted sooner. The apparatus configured by these images of violence and the terrorist machine, which drives it, no longer, constructs simply docile bodies but rather, manufactures bodies of violence. It becomes the ultimate example of desubjectification when this new emerging subject is now willing to give up his or her life to the demands imposed upon these newly fabricated selves.

The desubjectified subject of terrorism is fabricated by the apparatuses unleashed by the terrorism machine. Regardless the specific manifestation of this apparatus, be it photographic images, live video streaming, narratives of indoctrination, or specific constructions of shared lived-experience, the subject which often emerges is that of compliance and blind obedience. Social meaning and recognition become fundamentally driven by this process making it difficult to see anything other than perpetrators or victims. Taken from this perspective, the process of nomic ordering, as well as the specific ontic configuration of the they-self, both evoke powerful similarities with Agamben's configuration of the apparatus, and the fabricated "subjects" constructed by the same. Griffin (2012) describes an example of this process of nomic ordering in his important text *Terrorist Creed: Fanatical Violence and the Human Need for Meaning.*

---

[2] The notion of the unworthy self, the notion of the fabricated self of violent action, holds some similarities with Roger Griffin's construct of heroic doubling. Griffin (2012) describes this construct in the following way. "The heroic double empowered by a warrior ethos is an archetypal fantasy encountered in many epic cycles of the world's religious and oral storytelling traditions, of which the Greek legends, Norse myths, and the Hindu Mahabharata are just those better known in the West. But the heroic double also has affinities with the universal religious topos of the believer perfected through faith, devotion, and self-sacrifice, the Nietzschean 'superman,' and the 'new man' who has been the subject of totalitarian utopias of the left and right in modern times" (p. 98).

Nomic Ordering and the Fabrication of the Terrorist Self

In his text *Terrorist Creed: Fanatical Violence and the Human Need for Meaning*, Griffin offers a perspective on the understanding of radicalization and the fanatical violence this process evokes, by seeking to avoid the more familiar targets and conclusions on which more traditional studies of this topic seem to rely. Griffin (2012) observes:

> Radicalization is thus portrayed in these pages as a psychodynamic process of extraordinary intensity, transforming someone who initially feels powerless irrelevant in the face of an alien culture or a tyrannical state, or else hopelessly adrift on the boundless ocean of absurdity or decadence, into a fanatical devotee of a cause. (p. 8)

Griffin's focus on the "psychodynamic" effects of the radicalization process recognizes in the most fundamental way how individual experience and identity becomes transformed by the phenomenology this encounter evokes. However, it is also important to recognize that these experiences are not individually isolated events; rather, what becomes most transformative to this experience is the degree to which group identity recognizes the existing threat to the nomic order and seeks to act based on that realization.[3] As a result, this formerly "powerless," individual, overwhelmed by the relentless assault on social meaning and individual identity, becomes created a new, not as a singular superman, but as a warrior for a cause that transcends the facticity of his or her specific existence. Griffin situates this psychodynamic process of radicalization in the constructs of the Zealot and the Modernist.

Griffin begins his exploration of fanatical violence by situating terrorism as a type of religious zealotry, which is in the service of protecting a nomic structure under siege. Central to this phenomenological structure is the profound existential threat posed to both an existing manifestation

---

[3] Griffin's observation has some general similarities to Agnew's (2010) General Strain Theory approach to terrorism, to Moghaddam's (2018) construct of Mutual Radicalization, and the Object Relations approach offered by Jerrold Post (2008).

of the nomos—be this shared similarly by an entire culture or shared by a specific social group within the same—and those individuals whose identity is inseparably linked to the religious meaning it provides. As these threats to the existing nomic structure continue to escalate, threatening the collapse of this protective canopy, human meaning becomes similarly threatened given its inseparable connection to this network of social meaning. Griffin (2012) observes, "Most of all, the nomos protects them from the direct, unmediated and hence potentially shattering personal confrontation with the prospect of an ineluctable, absurd personal death, a realization which 'must be kept at bay at all cost'" (p. 25).

Taken from this perspective, Griffin's construct of the Zealot is one who seeks to both address the threat currently confronting the specific nomic structure to which they are inseparably tied, while also seeking to restore this process of nomic ordering to its past glory. When constructed in this way, the logic of this phenomenology is existentially rather clear: to restore the nomos, is to restore the protective canopy of meaning which the nomos provides to group identity and shared social existence. In the absence of this specific network of religiously constructed existential meaning and possibility, human existence is placed on the brink of existential annihilation. With no nomic structure to protect it, there is no longer a place of retreat, making the inevitability of a meaningless personal death unavoidable.

However, this perspective is not to argue that the loss of the religious nomos ushers in the annihilation of a given culture, though this certainly could be the result; rather, it is simply to observe that when the nomic order seeks to recreate itself, certain configurations of religious identity and practice may no longer be valued in the ways this faith community demands that it should. How this perceived threat of religious alienation is taken up will likely determine the degree to which the use of violence becomes a viable option by which to turn back this existential threat. If, for example, the emerging nomos expands in ways that continues to recognize more traditionally based religious belief and practice, while inclusively recognizing those not formerly validated by this process, then social calm may be possible. However, such a result can likely only be achieved in the absence of the demands of a very specific set of religious orthodoxy (Berger, 1967):

> Thus every nomos is an area of meaning craved out of a vast mass of meaninglessness, a small clearing of lucidity in the formless, dark, always ominous jungle. So profound is this terror of nothingness in the human psyche that, according to Berger, it produces a paradox which assumes considerable significance in understanding the radicalization process that leads to terrorism, especially martyr terrorism. (Griffin, 2012, p. 25)

If this experience of unresolvable meaninglessness is as central to this process as argued by Berger, then perhaps this paradox is neither surprising nor intolerable. What seems to be at question is not really the fear of death, but the fear of living a life so disconnected from the "sacral experience of the suprapersonal nomos," (Griffin, 2012, p. 25) that the "promise" of death offered in this religious context is no longer accessible. To give up one's life in the defense of the religious nomos is to die for a future "paradise" that the martyr will immediately experience as a reward for this act. What becomes far more intolerable for the followers of this nomic process is the confrontation of death absent the promise of paradise (Berger, 1967).

Griffin provides a variety of historical examples supporting the construct of the Zealot, who choose death over capitulation to the demands of a foreign nomos or they-self. Whether the Sicanians, the Assassins, or Chechens, all choose violent resistance or death, in their defense of their besieged nomos. In each of these examples, the attack on the nomos is the attack on the self and must be defended or risk the possibility of annihilation. To remove this cherished network of individual and social meaning is to remove the very ground on which the integrity of the self is based. For the Sicanians, who are confronted by the might of the Roman Empire, the presence of this foreign power threatens to destroy the very foundations of Judaic religious orthodoxy (Griffin, 2012). In the twelfth century, Hassan as-Sabbah, leader of the Nizari Ismailis, a branch of Shi'is Islam, used this period of conflict between Shi'ite and Sunni communities and Islam's fight against European Crusaders, to create an independent state, which would be able to free itself from the imposing influence of the Sunni nomos (Griffin, 2012). The Chechens, a more contemporary example of the construct of the Zealot offered by Griffin, seek to save their cultural nomos and Chechen identity by resisting the encroaching presence of Russian cultural and political power.[4]

What each of these examples help to clarify is the phenomenological process by which being-in-the-world and being-with takes up its lived-facticity. In the above examples, being-in-the-world-as-Sicanian, as-Assassin or as-Chechen, all reveal a specific point of access from which being-in-the-world finds itself and takes up the projects of its existence (Richardson, 2012). Though this Heideggerian read is clearly not Griffin's intent, this intervolvement between the nomos and individual identity is the general phenomenological structure for being-in-the-world-with-others. As a unified phenomenon, being-in-the-world-with-others reflects not only the inseparable relationship between individual being and social world, but the specific point from which human being finds itself along with those with whom this experience of the social is more or less shared.

As an ontological construct, being-in-the-world and being-with simply reflect the general "structure" for human being; however, as an ontological structure, it does not specify or determine the ontic characteristics or potentialities for the specific context from which being-in the-world finds itself. As a result, when being-in-the-world takes up the possibility of fanatical violence, it does so from a very specific cultural point of view, which greatly hinders any legitimate attempt to configure an understanding of terrorism that may be applied to all social contexts in the same way. Though certain general similarities may exist, their true significance can only be understood from the specific example of being-in-the-world from which they emerge. With each of the examples offered by Griffin, a very specific set of nomic threats are offered, which speak to the specific socio-religious context from which they emerge.

Griffin's configuration of the Zealot construct refers to an individual or group who employs fanatical violence, in an attempt to return the threatened nomos to its former place of social importance. Such a move is predicated upon the belief that a type of "nomic drift" has occurred which has weakened or perhaps even severed being-in-the-world's connection to

---

[4] Griffin provides a much richer historical discussion of these examples of the Zealot construct, but that detail is not necessary for the purposes of the current discussion. What is significant here is the general phenomenological structure which each of these versions of the Zealot provide and which helps to better reveal the constitutive power of the process of nomic ordering.

this life-affirming network of social and individual meaning. Taken from a Heideggerian perspective, this experience of "nomic drift" reveals the degree to which being-in-the-world has failed in its obligations to this religious manifestation of the they-self, and is now suffering the consequences for its lack of commitment to that responsibility. Those who feel complied to take up this struggle, seek to re-introduce those aspects of the nomic order, which they perceive as having been either displaced by the existing culture's unwillingness to remain faithful to this creed or by the threat posed by foreign attitudes and beliefs, which threaten to fundamentally transform the nomic identity of the current culture.

Regardless its specific manifestation, the construct of the Zealot is driven by a phenomenology of religious faith and existential necessity that demands the revitalization of an existing nomic structure. In the face of the type of alienation often experienced with the greater embrace of secular structures of meaning, be they foreign or domestic, the Zealot seeks solace in a construction of a religious past, whether actual or imagined, that will help to cease this perceived slid into a meaningless existence devoid of any connection with the sacred. A similar phenomenological structure is witnessed in Griffin's construct of the Modernist. However, unlike the Zealot, the Modernist is driven by the belief that the current nomos is no longer able to provide its necessary social functions and must be replaced.

One of the central themes related to the construct of the Modernist within Griffin's (2012) conceptualization of fanatical violence is the realization that the existing nomic structure is damaged beyond restoration. However, unlike the Zealot, the Modernist looks to the future and seeks to configure a new nomic structure more capable of providing individual identity with a more secure sense of self within the context of a more meaningful social existence. Though the Modernist may seek to restore certain aspects of the failing nomos, it will also include various attitudes and beliefs not formally contained in the former network of social meaning. Central to this process is the fact that formerly well-established structures of social meaning become so weakened by the onslaught of encroaching aspects of the modern world that they are no longer capable of proving a normative defense from these attacks and anomy is the result (Griffin, p. 51):

3 The Phenomenology of the Nomos

The most devasting nomocidal impacts of modernization have been experienced when it has been "exogenic", arriving as a by-product of imperial expansion or globalization imposed from without to impact cultures whose traditional religious nomoi were naturally evolving but intact. (Griffin, p. 52)

Griffin (2012) continues by observing,

Even where modernization is not resisted because it is an endogenic, homegrown force of change, contemporary modernity tends to erode held nomoi the possibility of communally while dissolving any prospect of metaphysical certainty. (p. 52)

Egypt[5] becomes a powerful example of Griffin's observations.

Hassan al-Banna created the Islamic Brotherhood (Ikhwan) in 1928 as a response to the "nomocidal impacts of modernization" represented by the increasing presence of British economic and cultural interests pursued by England and the subservient monarchy of King Farouk.[6] Banna feared that if these expanding cultural interests were left unchecked, the Islamic identity of Egypt as configured by the Ikhwan would be lost (Ali,

---

[5] The discussion offered here is not intended to offer a detailed historical exploration of the various developments and events, which helped to support the various manifestations of the Egyptian nomos during the periods discussed. Rather, its purpose is focused on briefly identifying the developing social phenomenology and its accompanying adumbrated variations to these competing nomic structures. For those seeking more historical detail, I would suggest some helpful texts toward that end: *The Society of the Muslim Brothers* by Richard Mitchell; *Making the Arab World: Nasser, Qutb, and the Clash that Shaped the Middle East* by Fawaz Gerges; *Muslim Extremism in Egypt: The Prophet and the Pharaoh* by Giles Kepel; *The Arab Predicament: Arab Political Thought and Practice Since 1967* by Fouad Ajami and *Black Wave: Saudi Arabia, Iran, and the Forty-Year Rivalry That Unraveled Culture, Religion, and Collective Memory in the Middle East* by Kim Ghattas, *The Muslim Brothers in Society: Everyday Politics, Social Action, and Islamism in Mubarak's Egypt* by Marie Vannetzel.

[6] It is also important to observe that the nomic structure of the Islamic Brotherhood is slightly different from the configuration of the Salifist Jihadi perspective of the same. The Islamic Brotherhood, though certainly very conservative in their interpretation of the Qur'an, differs with current examples of the Salifist Jihadi movement insofar as they are less "literal" than the Salafists in their understanding of an Islamic state or society. This version of the Islamist became more visible in Egypt during the 1970s, as a result of then President Sadat's more accommodational attitude toward the Brotherhood, which witnessed the emergence of Salifist attitudes within their ranks. It was also these more "radical" groups, who existed under the umbrella of the Ikhwan that ultimately would be responsible for the assassination of Sadat (Trager, 2016). Reem Abou-El-Fadl (2017) has observed that "Contemporary Egyptian Salafism traces its roots to Sheikh Hamid al-Fiqqi's establishment of Gam'iyyat Ansar al-Sunna in 1926" (p. 209).

2002; Gerges, 2018; Hamid, 2016; Mitchell, 1993; Trager, 2016). Concomitant with this development was the rise of anti-colonialist nationalist parties, particularly the group known as Young Egypt (Misr al-Fatat) who also wanted to put an end to British influence and the reign of King Farouk, and allow Egypt to be truly independent (Gerges, 2018; Mitchell, 1993). Though each of these groups often clashed over their conflicting views concerning the future of Egypt, they were both driven by the desire to remove Western influence and create an Egypt capable of pursuing its own interests. The domestic economic and political landscape continued to deteriorate throughout the 1940s, and with it, the legitimacy of the existing Egyptian political system; as this process of cultural unarrest continued to intensify, more radical voices of change began to gain political currency within the country (Ali, 2002; Gerges, 2018). During the last few years of the 1940s, a variety of events took place, which would fundamentally reshape the very core of Egyptian culture.

As clashes between the Ikhwan and the government of King Farouk become more and more frequent, and more and more violent in nature, al-Banna and his organization began to actively seek out military officers who shared some general agreement concerning the need to bring the reign of King Farouk to an end. In response to the emerging threat of the Islamic Brotherhood, then Prime Minister Nuqrashi demanded that the Ikhwan be disbanded in December of 1948, an order that resulted in his own death approximately two weeks later. Once a new Prime Minister was appointed, he was tasked with the job of overseeing the assassination al-Banna, which occurred in February of 1949 and was viewed as a revenge killing for the assassination of the former Prime Minister (Abed-Kotob, 1995; Ali, 2002; Gerges, 2018; Mitchell, 1993; Munson, 2001). During this same period, King Farouk in an attempt to elevate his own status in Egypt and the Arab world directed the Egyptian military to attack the new government of Israel in 1948; so sure was he of his military success that he promised victory to other Arab leaders within two weeks. However, the campaign was poorly executed, and the Egyptian military suffered a humiliating defeat; this defeat became one of the deciding factors that resulted in the Free Officers coup led by Gamal

Abdel Nasser in 1952, which successfully ended the rule of King Farouk (Gerges, 2018; Mitchell, 1993).

What the period between the introduction of the Islamic Brotherhood in 1928 and the Free Officers coup of 1952 reveals is the clash of three competing nomic structures, each of which seeking to establish its own cultural legitimacy within Egyptian society (Ali, 2002).[7] At the center of this triangulated nomic process was the existing monarchy of King Farouk, which was either viewed as a direct threat to the Islamic identity of Egyptian culture or as the political barrier to a truly independent Egypt. As a result, this reality made it much easier for the Islamic Brotherhood and certain segments of the Egyptian military as well as certain left-wing political interests to work together in ending the monarchy. However, even though each of these groups had a degree of shared purpose, particularly as this related to the removal of King Farouk; these overlapping interests were incapable of resolving the more obvious contradictions, which represented the core beliefs of each of these nomic structures.

Taken from the perspective offered by Griffin, two different manifestations of nomic ordering can be witnessed: the Zealot, presented by the increasing influence of the Islamic Brotherhood and their desire to return Egyptian culture to the authority of the Qur'an and Shari'a Law, and the Modernist, as witnessed by the secular vision of the Free Offers movement. What is perhaps one of the more interesting aspects of this process is the way in which each group sought to coop the assistance of the other, while believing that their partner in the end would recognize them as the ultimate power in Egypt. Though this shared partnership existed for a brief time during the post-coup period, this relationship quickly deteriorated when the Brotherhood realized that its vision of a "truly Islamic" Egypt was not to be (Gerges, 2018; Mitchell, 1993).

---

[7] This struggle between various iterations of the secular state and Islamism becomes possible in the twentieth century because of the perceived fading influence of Islam in those countries, which had been previously exclusively constructed by Islam and sharia. As Hamid (2016) observes in his text, Islamic exceptionalism: How the struggle over Islam is reshaping the world, "Islamism only made sense in opposition to something else—and that something else was secularism. Islam was no longer just a way of being. It was the natural order of things, and so it had to be reaffirmed and reasserted" (p. 79).

The relationship between the Brotherhood and the Nasser regime had so deteriorated that in 1954 the Nasser government banded the Ikhwan from all activities and made it illegal to be a member of that organization. The Brotherhood was demanding that the new regime be run in accordance to Shari'a Law, and the response of the regime was to ban the organization (Ali, 2002; Gerges, 2018). Much like their response to a similar order issued by then Prime Minister Nuqrashi in 1948, an attempt was made on Nasser's life, this time unsuccessful, resulting in the conviction and execution of the perpetrators and the incarceration of thousands of Muslim Brothers (Gerges, 2018). Over the next decade, many of the Brotherhood's leaders and supporters were forced to endure episodes of mass incarceration, torture, and execution.

In 1965, the regime uncovered another assassination plot targeting Nasser, resulting in the widespread incarceration, torture, and execution of Brotherhood members, the most notable of these being Sayyid Qutb, who was executed by the Nasser government on August 29, 1966 (Calvert, 2010; Khatab, 2006; Vannetzel, 2021). By 1967, the perception of Nasser as the protector of the Arab world comes to end with yet another defeat by the Israeli military (Ali, 2002; Kepel, 1993). Though now firmly within the Cold War embrace of the Soviet Union, Nasser's prestige was greatly diminished by numerous failures both domestic and international, and his combative relationship with the Brotherhood continued to intensify (Gerges, 2018) However, during the last few years of the 1960s some of this domestic intensity had diminished, but was not completely transformed until the death of Nasser in 1970 and the regime of Anwar Sadat. With Nasser gone, the Brotherhood once again dared to hope on the support of this new President (Ajami, 1992; Gerges, 2018; Kepel, 1993).

With the introduction of Anwar Sadat as the new President of Egypt in 1970, the Brotherhood was once again hopeful for the possibility of an Egypt that would embrace their call to return to the Qur'an. Sadat, in an attempt to remove himself from the legacy of the Nasserist state, sought to embrace his religious faith, while moving away from certain aspects of Arab nationalism, as a way to address the lingering fractures within the Egyptian social order in the wake of Nasser's death (Gerges, 2018; Vannetzel, 2021). Gerges (2018) describes this period as the re-Islamization of the Egyptian state, which witnessed the release of members of the Ikhwan from Egyptian prisons along with the ability to rebuild their organization and once again publish and distribute religious materials to the community at large.

During this same period, Sadat also began to end his country's relationship with the Soviet Union and began to actively move toward the U.S. He also initiated domestic economic programs focused on developing free market strategies that appeared to appeal to both his political and religious supporters. Most importantly, Sadat decided to break with his Arab allies and pursue peace with Israel in the late 1970s. During the 1970s, Sadat was able to use the status of the Brotherhood to check the continued political influence of the Egyptian left; however, over the course of that decade, Islamist support for Sadat gradually decreased, resulting ultimately in his assassination in the Fall of 1980. However, as Fouad Ajami observes in his text, *The Dream Palace of the Arabs*, the assassination of Sadat was more a warning to those who would follow and not actually an overt attempt to topple the existing power structure of the Egyptian state:

> Sadat's inheritors, the assassins hoped, would be humbled by what they had seen; they would refrain from playing with fire and from the kinds of violations Sadat (and his wife Jihan) committed against the mores of the land. (Ajami, 1999, p. 201)

In the aftermath of the assassination of Sadat, his predecessor Hosni Mubarak began his regime with a more tolerate attitude toward the Islamic Brotherhood, and appeared to heed the warning imposed by Sadat's killers. Campagna (1996) observed that Mubarak began his regime with an attitude of "accommodation" toward the Muslim Brotherhood, which seemed to exist for most of the 1980s:

> This policy, in the past, had afforded the organization wide berth to function as a technically illegal, but widely recognized, political entity, allowing the group's indirect participation in parliamentary elections and the growth of its operations in the field of social services throughout the country. (Campagna, 1996, p. 279).

However, as the Ikhwan made more vocal claims concerning their direct participation in the general election process, Mubarak gradually returned to the strategies of incarceration, torture, and execution so "effectively" used by Nasser, by which to squash these goals. (Campagna, 1996; Gerges, 2018; Kepel, 2020).

Whatever the lesson Sadat's assassins were trying to convey, Mubarak clearly did not heed it and if anything, provided him the excuse to respond to the Brotherhood with a now all too familiar iron hand. Though a great deal of internal conflict ensued within the Ikhwan community after the assassination of Sadat, Mubarak did not intend to make his predecessor's mistakes. His authoritarian regime confronted the continuing presence of the Brotherhood with brutal regularity, while also successfully side-stepping charges of human rights violations by "rationalizing" his tactics, as a necessary strategy by which to confront the domestic and international threat these individuals posed to Egypt and the world (Ajami, 1999; Campagna, 1996; Ghattas, 2020). However, this all ended when the Arab Spring reached Egypt, after a brief period of rising civil unrest, Mubarak was removed from power by The Supreme Counsel of the Armed Forces in 2011.

In the aftermath of the removal and arrest of Hosni Mubarak, The Supreme Counsel of the Armed Forces led by General Hussein Tantawi began the process by which parliamentary and presidential elections would be held (Kepel, 2020; Trager, 2016). Though this announcement was positively greeted by the Muslim Brotherhood, it was negatively perceived by many of the competing political parties, who would not be able to match the organizational and financial strength enjoyed by the Ikhwan:

> Building on their religious appeal and long-standing social networks, Islamists dominated Egyptian politics after the uprising. They established new parties, participated ardently in elections, and became heavily involved negotiating the road map of the transition with the military. (al-Anani, 2015)

As a result, Mohamed Morsi, a longtime member of the Islamic Brotherhood and candidate for the newly created Freedom and Justice Party, became the first freely elected president of Egypt approximately one year later (Trager, 2016; Vannetzel, 2021). Once in power, the Ikhwan under the rule of Morsi sought to incorporate a wide variety of social changes reflected in their interpretation of the Qur'an and place all of the Egyptian legal system under the authority of Shari'a Law (Gerges, 2018; Kepel, 2020; Meital, 2013; Perlov & Winter, 2019; Trager, 2016). However, within a span of approximately twelve months, the very same political headwinds that delivered Morsi to the presidency were used by the Supreme Counsel of the Armed Forces, as the "rationale" by which to remove him from the office of the presidency. In July of 2013, Morsi was replaced as president by General Abdel Fattah el-Sissi, who Morsi had appointed as Defense Minister after his electoral victory in June of 2012. Morsi was subsequently tried and convicted on numerous charges and was sentenced to a lengthy prison term. In 2019, Morsi died of a heart attack while in court during the retrial of his case.

The events in Egypt over the last nine years, though specific to their own historical moment, share a great deal of similarities to the very brief history offered above, which began in 1928. With each iteration of this conflict of clashing nomic structures, some manifestation of the Modernist position was able to prevail over its Zealot alternative but was never able to completely quell the powerful connection this nomic structure provides those still faithful to this canopy of meaning. Though each emerging political regime sought in their own way to find some degree of accommodation with the Islamic Brotherhood, these straggles ultimately failed, resulting in the use of brutal repression by which to confront this challenge.

As was stated above, the simultaneously emerging nomic structures of the Zealot nomos represented by the Ikhwan and the Modernist nomic manifestation of the Free Officers revolution evoked a powerful cultural tension between these two-competing meaning-generating processes that offered two very different visions for the Egyptian culture. Through all of its developmental iterations, the Brotherhood actively pursued a nomic process, which situated their transformational aspirations of Egyptian society on what they viewed as a "legitimate" return to the Qur'an. Consistent with Griffin's conceptualization of the Zealot, the Brotherhood viewed the continuing encroachment of Western political ideas, be these of liberal democracy, Nasserism, and the socialist state, as the fundamental threat to the Islamic soul of the Egyptian culture. Any prospect for change, which did not embrace this goal of the return to Shari'a Law must be confronted, even if this meant incarceration and death, which it clearly did for literally tens of thousands members of the Muslim Brotherhood over the life of this organization.

The Modernist iterations of this nomic ordering begin to coalesce around the crumbling structure of the Farouk monarchy and with it the old political benefactors of that system. With the subsequent regimes of Nasser, Sadat, and Mubarak, a variety of secular nomic structures were offered to the Egyptian people by which a new manifestation of Egyptian identity could be pursued. With the emergence of each new regime, a process of nomic ordering was pursued, which sought to correct the errors of the past, while also attempting to introduce a new path for Egyptian society. Though Sadat attempted to offer a hybrid variation of these two competing nomic structures, he was ultimately unable to control the powerful forces his initial attempts of reconciliation with the Brothers would evoke and he paid for that mistake with his life.

However, the observation of Sadat's assassins provided by Ajami helps to illuminate the degree to which any nomic reconciliation of this clashing nomic structures will be possible. If Ajami's observation concerning Sadat's killers is correct, their hope becomes based on the belief that the act of assassination would transform the state in ways that the Islamic Brotherhood as a group was powerless to achieve. The humbling imposition of individual fear and not the legitimate threat of revolution was deemed the more powerful weapon against the further violation of Egyptian mores. Such a conclusion has proved to be tragically incorrect.

As was witnessed with the brutal repression of the Islamic Brotherhood by Hosni Mubarak and the rise to power of General Abdel Fattah el-Sissi, the lesson to be learned was not to be humility, but the exacting power of the state willing to employ violence when revolutionary change threatens its very existence. Though the nomic strength of the most extreme iterations of the Islamic Brotherhood remains a powerful force within Egyptian society, it has proven to be incapable of supplanting the Modernist nomic structure currently in place under the regime of General Sisi. The Brotherhood seemed to misread the depth of their electoral victory, even as their popular support seemed to erode at an increasing pace.

Each new edict from President Morsi, seeking to further Islamize Egyptian society, was resisted by larger and larger groups within the country, ultimately becoming the rational for Morsi's removal from office (Kepel, 2020; Trager, 2016; Vannetzel, 2021). Finally, the issue here does not end in the existing space separating these two nomic positions; rather, it reveals the possibility of a true hybrid manifestation of a nomic order that is capable of bridging this gap.

Nomic Ordering and the Return of the Repressed

This notion of nomic ordering and the "return of repressed" has been of interest to me for some time and seems to be a core part of the phenomenology of radicalization and terrorism. As has been argued in various ways throughout the previous two chapters, the manifestation of a specific nomic structure emerges as a co-constituting process of social meaning and identity formation. As aspects of this structure are recreated, certain closely held social beliefs formally central to this nomic process may now no longer be valued as they once were and, in some instances, may be completely invalidated by this emerging structure of social meaning. "One may add that the individual appropriates the world in conversation with others and, furthermore, that both identity and world remain real to himself only as long as he can continue that conversation" (Berger, 1967, p. 16). However, what occurs if that conversation is no longer allowed?

As nomic structures evolve and recreate the possibilities for individual identity, certain formally embraced aspects of social meaning and validation recede into the social unconscious of a given society. As a result, those aspects of the former nomic structure are either suppressed or repressed for this evolving structure of meaning, seemingly legitimating the belief that this material has now been effectively eliminated from this newly configured nomic structure. However, as it is with any material of this psychological type, it does not go away. One may conveniently attempt to embrace the strategy of "out of sight, out of mind"; but such a strategy is often unsuccessful: The repressed always returns.

It will be recalled that this phrase, the return of the repressed, was initially coined by Freud and subsequently reintroduced by Jacques Lacan. The phrase is concerned with the process by which formerly repressed unconscious material finds its way back into the conscious awareness of the individual (or nomic structure) who must now attempt to resolve the conflict this formerly repressed material now presents (Fink, 1997; Laplanche & Pontalis, 1973). In its most traditional understanding, the process of repression works as a defense mechanism, which shelters waking consciousness from the psychological implications this material threatens to impose on the now unprotected ego of the individual. The strategy employed to confront this material is rather straight forward (1) confront the contradictions which it poses to waking consciousness and resolve the conflict or (2) find a more effective strategy that will allow this material to be returned to the confines of the unconscious.

For example, we all have heard bystanders proclaim their shock and surprise to interviewing news reporters that such a violent event or crime spree could possibly happen in their neighborhood or community. The possibility for such an event(s) is repressed given that it generally does not occur there. However, when it explosively reveals itself, it is met with a sense of shock or surprise given that the "types" of people who act in this way are not part of this community. Similar attitudes were offered in the aftermath of the bombing of the Alfred P. Murrah Federal Building in Oklahoma City, where it was initially believed that the perpetrators of this offense were certainly of Arab origin; in fact, two individuals of Iraqi decent were initially taken into custody for this attack. Another more recent example can be witnessed in the Black Lives Matter Movement, which has successfully prevented these episodes of police violence to once again recede back into the unconscious of white America. When situated within the context of radicalization and terrorism, a similar dynamic can be witnessed.

What seems most significant to the phenomenology of radicalization and fanatical violence is the degree to which individual experience can situate its own biography within the evolving nomic structure. As the process of nomic ordering re-creates itself, it will likely provide new validity to formally marginalized human experience, while at the same moment, potentially devalue formerly accepted aspects of social behavior and social discourse. For the individual suddenly cut off from his or her former connection to this network of social meaning, the existential need for a shared relationality still must be satisfied. Regardless the degree to which the former nomos evolves, those discarded aspects of social meaning remain intact and do not disappear, simply because they are no longer valued in the same way.

As was observed above, this process can often result in the fragmenting of this nomic structure, which becomes a haven for those now "disenfranchised" social identities, who no longer feel as securely connected to the social order as perhaps they once did. Whether these examples of a fragmenting or co-occurring nomic structure are situated within the context of a Zealot typology, which seeks to regain one's connection to the sacred or a Modernist typology, which seeks to reincorporate the narratives of Fascism, anti-Semitism, or racism as a way to reclaim and re-vision their understanding of ethnic and religious superiority, they remain actively present regardless the actual pace of social change. However, what often occurs, particularly when these advances are now believed to be firmly entrenched within this new evolving structure of social meaning, is that these former attitudes, because of this process of nomic transformation beliefs no longer exist. Unfortunately, this belief is almost never true or at the very least, not true in the way that it is often perceived.

However, as depth psychology observes, much more is required than simply relegating undesirable material back into the confines of the individual unconscious, or the social unconscious of a given culture (Fink, 1997; Samuels, 1993, 2018; Zizek, 2008, 2016). The sudden manifestation of such materials implies that one's previous psychological defenses are no longer sufficient to contain the threat, which now confronts the core meaning of individual and social identity.[8] Though such a process is far more complex when applied to society as a whole, it can be used to

---

[8] This observation is particularly salient currently in the U.S., where issues of racism left long unresolved since its inception refuse to go away. More traditional societal distractions like professional sports are no longer willing to be used as an apparatus for this process and is now demanding that these issues finally be legitimately addressed.

help explore possible solutions to these issues. The failure to do so seems obvious.

With the powerful emergence of terrorist groups from both the alt-right and extremist versions of fundamentalist Islam, it has become abundantly clear that the emerging tensions evoked by this clashing of nomic orders must be addressed. How these tensions are resolved will determine the degree to which social calm is even possible. Such a goal will be difficult to achieve. It should be observed that the Muslim Brotherhood has been able to survive nearly ninety years of brutal repression at the hands of every regime in Egypt since the inception of that organization. In spite of this reality, the Brotherhood remains a powerful presence in that country.[9] Similarly, the reemergence of the Modernist configuration of the alt-right, has shown the same type lasting resilience, in the face of mounting "setbacks" and outright social rejection of their beliefs.

The reemergence of the alt-right, both in Europe and the U.S., reflects the "return" of certain repressed configurations of social experience that were believed to be "finished" and relegated to the confines of our social past. As the contemporary Modernist iteration of Griffin's example of fanatical violence, the alt-right in all of its various manifestations represents a network of socially shared perceptions, which are focused on specific constructions of ethnicity, gender, political orientation, and religious affiliation, to which they feel most threatened. As the process of nomic ordering drifts farther and farther away from the core beliefs of this marginalized nomic structure, those identities most firmly connected to this network of social meaning have often responded with increasing attacks of violence over the last three or four decades. As such, the targets of these attacks have been directed toward those groups deemed most responsible

---

[9] It should also be noted that even though this manifestation of the Islamic nomos remains a viable presence within Egyptian culture, it has been unable to attract sufficient levels of support, by which to replace the various iterations of the Modernist nomos that has been able to prevent its further rise to power. Though it is certainly true that one of the reasons for this failure is directly related to the levels of state repression, which ensued once this group threatened the existing structures of power in that country, it is also true that even in the aftermath of their electoral success, their support quickly evaporated once the specific aspects of their religious agenda were put into place. Once popular unrest rose to "appropriate" levels of dissatisfaction with the direction of the country under their leadership, the Supreme Counsel of the Armed Forces used this as the rationalization by which to bring their rule to an end.

3 The Phenomenology of the Nomos

for the eroding levels social currency, this manifestation of the Modernist nomos once enjoyed (Griffin, 2012; Jardina, 2019; Perliger, 2020). Though it may not be literally correct to identify this material as technically repressed, given that these ideas never completely receded from social consciousness, the powerful contradictions they evoke must be confronted and resolved.

The horrific episodes of Modernist fanatical violence, exemplified by such individuals as Anders Behring Breivik, Dylann Roof, Robert Bowers, Brenton Tarrant, or Philip Manshaus,[10] to name just a few, all represent various manifestations of the type of fanatical violence directly employed by those who feel most "compelled" to confront this perceived threat. What is shared by the attackers in each of these terrorist killings is the belief that the targets of these attacks represented those most responsible for the current conditions confronting the recreation of this Modernist nomic structure, therefore, making their deaths "justifiable" (Archer, 2013; Jardina, 2019; Perliger, 2020; Polizzi, 2020).

Taken from the perspective of this phenomenological process, being-in-the-world-as-white-supremacist becomes "informed" and "validated" by this manifestation of the they-self, which recreates the possibilities for being-with by invalidating the very existence of those targeted for death. As these formerly "repressed" or "marginalized" racist attitudes become reconfigured within this emerging nomic structure, so does the very possibility for certain examples of human relationality.

What the phenomenology of the nomos reveals is the way in which the structure of social meaning becomes configured within the context of

---

[10] Anders Behring Breivik on July 22, 2011 killed 77 people in two different attacks in Norway and was subsequently convicted of those crimes. Dylann Roof on June 17, 2015 entered the Emanuel African Methodist Episcopal Church in Charlestown, SC and killed nine individuals and wounded eleven during an evening Bible study class he attended at that church. Robert Bowers on October 11, 2017 entered the Tree of Life Synagogue in Pittsburgh PA. and killed nine people and wounded seven others during Saturday worship services at that Synagogue. Brenton Tarrant on March 15, 2019 entered the Al Noor Mosque and the Linwood Islamic Centre in Christchurch, New Zealand during Friday prayers and opened fire on those congregations. The attacks on these two Mosques left fifty-one dead and forty injured. Even more shocking was the fact that Tarrant actually livestreamed the initial portion of the Al Noor Mosque attack and made it available on the internet. Philip Manshaus on August 10, 2019 entered the Al-Noor Islamic Centre in Oslo, Norway motivated by the terrorist attack, which occurred in Christchurch, New Zealand in March, but was apprehended upon entering that Mosque and before anyone was injured in this attack.

individual identity and experience. If this example of being-in-the-world (i.e., nomic ordering and individual experience/identity) remains intact, the social world and individual identity continue as a "unified phenomena," and human experience remains capable of pursuing its projects. However, in moments of transformation or threat, this "unified phenomena" can become fractured or fragmented and is experienced as being no longer capable of providing the same degree of psychological security, which it once did. It is in these moments when fanatical violence becomes possible.

Whether this experience of nomic threat is configured from a Zealot or Modernist perspective, both share one aspect of this process: the existing nomic structure has been so damaged that it must be either rigorously strengthened or completely reconstructed. How being-in-the-world perceives and takes up this threat will obviously be predicated upon the specific contextual aspects of this experience. These threats are experienced as so perilous given that the collapse of the nomos is also the collapse of the self and the very ground from which individual identity and meaning become possible.

References

Abed-Kotob, S. (1995). The accommodationists speak: Goals and strategies of the Muslim Brotherhood of Egypt. *International Journal of Middle East Studies, 27*, 321–339.

Abou-El-Fadl, R. (2017). Between Cairo and Washington: Sectarianism and counter-revolution in post-Mubarak Egypt. In R. Abou-El-Fadl (Ed.), *Revolutionary Egypt: Connecting domestic and international struggles* (pp. 205–231). London & New York: Routledge.

Agamben, G. (2009). *What is an apparatus? And other essays* (D. Kishik & S. Pedatella, Trans.). Stanford University Press.

Agnew, R. (2010). A general strain theory of terrorism. *Theoretical Criminology, 14*, 131–153.

Ajami, F. (1992). *The Arab predicament: Arab political thought and practice since 1967*. Cambridge University Press.

Ajami, F. (1999). *The dream of the palace: A generation's odyssey*. Vintage Books.

al-Anani, K. (2015). The rise and fall of Egypt's Muslim Brotherhood. *The Middle East Journal, 69*, 527–543.

Ali, T. (2002). *The clash of fundamentalisms: Crusades, jihads and modernity*. Verso.

Archer, T. (2013). Breivik's mindset: The counterjihad and the new transatlantic anti-Muslim Right. In M. Taylor, P. M. Currie, & D. Holbrook (Eds.), *Extreme right-wing political violence and terrorism* (pp. 169–185). Bloomsbury.

Berger, P. (1967). *The sacred canopy: Elements of a sociological theory of religion*. Anchor Books.

Calvert, J. (2010). *Sayyid Qutb and the origins of radical Islamism*. Columbia University Press.

Campagna, J. (1996). From accommodation to confrontation: The Muslim Brotherhood in the Mubarak years. *Journal of International Affairs, 50*, 278–304.

Fink, B. (1997). *A clinical introduction to Lacanian psychoanalysis: Theory and technique*. Harvard University Press.

Gerges, F. A. (2018). *Making the Arab world: Nasser, Qutb, and the clash that shaped the Middle East*. Princeton University Press.

Ghattas, K. (2020). *Black wave: Saudi Arabia, Iran, and the forty-year rivalry that unraveled culture, religion, and the collective memory of the Middle East*. Henry Holt & Company.

Griffin, R. (2012). *Terrorist creed: Fanatical violence and the human need for meaning*. Palgrave Macmillan.

Hamid, S. (2016). *Islamic exceptionalism: How the struggle over Islam is reshaping the world*. St. Martin's Press.

Heidegger, M. (2010). *Being and time* (J. Stambaugh, Trans.). SUNY Press.

Jardina, A. (2019). *White identity politics*. Cambridge University Press.

Jefferson, T. (2019). The Declaration of Independence. In Founding Fathers (Ed.), *The Declaration of Independence and the Constitution of the United States of America* (pp. 53–62). SoHo Books.

Khatab, S. (2006). *The Power of sovereignty: The political and ideological philosophy of Sayyid Qutb*. London & New York: Routledge.

Kepel, G. (1993). *Muslim extremism in Egypt: The prophet and pharaoh*. University of California Press.

Kepel, G. (2020). *Away from chaos: The Middle East and the challenge to the West*. Columbia University Press.

Laplanche, J., & Pontalis, J.-B. (1973). *The language of psycho-analysis* (D. Nicholson-Smith, Trans.). W.W. Norton & Company.

Meital, Y. (2013, July 13). Morsi's ouster and the struggle to revive the Egyptian revolution. (Institute for National Security Studies) *INSS Insight*, No. 443.

Mitchell, R. A. (1993). *The society of the Muslim Brothers*. Oxford University Press.

Moghaddam, F. M. (2018). *Mutual radicalization: How groups and nations drive each other to extremes*. American Psychological Association.

Munson, Z. (2001). Islamic mobilization: Social movement theory and the Egyptian Muslim Brotherhood. *The Sociological Quarterly, 42*, 487–510.

Perliger, A. (2020). *American zealots: Inside right-wing domestic terrorism*. Columbia University Press.

Perlov, O., & Winter, O. (2019, July 1). Mohamed Morsi: Martyr or traitor? (Institute for National Security Studies) *INSS Insight* No. 1183.

Polizzi, D. (2020). Righteous slaughter and the phenomenology of the assailed self. In D. Polizzi (Ed.), *Jack Katz: Seduction, the street and emotion* (pp. 57–72). Emerald Publishing.

Post, J. (2008). *The mind of the terrorist: The psychology of terrorism from the IRA to al-Qaeda*. New York: St. Martin's Griffin.

Richardson, J. (2012). *Heidegger*. Routledge.

Samuels, A. (1993). *The political psyche*. Routledge.

Samuels, A. (2018). *A new theory for politics*. Routledge.

Trager, E. (2016). *Arab fall: How the Muslim Brotherhood won and lost Egypt in 891 days*. Georgetown University Press.

Vannetzel, M. (2021). *The Muslim Brotherhood in society: Everyday politics, social action, and Islamism in Mubarak's Egypt*. The American University Press of Cairo.

Zizek, S. (2008). *The plague of fantasies*. Verso.

Zizek, S. (2016). *Refugees, terror and other troubles with the neighbors: Against the double blackmail*. Melville House.

4

Toward a Phenomenology of Jihad: Salifist Jihadi Perspectives

The Competing Constructions of Jihad

Perhaps no single concept within the lexicon of the phenomenology of Islamist radicalization and terrorism carries more importance or misunderstanding then does the construct of jihad. Though such disagreement over the exact meaning of a theologically structured term is certainly not a new phenomenon, these disagreements take on a very specific significance when situated within the context of the phenomenology of radicalization and terror-driven violence (Cook, 2015; El Fadl, 2007; Gerges, 2009; Juergensmeyer, 2017; al-Qaradawi, 1991). El Fadl observes:

> It won't come as a surprise that the positions of moderates and puritans on this issue are worlds apart. The problem is that the puritans speak much louder than the moderates. Puritans speak with guns; what weapons to moderates possess? (El Fadl, 2007, p. 221)

In fact, what these disagreements reveal is not simply a disagreement concerning the appropriate understanding of religious terminology; rather, they reflect in the most profound ways, the degree to which these religious claims, and the behavioral practices they validate, actually reflect the sacred authority upon which their theological legitimacy depends.

In his text, *The Great Theft: Wrestling Islam from the Extremists*, El Fadl (2007) observes:

> Jihad is a core principle in Islamic theology; the word itself literally means "to strive, to apply oneself, to struggle, to persevere. In many ways, jihad connotes a strong spiritual and material work ethic in Islam." (El Fadl, 2007, p. 221)

Mohammad in his article, The Doctrine of Jihad: An Introduction, provides a similar understanding:

> Jihad means struggle or exertion of one's power in Allah's path against that which is evil; its goal is to destroy evil, to spread belief in Allah and make His words supreme in this world. (Mohammad, 1985, p. 385)

Mohammad[1] (1985) continues his description of jihad as that which evokes the demand of self-sacrifice in the fight for "God's causes" (p. 386). He concludes by observing, "Mere brutal fighting is opposed to the whole spirit of *Jihad*" (p. 386). However, his claim represents one of the main disagreements related to the "phenomenology" of jihad.

Though certain agreement can be found concerning the belief that jihad means struggle, that same agreement becomes more difficult to achieve when one attempts to define actually what this understanding of struggle implies (Cook, 2015). Is this struggle a defensive struggle, such as the attack on the religion or the attack on a Muslim country; or is the struggle an offensive struggle directed toward the spreading of Islam to the non-believers and all those who have not accepted sharia as God's law? On the other hand, does Jihad reflect the personal struggle with sin and the path from which one becomes closer to God?

---

[1] Mohammad (1985) also explores the practice of jihad as described in the Hadith, which he identities as "the tradition or practices laid down by the Prophet" (p. 389). He further observes that "this struggle or exertion is not limited to the battlefield. Muslim jurists have also spelled out four ways to perform the Jihad obligation. These are: 1) by heart, 2) by tongue, 3) by the mind, and 4) by the sword" (Mohammad, 1985, p. 389).

4 Toward a Phenomenology of Jihad: Salifist Jihadi Perspectives

How this question is answered is as much focused upon the textual interpretation of the Qur'an, as it is on the specific phenomenology, which it evokes for the lived-experience of these faith communities. Though a variety of different, theological strategies exist by which to construct a specific meaning for jihad, a number of important theological distinctions have been identified by scholars seeking to address the misunderstanding of this religious duty. These distinctions include: is the duty of jihad defensive, or does it also require an offensive strategy that is concerned with bringing God's law to all non-believers; is the call to jihad an individual duty to address one's sins, so as to be more worthy of God's mercy or is it broader to include the sins of the community and those areas not currently under Islamic rule; is jihad an individual duty, regardless the larger opinion of the ummah, or is the call to jihad only legitimate when the faith community agrees; can jihad be called by individuals or does it remain the sole responsibility of the religious authority and caliph to determine the legitimacy of this call; and lastly, is the call to jihad a spiritual duty, also identified as The Greater Jihad, exclusively, or does the Greater Jihad and the Lower Jihad, offensive strategies designed to send God's Law, represent the complete structure of this religious duty (Cook, 2015; Gerges, 2009; Heck, 2004; Hegghammer, 2020; Juergensmeyer, 2017; Kafrawi, 1998; Mohammad, 1985; Moniruzzaman; 2008; Wagemakers, 2012).

Perhaps the most important issue to be addressed concerning this list of competing theological distinctions is concerned with how the construct of jihad is to be defined and established. Are the textual descriptions provided by the Qur'an concerning the duty of jihad a "finished" construct, therefore, requiring no further theological validation or is it dependent upon the various developmental iterations of this practice since its inception, which have changed over time? A number of religious scholars have attempted to argue that the current understanding of jihad should be focused almost exclusively on the spiritual aspects of this religious concept, while rejecting all attempts to view this process as an offensive practice. However, for Salafists and Islamists of various strips, such an interpretative process is coined as "innovation," which from this perspective is viewed as the attempt by religious authorities to usurp the textual integrity of the Qur'an and God's law, while seeking to impose their own definitional authority on this practice.

Taken from this perspective, what becomes powerfully clear is that the real disagreement concerning the practice of jihad across a variety of Islamic faith communities is not misunderstanding; rather, it is more specifically focused upon whether the Qur'an must be interpreted literally, as it is to a large degree by Salafist and Islamist groups or constructed as a topical interpretation, which is informed by historical development of the topic over time. (Kafrawi, 1998). As a result, a number of religious scholars have attempted to trace the theological development of the practice of jihad, as a strategy by which to invalidate the claims made by those, who would use this concept as a way to legitimize the violence they evoke in its name (Cook, 2015, Gerges, 2009; Juergensmeyer, 2017; Kafrawi, 1998). Though such an approach is focused upon separating the practice of jihad from the types of religious violence often attributed to it, isn't it also true that such an interpretive strategy must also remove itself from the Qur'an's specific history as well? If Islam has always been a religion of peace, how does one reconcile the violent conditions and strategies employed during its initial history? If jihad has always been viewed as defensive, how does one reconcile its spread during its formative years and how does one confront that history when attempting to invalidate those claims made by Salafist and Islamist interpretations of this practice?

One of the main claims by Salafist and Islamist believers is that it is impossible to separate the practice of jihad from its offensive applications. This position is further strengthened by the fact that ample historical evidence is provided in both the Qur'an and Hadiths, which seems to support this belief. Religious scholars such as David Cook (2015) and Mark Juergensmeyer (2017) have argued that such a history has existed almost from its beginning and was an important strategy by which the spread of Islam took place over the first seventy years of its existence. Cook (2015) observes that though one can find textual evidence concerning the nonviolent nature of this internalized spiritual warfare, "the Qur'an cannot support a reading that would make fighters and noncombatants spiritual equals" (pp. 32–33). The distinction to which Cook eludes is focused on what is identified in the Qur'an and Hadiths as the Greater and Lesser Jihad.

The constructs of Greater and Lesser Jihad reflect the spiritual and "militarist" aspects of this practice. The Greater Jihad is focused on one's

4 Toward a Phenomenology of Jihad: Salifist Jihadi Perspectives

spiritual struggle that is viewed as nonviolent and targeted toward inward concerns. However, Cook (2015) observes:

> Traditions indicating that jihad meant spiritual warfare, however, are entirely absent from any of the official, canonical collections (with the expectation of that of al-Tirmidhi, who cites "the fighter is one who fights his passions"), they appear most often in collections of ascetic material or proverbs. (p. 35)

Cook continues by observing:

> One might reasonably infer from this that the *hadith* collectors construed as illegitimate the entire line of thought lending to the conclusion that spiritual warfare is part of or equivalent to aggressive jihad. Therefore, they did not include these traditions in their collections or rate them as "sound" (meaning that a Muslim can rely upon them as authority. (p. 35)

Taken phenomenologically, one's perceived duty to jihad constructs a type of being-in-the-world-as-Muslim that also determines the types of projects that will be pursued. If one configures the duty of jihad as described in the Qur'an from a literal interpretative frame of reference, it becomes much more difficult to invalidate the offensive aspects of this construction. As a result, being-in-the-world and its projects become validated by a manifestation of an Islamic they-self, which structures the practice of jihad as both defensive and offensive in nature. Though any number of scholarly critiques have deemed the Salafist or Islamist stance invalid or illegitimate based upon their method of the topical interpretation of the Qur'an, this theoretical fact has not been terribly effective in convincing those who embrace this type of being-in-the-world-as-Muslim (Cook, 2015; Heck, 2004; Kafrawi, 1998; Moniruzzaman, 2008). When viewed from the perspective of being-in-the-world-as-Salafist, the failure to pursue offensive jihad becomes a neglected duty, which must be addressed and corrected (Juergensmeyer, 2017), just as the Prophet and his companions fought to spread God's Law across the globe, current Muslims are no less charged with the same duty.

It is also perhaps not surprising that the literal interpretative stance taken by the perspective of being-in-the-world-as-Salafist-Islamist also conveniently "invalidates" or seeks to "invalidate" any competing interpretation of the Qur'an, which disagrees with this position. As such, the manifestation of the Salafist/Islamic they-self determines what will be validated and what will not and what will be granted success and what will not (Heidegger, 2010; Richardson, 2012). Concomitant with this phenomenological structure is the way in which being-in-the-world finds itself in relation to this perception of neglected duty:

> Self-finding is the way we are affected or acted upon, in contrast with the way we reach out to act. But—critically—it is this being-affected as an element (or structure) within our intentionality, and not as an objective property. It's not that I *am in fact* determined by the past, but that I have a sense of myself as pressing ahead towards ends, as well as my sense of things as "there for" these ends. (Richardson, 2012, p. 108)

Taken from this perspective, the phenomenology of self-finding as described by Richardson (2012) becomes the ways in which we feel affected within the immediacy of our intentional relationship to our projects and social world. For being-in-the-world-as-Salafist/Islamist, the sense of being-affected becomes manifested through this notion of neglected duty, which in turn configures the thrown nature of this type of experience. "I find myself as thrown, i.e. as thrust into my present intentional situation ('the there') by forces outside and behind me" (Richardson, 2012, p. 110). Richardson (2012) continues by observing:

> I find myself not just as acting but as being-affected, as made to be in some particular way. I find myself so, precisely because the finding occurs in feeling: the manner dictates the content. (p. 110)

To find one's self thrown from the Salafist/Islamist perspective is to find one's self as being-affected by a social context that rejects the type of being-in-the-world which they embrace. Once so configured, it almost doesn't matter how this understanding is constructed. When placed in the context of defensive jihad, the need to respond violently becomes justified as a defense of Islam and a defense of ummah, which is prevented from practicing their religion as their interpretation of the Qur'an demands. If viewed from the context of offensive jihad, being-in-the-world-as-Salafist/Islamist becomes situated within the context of spreading God's Law to all communities of non-believers. As such, the notion of neglected duty becomes manifest within not only the specific understanding of jihad, but as a fundamental neglect to religious life itself.

As a result of this rigid and unbending fidelity to the Salafist/Islamist they-self, any type of theological contradiction may be offered and defended. Whether this defense be situated within the Qur'anic prohibition against executing women and children, the killing of enemy combatants that are no longer a threat on the battlefield, the prohibition against suicide or the rejection of the need for a caliph to declare jihad, all become validated within the rationale this perspective of the they-self provides. Though such theological interpretations may indeed be misunderstandings of the text of the Qur'an, those "mistakes" of interpretation have not lessened the strength these manifestations of the Islamic they-self continue to enjoy.

This discussion will now move to the phenomenology of jihad as reflected in the various texts of those individuals most influential to this religious perspective. Though this analysis will not be able to include every theological perspective related to this process, it will focus on small group perspectives that are viewed as significance voices of this specific manifestation of the Islamic they-self.[2] We will begin with a discussion of the theological perspective offered by ibn Taymiyya.

Ibn Taymiyya[3] and the Construct of Offensive Jihad

Ibn Taymiyya was a medieval theologian (1263–1328) who has become identified as one of the more influential voices of the Modern Islamic Reform Movement, which began with the introduction of Wahhabism

---

[2] Please note that leaders of al-Qaeda and ISIL, ISIS, IS, and Daesh will be included in those chapters discussing al-Qaeda and the Islamic State.

[3] The brief description related to ibn Taymiyya's influence on the Salafist movement is simply to observe the way in which current Salafist and Islamist groups have relied upon his focus on the concept of the salaf and what has come to be known as the enemy near to justify their own armed struggle against Arab governments deemed to be viewed as non-Muslim in nature. Rapoport

by Muhammad ibn Abd al-Wahhab on the Arabian Peninsula in 1734 and continues to the present day. Though almost completely ignored during his own life, as well as by Islamic scholars for literally hundreds of years after his death in 1328, Taymiyya has become recognized as one of the most currently cited authors from the medieval period (Rapoport & Ahmed, 2010). His influence has been most specifically identified within the Salifist/Islamist movements of the twentieth century, who have used certain "select" aspects of his enormous written corpse to justify the legitimacy of violent jihad (Barkindo, 2013; Benjamin & Simon, 2002).

Ibn Taymiyya's most significant influence on Salafist and Islamist groups in the twentieth century has been specifically focused on his conceptualization of the salaf and the fatwas or legal opinions he issued in the aftermath of the Mongol invasion of Syria early in the fourteenth century (Adraoui, 2019; Bori, 2010; Rapoport & Ahmed, 2010). For Taymiyya, the salaf or earliest generations of the Islamic faith community represent for him the most definitive perspective concerning the meanings for Holy Scripture (Rapoport & Ahmed, 2010):

> Instead of an encyclopedic search for the possible meanings of the Divine word, Ibn Taymiyya suggests that one should only look to the interpretations of the Qur'an transmitted by the members of the early community. As the *salaf's* understanding of the Prophetic message was by necessity superior to that of later generations, one need only verify that the report attributed to the salaf is indeed authentic for it to become authoritative. (Rapoport & Ahmed, 2010)

As a number of scholars have observed (Bori, 2010; Hoover, 2010; Rapoport & Ahmed, 2010), ibn Taymiyya's focus on the salaf sought to undermine the existing religious authority of his day and his rejection of that authority has been used by current Salafist and Islamist groups to reject current religious authority in similar ways.[4] As will be seen in the

---

and Ahmed (2010) have observed that "Yet ibn Taymiyya is more often cited than understood, constantly evoked and not sufficiently studied" (p. 4). The authors add that given the scope of this corpse, which spans thirty-five volumes, it is impossible to reduce its complexity into singular conclusions.

[4] A number of the quoted authors included in this section would likely take some issue with the accuracy of any direct connection between ibn Taymiyya and the way in which his work is currently

4 Toward a Phenomenology of Jihad: Salifist Jihadi Perspectives

discussion that follows, much of the disagreement directed toward existing Arab states by these Salafist groups is focused on this notion of interpretative innovation, which views any attempt to ignore or move away from the initial interpretations of the salaf as anti-Muslim and it is from this position that the notion of the enemy near appears to emerge (Kepel, 1993).

The notion of the enemy near seems to borrow from ibn Taymiyya legal options, which ruled that non-Muslim governments should not govern Muslim communities:

> Ibn Taimyya[5] legitimated what has been called "*jihad* within the community", stating: "It is established by the Qur'an, the Sunna, and the ijma' that one must combat whosoever departs from the law of Islam, even if he pronounces the two professions of faith." (Kepel, 2005, p. 203)

Kepel (2005) continues by observing that Egyptian jihadist Abd al-Salam Faraj used these more obscure legal rulings by which to justify the assassination of President Anwar Sadat. From Farja's perspective, the regime of Sadat was viewed as similar to the Mongol invaders from Taymiyya's time, who like Sadat were Muslim in name only:

> And just as Ibn Taimyya issued a *fatwa*—juridical ruling based on the Book—that Commanded jihad against the prince who governed according to the principles of the Mongols, so Faraj ordered a holy war against a regime that did not govern according to the shari'a alone but instead applied a legal system adulterated by Western legislation. (Kepel, 2005, pp. 200–201)

---

interpreted. However, regardless the specific scholarly accuracy of such claims, Salafis and Islamist groups of various strips have employed this work, regardless how piecemeal in its approach, to justify their current actions. A thorough exploration of these very complex issues can be found in *Ibn Taymiyya and his Times* edited by Yossef Rapoport and Shahab Ahmed on which this section has relied.

[5] I would like the reader to be aware that there appears to be a variety of different spellings for Taymiyya's name depending upon the specific author in question. Rather than use one specific spelling, the following will be used: In the material discussed in the body of the text, but not attributed by a direct quote, ibn Taymiyya or Taymiyya will be used as the source name for that material; in all other direct quotes, the spelling provided by the author will be used.

Though more could be discussed concerning ibn Taymiyya's influence on contemporary Salafist and Islamist groups and the various ways in which his work has either been taken out of context, as some scholars have alleged (Rapoport & Ahmed, 2010) or, simply superficially applied, but that to some degree actually misses the point. Academic rigor is certainly important, particularly when employed to interpret such a complex corpse as the one left by ibn Taymiyya, but I'm not certain that intellectual accuracy is the actual goal of those individuals or groups, using his work to justify their perspectives and actions. The "how" of this process is far more psychologically significant than is any authoritative scholarly determination concerning the accuracy of these interpretations. In fact, it almost becomes self-defeating given that these authoritative renderings, regardless their accuracy come from the very sources that these groups seek to invalidate. This discussion will now move to the Salafist theories of the twentieth century, beginning with the work of Mawlana Mawdudi of Pakistan.

Mawlana Mawdudi and His Islamic Revivalism

Mawlana Mawdudi, a journalist and political theorist by training and education, was born in 1903 to a religious family in the Muslim region of Hyderabad Deccan, India, and would later come to be known as one of the most influential Islamic thinkers of the twentieth century (White & Siddiqui, 2018). Mawdudi's intellectual and theological development takes shape within the context of what he called the need for a return to the original tenets of Islam. Central to Mawdudi's goal of Islamic revivalism was his desire to resuscitate the diminishing faith of the Muslim community in Islam, which he witnessed all around him. He rationalized that if he could revitalize Muslim faith, it would also help to address the declining state of Muslim power in India as well (Nasr, 1996).

Mawdudi began his project of Islamic revitalization in the late 1930s where political discontent over English colonial rule was on the rise. However, the main forces behind this discontent were driven by Hindu

4 Toward a Phenomenology of Jihad: Salifist Jihadi Perspectives

and Muslim leaders seeking to end British rule in India, but who did not share the revivalist vision which Mawdudi hoped to pursue (White & Siddiqui, 2018):

> He remained pointedly opposed to the political visions of both the Indian National Congress and the Muslim League, declaring that Muslims had little in common with the Hindus of India, while at the same time decrying the Muslim League's nationalist vision as an un-Islamic substitute for true religious devotion. (White & Siddiqui, p. 45)

Finding little commonality with the existing political system of India, Mawdudi created the Jama'at-i Islami party in 1941.

Though Mawdudi's perspective is often contextualized as an example of political Islam, a closer look at his work seems to contradict such a conclusion.[6] For Mawdudi, the goal was not simply to participate in the evolving political process of then India and later Pakistan; rather, it was to pursue a project of Islamic revitalization, which "allowed no distinction between the public and private spheres and was structured as 'an all-embracing social order where nothing is superfluous or nothing is lacking'" (White & Siddiqui, 2018, p. 47). To achieve this goal, Mawdudi sought to borrow from certain aspects of the liberal democratic traditions of the West and reincorporate these ideas within the context of his interpretation of Islam (Nasr, 1996). However, unlike other Salafist theoreticians, Mawdudi believed that the rejection of modernity was the very thing that prevented Muslim societies from regaining the glory of Islam's past:

> According to Mawdudi, modern science was not based on any particular philosophical perspective, nor did it promote a set of values or require an attitude from Muslims that could interfere with their faith. Modern science was a "body" that could accommodate any "spirit"—philosophy or value system—just as a radio could broadcast Islamic or Western messages with equal facility. (Nasr, 1996, p. 53)

---

[6] The construct of political Islam seems incapable of resolving the obvious challenges to its accuracy when situated within the context of Salafist or Islamist perspectives. As will be seen, Mawdudi's Jama 'at-I Islami party was created for the purpose of instituting the Islamic revitalization of Muslims in India and later Pakistan and was fundamentally driven by the desire to create an Islamic State. Most importantly, the employ of the political should be seen as a function by which to achieve that end, and not as an end it itself.

Mawdudi was astutely aware of the advantages Western modernization offered to what he observed as backward Muslim societies; however, he failed to accept that such an accommodation would somehow prevent the type of Islamic society he envisioned. Mawdudi simply saw no contradiction between modernization and Islamic faith. "We Muslims are therefore determined to make full use of modern knowledge but for our purposes which will be in conformity to our cultural values and ideals" (Jameelah, 1969, p. 42 as quoted in Nasr, 1996, p. 52). From this perspective, modernization simply was viewed as the vehicle by which his project of Islamic revitalization would be achieved. But make no mistake, Mawdudi's Salafist vision remained intact and without compromise.

Though Mawdudi argued for the necessity of the modernization of Islamic society, this belief was firmly situated within an interpretation of Muslim faith that connected the current historical moment to the glorified times of the Prophet and the Salaf. Central to Mawdudi's strategy of revitalizing Islam was the need to reexamine the basic structure of Islamic faith (Nasr, 1996). At the core of this reexamination of faith was the need for man's exclusive submission to God (Mawdudi, 1980):

> Islam does not consist merely in bowing [ruku'], prostration [sujud], fasting [sawm] and pilgrimage [hajj]; nor is it found in the face and dress of a man. Islam means submission to God and the Messenger. Anyone who refuses to obey them in the conduct of his life-affairs has a heart devoid of the real Islam—"faith has not yet entered their hearts." His Prayers, his Fasting and his pious appearance are nothing but deception. (Mawdudi quoted in Nasr, 1996, p. 58)

Mawdudi's call for a return to the real Islam is a call which seeks to reconstruct Muslim identity and social experience in such a way that the presence of Islam permeates every aspect of social existence; this approach, however, was viewed by domestic critics of his project as an attack on centuries of Islamic tradition. Nasr (1996) argues that Mawdudi's claim for the inseparability of religion and politics was simply not supported by centuries of Islamic tradition, which deemed this separation as a fact of history which occurred due to God's will and, therefore, divinely sanctioned. "The inseparability of religion and politics has been a part of the

4 Toward a Phenomenology of Jihad: Salifist Jihadi Perspectives

teachings of all schools of Islamic law and theology; however, it has not necessarily been maintained in Islamic history" (Nasr, 1996, p. 60). As a result, the existing religious authority in India/Pakistan during the initial stages of Mawdudi's pursuit of Islamic revitalization viewed his approach as fundamentally breaking with established Islamic tradition and viewed this approach as a new interpretation of Islam. However, for Mawdudi, his approach was "simply" seeking to address centuries of religious "innovation" that allowed for the acceptance of this illegitimate separation of the religious and political to take place; a position that places him firmly within purview of many contemporary Salafist thinkers.

The religious phenomenology which Mawdudi's project of revitalization intended was to deconstruct the very being of the contemporary Muslim subject of his day, by removing those calcified aspects of religious meaning which had become barriers to the return to God. Mawdudi also recognized that the vehicle for this return could be achieved by the appropriation of Western liberal democratic ideals, which could be reconfigured with Islamic beliefs and values, which in turn would establish an authentic Islamic state. Such a conclusion, however, seems inappropriately labeled as an example of Political Islam, for the simple reason that Mawdudi's intention was to "heal the split," which Islamic history allowed to remain unattended. Though Mawdudi's unapologetic embrace of modernism and Western political ideas cannot be legitimately contested, neither can it be legitimately denied that his easily established Salafist perspective viewed the political as the vehicle by which his religious vision was to be achieved.

In his text, *First Principles of Islam*, Mawdudi makes the following observation concerning the relationship between faith, politics, and society:

> It [the Quran[7]] is the first and primary source [of the Islamic constitution], containing as it does all the fundamental directions and instructions from God himself. The directions and instructions cover the entire gamut of

---

[7] The spelling of the term Qur'an will appear differently based on the specific author. All in-text spellings of the term that are not part of a direct quote will be spelled "Qur'an." All other spellings of the term "Qur'an" will be spelled as they appear in the quoted material provided or how it appears in the title of a published article or book.

man's existence. Herein are to be found not only directives related to individual conduct but also principles regulating all aspects of the social and cultural life of man. It has also been clearly shown therein as to why should Muslims endeavor to create and establish a State of their own. (Mawdudi, 1967 as quoted in Jackson, 2013, p. 110)

Jackson (2013) continues by observing that Mawdudi's quote seems to imply that a theocracy is the only possible alternative to the secular state; however, in his text, *Islamic Rule*, published in 1968, Mawdudi seems to take a different position:

Islamic theocracy is not controlled by a special religious group of people but by ordinary Muslims. They run it according to the Qur'an and Sunna. And if I am allowed to coin a new word, I would call it "theo-democracy". It would grant limited popular sovereignty to Muslims *under the paramount sovereignty of God* (emphasis added). (Mawdudi, 1968 as quoted in Jackson, 2013, p. 110)

Though Mawdudi's claim that religious authority would not control his Islamic theocracy, it is indeed different from the conventional sense of this term as Jackson contends (2013), but it is still a theocracy, nonetheless. By removing what he viewed as the autocratic rule by religious elite, he seeks to democratize the process of Qur'anic interpretation by giving that responsibility to the Muslim community, while retaining what seems most central to his position: the sovereignty of God. It is also interesting that Mawdudi's position is in some ways similar to the one offered by ibn Taymiyya, insofar as Taymiyya was also often contemptuous of the existing religious authority of his day and viewed them as an obstacle to his own desired return to the Qur'an. Since Mawdudi viewed the current structure of the existing religious authority of his day as a barrier to his project of Islamic revitalization, it should not be at all surprising that the theocratic model which he offers seeks to neutralize that authority.

Mawdudi's narrative of Islamic revitalization may be viewed as the apparatus employed by the Salafist-machine to re-fabricate both the Muslim subject and the social world it inhabits. By reconfiguring the

4 Toward a Phenomenology of Jihad: Salifist Jihadi Perspectives

process of nomic ordering, this new manifestation of the Islamic State and the Muslim subject encourages a return to the origin "spiritual" context of the Qur'an and Sunna, while employing modern aspects of Western-inspired liberal democratic ideas by which to bring about this transformation. Too often, the distinction concerning the mingling of the religious and the political aspects of this process gets confused by the conclusion that such a process of nomic ordering provides equal weight to both of these theoretical concepts. It simply does not. The fabrication of this revitalized Muslim subject is the result of human being's struggle with the apparatus of the sacred text of the Qur'an, which allows for the negation of the sin of failed faith and restores the individual under this submission to God's law.

Most important to this process of subjectification, which the apparatus of the Qur'an provides to this newly fabricated Muslim self, is the promise of redemption. "Indeed, every apparatus implies a process of subjectification, without which it cannot function as an apparatus of governance but, is rather reduced to a mere exercise in violence" (Agamben, 2009, p. 19). Taken from this context, redemption becomes possible as a result of the negation of the former Muslim self, which has fallen into sin. Much like Agamben's example of the Catholic confessional, this revitalized Muslim self is able to negate the former self of disbelief and sin, and once again embrace the promise of the Qur'an. Agamben (2009) observes, "The split of the subject performed by the apparatus of penance resulted therefore, in the production of a new subject, which found its real truth in the nontruth of the already repudiated sinning" (p. 20).

The reconnection to the truth of the Qur'an becomes for Mawdudi, the strategy he will employ to confront the violence evoked by the apparatuses of diminishing belief and fidelity to the sacred texts of Islam, which continue their assault on the structures of Muslim faith. The goal of this process seeks to free the Muslim self from the violence of desubjectification and by so doing return it to the promise of redemption offered by the Qur'an. The discussion will now move to the Salafist perspective offered by the Egyptian theorist Sayyid Qutb.

Sayyid Qutb: Submission, Jahiliyyah, and Jihad

Of all of the twentieth-century voices calling for a revitalization of Islam, the voice of the Egyptian Islamist Sayyid Qutb has perhaps been its most influential (Calvert, 2010; Cook, 2015; Haddad, 1983; Moussalli, 1992). Qutb witnessed what he perceived as the profound deterioration of Egyptian culture during the 1940s and blamed this failure on the secular apparatuses of societal governance, which he identified as being responsible for that decline. Significantly influenced by the work of Hasan al-Banna and Mawlana Mawdudi, Qutb believed that the solution for the cultural problems he perceived in Egyptian society could only be remedied by a return to the Qur'an. For Qutb, the Islamic society, which he envisioned, was one based on the example of the first generation of Muslims, who were able to construct a social order based upon the normative and religious values offered in the Qur'an. Qutb observes:

> [W]hat an amazing phenomenon in the history of mankind: a nation emerging from the text of a Book, living by it, and depending on its guidance as its prime source!, by which he is referring to, "the first group of Muslims {who} molded their lives according to this concept which comes directly from the Qur'an. They led mankind in a manner unparalleled in history, either before or after {but then} …later generations drifted away from the Qur'an, … {such that} today we see mankind in a miserable condition." (Qutb, as quoted in Bergesen, 2008, p. 14)

The distinction, which Qutb makes concerning the relationship between the political and the religious seems unmistakable in its structure in the above quote; the political becomes the manifestation of the Qur'an in day-to-day practice and behavior. Politics is guided and informed by the Qur'an, which is identified as the exclusive source by which this process of social ordering is to be constructed and lived. For Qutb, the distinction between an unparalleled history and the current miserable condition of humanity becomes fundamentally predicated upon the degree to which humanity has drifted from Qur'anic guidance.

4 Toward a Phenomenology of Jihad: Salifist Jihadi Perspectives

However, before a more thorough discussion of Qutb's ideas is offered, it will perhaps be helpful to explore the developmental process, which influenced Qutb's journey back to the Qur'an.

In his autobiographical text, *Child from the Village*, Qutb documents what Calvert (2010) has described as Qutb's "'awakening' from the unreflective slumber of customary rural life to a new kind of existence lived within the problematic context of the modernizing nation-state" (p. 37). Calvert (2010) continues by observing that Qutb unlike others in Egyptian society, who seemed to gravitate toward the cultural ideas of the West, sought to envision a "modernized and reformed version of the Egyptian national community," which took its inspiration from Islamic history and culture. (pp. 37–38). It was also during this period which Qutb eagerly began studying the scholarly tradition of Islam (Bergesen, 2008; Calvert, 2010; Haddad, 1983; Moussalli, 1992).

As Qutb matured both intellectually and religiously, he found himself in regular disagreement with both the governmental authorities of then King Faruq and the Western interests he supported along with the government instituted by the Free Officers coup of 1952, which ended monastic rule in Egypt (Bergesen, 2008). Initially viewed, as a go between for the Nasser regime and the Islamic Brotherhood, which he joined in 1951, Qutb believed that the Free Officers coup represented a real opportunity to realize his version of the revitalization of Islam in Egypt (Calvert, 2010; Gerges, 2018; Mitchell, 1993). However, as it become clear that there would be no return to Islam in the way he envisioned under Nasser, animosities between the Brotherhood and the regime grew, culminating in the attempted assassination of Nasser in 1954, which was met with brutal repression, incarceration, and execution of Brotherhood members believed to be part of that attempt; Qutb was one of those arrested and identified as one of the main instigators of the attempt on Naser's life. Qutb was incarcerated for approximately ten years where he wrote *In the Shadow of the Qur'an* and *Milestones*. After his release in 1962, he was rearrested and subsequently executed in August 1966 (Calvert, 2010; Gerges, 2018; Kepel, 1993; Mitchell, 1993).

Though such a short historical account of such a complex figure as Sayyid Qutb cannot do justice to that complexity,[8] its intent is simply to introduce albeit in a very limited the core ideas of his work, which still enjoys a great deal of significance today. We will now move to a discussion of Qutb's interpretation of the Oneness of God (*tawhid*) and God's Sovereignty, both of which play a fundamental role in his description of Jahili societies and his call to jihad by which to address that condition.

For Qutb, the Islamic construct of the Oneness of God seems central to the interpretative structure, which follows. Qutb defines his understanding of the Oneness of God in the following way: "The Islamic concept rests on the principle that the Divine Being is distinct from his creation. Divinity belongs exclusively to Allah Most High, while creatureliness is common to everyone and everything else" (Qutb as quoted in Bergesen, 2008, p. 15). Qutb continues by observing:

> The relationship between Allah and everything else is that of the Creator to His creatures and of the Lord to His servants. This is the first principle of the Islamic concept and all other principles follow from it. Because the Islamic concept rests on this basic principle, the Oneness of God is its most important characteristic. (Qutb as quoted in Bergesen, 2008, p. 15)

By making the distinction, which he does concerning God's relationship with everyone and everything else, Qutb constructs a very specific phenomenological relationship between God and his law and "creatures" which must submit to that law. God's Oneness is absolute, and all knowledge comes from that understanding. To submit to God is to accept the fact of His Oneness, and to enjoy the benefit that Oneness provides (Haddad, 1983; Khatab, 2006). From this perspective submission becomes a duty, which should not be questioned or examined by reason (Moussalli, 1992). Taken phenomenologically, being-in-the-world-as-Muslim from the perspective offered by Qutb becomes the point from

---

[8] For a very thorough exploration of Sayyid Qutb and his significance to the Islamist movement, I would suggest the following texts, which have been relied for this discussion: *The Sayyid Qutb Reader: Selected Writings on Politics, Religion, and Society*; *Milestones*, *In the Shadow of the Qur'an*; *Sayyid Qutb and the Origins of Radical Islam* by Jon Calvert; *Radical Islamic Fundamentalism: The Ideological and Political Discourse of Sayyid Qut*b by Ahmad Moussalli; *The Political Thought of Sayyid Qutb: The Theory of Jahiliyyah* by Sayed Khatab.

4 Toward a Phenomenology of Jihad: Salifist Jihadi Perspectives

which human being finds itself and from which its projects may be "legitimately" pursued. The significance of this stance for Qutb, and other thinkers who have argued similarly, should not be underestimated.

Perhaps most importantly, to be in the world as submissive-to-God and the exclusive knowledge that only he can provide is also to delegitimize any authoritative call or ideological perspective, which does not begin with this required duty. As a result, this call to once again submit to the Oneness of God or *tawhid* not only helps to revitalize diminished individual faith, but also challenges the very legitimacy of those social structures, which do not reflect the prescribed practices and values outlined in God's sacred text. As Moussalli (1992) observes, submission to God is the duty and practice, which informs man of its proper place. "For knowing man's place, goal, and role in this universe helps man to define his proper social and political approach and method (al-manhaj) in life" (Moussalli, 1992, p. 70).

Taken phenomenologically, "knowing man's place," evokes a very specific relationship to this sacred they-self, which determines what will be legitimized and granted success and what will not. When situated in this way, one's duty to submission is reflected in the ways in which being-in-the-world pursues its projects. However, these are not any projects, and as a result must reflect what God's law demands both individually and socially. From this perspective, every moment of existence must be focused on God's law, a demand that fundamentally removes the gap between individual and social experience. For Qutb there is none!

> What becomes actually important is not whether an act is personal or public but whether that act is in conformity with the Holy *Qur'an* and the divine law (*the shari'ah*) whose fountainhead is *tawhid*. Submission to God, therefore, is not a personal or public act but is the focal point which engulfs the Muslim society in its legislation, governance, and life. (Moussalli, 1992, p. 75)

As a "focal point which engulfs Muslim society," submission becomes the artifact which emerges from the in-between of the struggle which human being experiences when confronted by this powerful sacred apparatus and frees it from its state of desubjectification. The promise of redemption, therefore, which is predicated upon the fidelity to submission, becomes possible once the Muslim subject is freed from the debilitating process of desubjectification fabricated by innovation and the secular ideologies of the West. Once these barriers have been removed, Qutb's vision of Islam becomes possible.

Though Qutb's (2002) focus on the concepts of *jihad* and *jahili* society is perhaps better known, his understanding of *tawhid* becomes the essential foundation from which these concepts emerge. Once established, Qutb's interpretation of the Oneness of God and the relationship it creates with the Muslim subject can then begin to address those barriers which prevent this vision from coming to fruition. His deontological strategy, by which he constructs the Muslim subject, is able to reject Western secular ideological approaches to governance on the grounds that they are ill-suited for Islamic societies, while also rejecting any attempts to split the demands of religious duty into separate spheres of individual and public experience. However, given that Qutb believed in the universal legitimacy of the Qur'an, the possibility of "re-imaging" these secular ideologies remained a legitimate strategy as long as this structure of governance and the law reflected the practices and values outlined in the Qur'an (Calvert, 2010; Moussalli, 1992; Qutb, 2002).

If the Oneness of God required a submission to God's Holy text, then fidelity to any other system of living would be viewed as a violation of that duty (Qutb, 2002). It is from this vantage that Qutb can chastise jahili society,[9] while evoking the call to jihad by which to confront the conditions which this ignorance of God's law must evoke. Given that there is only one God and all fidelity must be given to him, any other established authority not divinely informed by the knowledge offered in the Qur'an is illegitimate and must not be obeyed. Qutb used this perspective to attempt to neutralize the existing religious authority and secular rule in Egypt by defining it as non-Muslim and an example of jahili society.

---

[9] Jahili society or Jahiliyyah is referred to in the Qur'an as the period of ignorance, which existed prior to the time of God's revelation to man as dictated in the Qur'an. Lay theologians like Qutb have used these passages as way to legitimize their critical view that contemporary Muslim societies are similarly inflicted by a condition of jahiliyyah.

4 Toward a Phenomenology of Jihad: Salifist Jihadi Perspectives

In his well-known text, *Milestones*, Qutb (2002) describes his interpretation of jahili or Jahiliyyah. For Qutb, jahili culture represents any authority, be that secular or religious, which fails to recognize and submit to the universal authority of God and his laws:

> Man cannot change the practice of God in the laws prevailing in the universe. It is therefore desirable that he should also follow Islam in those aspects of his life in which he is given a choice and should make the Divine the arbiter in all matters of life so that there may be harmony between man and the rest of the universe. (Qutb, 2002, p. 46)

When human being fails in this choice, it falls into what Qutb describes as jahiliyyah. In describing the phenomenology of this process, Qutb observes:

> It always takes the form of a living movement in a society which has its own leadership, its own concepts and values, and its own traditions, habits and feelings. It is an organized society and there is close cooperation and loyalty between its individuals, and is always ready and alive to defend its existence consciously or unconsciously. It crushes all elements which seem to be dangerous to its personality. (Qutb, 2002, p. 46)

Qutb's description of Jahiliyyah has a variety of similarities to Heidegger's construct of the they-self and Agamben's construct of the apparatus.

What Qutb describes is a phenomenological structure of nomic ordering that provides a proscribed meaning for individual experience, which in turn identifies the type of human being that will be allowed success and the type that will not. However, the phenomenology of such a society—that is, a "living movement" which follows manmade concepts, values, and traditions—is a society that is non-Muslim in nature given its unwillingness to submit to the divine authority of God. For Qutb (2002), such contemporary societies reflect similarly to those confronted by the Prophet Muhammad and the other great divine prophets of the Book, who confronted these faithless cultures when attempting to spread God's word. From this perspective, faith is not witnessed within the performance of specific religious rituals exclusively; rather, it becomes manifest through those practices which are formed by the community

> into an active group, and makes this faith the sole basis for the relationship between individuals and this group, its ultimate aim is to awaken the "humanity of man", to develop it, to make it powerful and strong, and to make it the most dominant factor among all aspects found in man's being. (Qutb, 2002, p. 48)

By beginning with the universal authority of God's law and sovereignty, Qutb is able to address what he perceives as two of the most detrimental aspects of the Egyptian society of his day: the continued faith in manmade authority and the failure to submit to God's law. Qutb is also able to deflect certain criticisms of his approach by claiming that the universal authority of God's law was as legitimate today as it was in the time of the Prophet. The Islamic community created by the Prophet and his compassions, therefore, becomes the universal example for all such communities to follow and not simply the example of a socio-religious arrangement that applies exclusively to its own period in history. Haddad (1983) observed that "For Qutb, Islamic society is 'not a mere historical form that is hidden in the memories of the past, it is the demand of the present and the hope of the future'" (p. 87). Qutb believed that the only requirement of the Islamic State was that it recognizes the exclusive sovereignty of God and one that rejects the possibility of the enactment of manmade law (Calvert, 2010; Haddad, 1983; Moussalli, 1992):

> For Qutb, Islamic law is not a social phenomenon but an eternal manifestation of God's will defining the duties and rights of individuals as well as the state. What this means is that legislation of the basic principles of authority, right or wrong or legality or illegality are set forth and sealed from human consideration. No matter what individuals or societies think, they cannot—or do not have the right to—make what is right wrong or what is wrong right. (Moussalli, 1992, p. 149)

As a result, Qutb is able to connect his interpretation of the Oneness of God to his "diagnosis" of jahili society, which in turn requires a return to his understanding of jihad by which to address this problem. Generally speaking, Qutb's configuration of jihad is structured to achieve two immediate and very specific goals: confront the conditions of jahili society as present in the Egypt of his day and by so doing, reestablish the authority of God's law. By configuring the "problem" in this way, Qutb constructs an alternative nomic structure, which if accepted, fabricates a new Muslim self or identity that will be employed to bring about the transformation of Egyptian society. Central to this new manifestation of the they-Self, is a version of being-in-the-world -as-Muslim that is now duty bound to submit totally to the authority of God, and to defend God's religion, which is currently under attack by the supporters of Jahiliyyah (Qutb, 2002).

Qutb views the presence of jahili society as the fundamental barrier to the enactment of God's exclusive sovereignty and sees jihad as the fundamental duty of all Muslims as the strategy by which these conditions must be addressed. In discussing this duty, Qutb observes that preaching and persuasion become the method employed to address what he identifies as incorrect or false belief; whereas jihad is employed to confront and destroy the culture of Jahili, which is imposed upon the ummah and forces it to obey the laws of man rather than the laws of God (Qutb, 2002).

Taken from the perspective offered by Qutb, the specific duties of jihad become the way in which being-in-the-world-as-Muslim finds itself and by which its projects are defined. When viewed in this way, jihad becomes an all-encompassing engagement with the social world that is exclusively focused on the submission to God's authority and the duty to spread his Holy Law. Here, there is no distinction between defensive jihad—jihad waged in the defense of Muslims or Islam—or offensive jihad—jihad waged to spread God's word and obtain more territory for Islam—there is simply a duty to jihad as described in the Qur'an (Cook, 2015). Qutb (2002) insists that if jihad is to be exclusively identified as a defensive response, then it must be viewed as a defensive act for all humanity and in turn, must reference all aspects of jahili society that limits human freedom. When defensive is defined in this way all distinctions simply fall away.

Qutb's interpretation of the "defensive" nature of jihad becomes the rationale employed in his critique of Egyptian secular and religious authority. The defense of man, which in this case becomes the defense of the people of Egypt, demands the call for jihad given that the Egyptian citizenry are forced to live under the freedom limiting authority of both the political and religious establishments of that country. When viewed from this perspective the duty of the faithful becomes clear: remove the barriers constructed by jahili attitudes and beliefs so as to liberate the people and allow for their return to God. To deny such a call to duty or to make distinctions concerning how and when this jihad should be waged is viewed as either a capitulation with jahili ideas and values or an attempt to impose manmade innovations[10] to God's law, which seeks to undermine God's exclusive sovereignty over man.

When constructed from this vantage point, being-in-the-world-as-Muslim is charged with the near exclusive duty of preaching, persuading, and physically confronting all aspects of jahili society, which have been viewed as barriers to God's rule:

> Islam is not a theory to be believed and practiced by its adherents while they continue to live in a *jahili* society. Should they continue to dwell in such a system they will compromise Islam's very existence by consciously or inadvertently defending it against outside threats. Islam and *jahiliyyah* cannot coexist; Muslims must consciously separate themselves from the prevailing social order and seek to eradicate it. (Haddad, 1983, pp. 88–89).

Submission to God, then, becomes an active engagement with the existing conditions of jahili society that requires not only this version of religious piety, but includes the call to action by which these conditions may be eradicated.

As was discussed in the previous chapter, this call to action has been exemplified within Egyptian society since the 1940s; this call to wage jihad against governmental leaders and other religious faiths in Egypt

---

[10] The construct of innovation(s) is often employed by Salifist Jihadi or Islamist thinkers as a type of hermeneutic process, which has covered over the original meaning of the Qur'an. For example, central to most if not all of these interpretations of Islam is the significance given to the years of the Prophet and his companions. Anything after the first seventy or eighty years of the religion is considered suspect and often constructed as innovation, which implies a move away from the authority of the early period of Islam; it also has the important result of delegitimizing the interpretative tradition of the Qur'an that has developed since its introduction on the Arabian Peninsula.

violently targeted various groups and government leaders within that country, who have been identified as supporters of jahili values. Whether these acts were directed toward leaders within the regime of the former monarchy, which ruled Egypt up until 1952, the two failed attempts on the life of then President Nasser in 1954 and 1965 or the more contemporary examples of violent attacks on Coptic Christians and former President Hosni Mubarak, all were driven by the main goal of eradicating the voices of Jahiliyyah from Egyptian society. The most successful example of these attacks on jahili culture was the assassination of then President Anwar Sadat on October 6, 1981 by al-Jama'at al-Jihad (The Jihad Group).

Though Sadat was assassinated in 1981, the beginning motivation for this action can be found in the takeover of the Technical Military Academy located in Cairo in 1974 (Calvert, 2010). Salih 'Abdallah Siriyya, a strong supporter of Qutb's understanding of jihad, and his followers believed that their attack on the military academy would be the first step in overthrowing the Egyptian government. Their attempt was unsuccessful. Siriyya was arrested and subsequently executed for his actions, which Calvert (2010) believes became the motivating event that would culminate in the assassination of Sadat approximately seven years later.

During this same time frame, the group al-Jama'at al-Jihad started to gain in prominence and sought to pursue Qutb's call to action. Most prominent in this group was 'Abd al-Salem Faraj, whose pamphlet, *The Neglected Duty*, which was written in 1979, was a call to action for all Muslims to perform jihad:

> Jihad for God's cause, in spite of its extreme importance and its great significance for the future of the religion, has been neglected by the 'ulama of this age. They have feigned ignorance of it, but they know that it is the only way to the return and establishment of the glory of Islam anew. (Faraj, 2009, p. 327)

Faraj, greatly influenced by the writing of Sayyid Qutb, viewed the existing Egyptian government of Anwar Sadat as being similar to the Mongol rulers of ibn Taymiyya's time and believed that this infidel government needed to be overthrown (Calvert, 2010; Kepel, 1993, 2005; Moussalli, 1992). Though ultimately successful in his desire to kill Pharaoh, he was ultimately arrested and executed. To prove his fidelity to this religious they-self, Faraj, much like his mentor Qutb, chose martyrdom over any attempt to ask the Egyptian Courts to spare his life.

What is clearly witnessed in the writings and actions of Sayyid Qutb, and those individuals who sought to pursue his call after his execution in 1966, is the process by which the Egyptian self becomes transformed by these texts into the Holy Warriors of jihad. If these interpretations of the Qur'an become the manifestation of this Islamic, they-self, then these newly configured Holy Warriors become the artifact of this identity-creating process. As a result, the experience of desubjectification evoked by the apparatuses of secular Western ideologies and failed Islamic innovation frees this re-imagined version of the Muslim subject from the veil of humiliation and inferiority imposed by these jahili societies. Even if this call to action results in death, as it did for Qutb, Siriyya, and Faraj, and many members of the Islamic Brotherhood, redemption remains its promise.[11] We will now explore the concept of jihad as offered by the Palestinian Islamist Abdallah Azzam, known as the father of contemporary jihad.

Abdallah Azzam: The Contemporary Father of Global Jihad

Thomas Hegghammer (2020) in his recent text, *Abdullah Azzam and the Rise of Global Jihad*, provides a powerful biographical account of the Palestinian Islamist ideologue Abdullah Azzam, and the role he played in the recruitment of Afghan Arab fighters seeking to end the Soviet occupation of Afghanistan. In the introduction of that text, Hegghammer (2020) observes:

---

[11] The relationship between martyrdom and redemption remains a contested idea within Islamic discourse. Though this relationship for the Salifist Jihadi/Islamist machine remains of central importance to its theological interpretative process, it clearly represents a much smaller degree of acceptance generally within the faith. The concept of offensive jihad and the active pursuit of martyrdom as witnessed in the act of suicide bombing is often rigorously rejected by many clerical voices within the religious establishment of Islam (Cook, 2007, 2015; Moussalli, 1992).

4 Toward a Phenomenology of Jihad: Salifist Jihadi Perspectives

> The Afghan jihad is widely recognized as the Big Bang in the globalization of jihadism, but we have not really understood why the Arabs joined it. The deep answer, as well shall see, lies neither in Islamic theology nor in international politics, but in the domestic politics of the postwar Arab world. (p. 1)

Before this discussion moves to Azzam's specific interpretation of jihad, it will perhaps be helpful to begin with a discussion of some of the points observed by Hegghammer in the above quote.

As Hegghammer (2020) observes, the life journey which ultimately led Azzam to pursue jihad against the Soviets in Afghanistan would also prove to be perhaps one of the most important developmental periods for the global jihad movement. But as Hegghammer also observes, why Afghanistan? Any number of credible scholarly opinions have offered an answer to this question: some have emphasized the role of geopolitics and the financial support from the Saudi government (Gilles Kepel and Peter Mandaville); while others (Fawaz Gerges and Bernard Rougier) have focused on the fact that Afghanistan offered a degree of "safety" for those domestic Islamist fighters who were finding it much harder to act freely in their own country (Hegghammer, 2020). Taken from the later perspective, the pursuit of jihad in Afghanistan should be viewed as the simple extension of the ideas of Sayyid Qutb. However, as Hegghammer (2020) recognizes, global jihad was really not the specific focus of Qutb's thinking; even though one could reasonably witness a global aspect to Qutb's interpretation of jihad, his was more predominately focused on regime change in Egypt. In fact, for Hegghammer (2020), the experience of foreign fighters pursuing jihad in Afghanistan represents a fundamental change from the perspective offered by Qutb: rather than fighting various manifestations of jahili Arab regimes, the focus would now be on the invasion of a Muslim non-Arab country by a non-Arab invader.

Such a change of focus within Islamist practice and strategy provided for the opportunity to wage jihad within a political context that could be more successfully described as a legitimate defense of Muslims and Islam. Concomitantly, this approach to jihad also made it possible to use Afghanistan as a type of staging ground that would attract Islamists from all over the world and, which in turn, would create a network for jihadist fighters worldwide. As individuals like Hegghammer (2020) and Anas and Hussein (2019) have specifically documented, the contingent group of foreign fighters commonly identified as Afghan Arabs, was initially rather small, and probably numbered no more than approximately 400 jihadist volunteers, who due to their total lack of military experience saw very little combat duty against Soviet and government forces; as a result, these volunteers were often overlooked by various factions of the Afghan resistance during this time due to this inexperience. However, these were not the only differences which existed between the Afghan resistance and those foreign Muslims fighters who came to Afghanistan to wage jihad against the Soviet occupation.[12]

Given that Azzam viewed the Soviet invasion of Afghanistan as an opportunity by which to unify the various groups of jihadi fighters under the single banner of Islam, his initial strategy was focused on identifying and addressing specific areas of conflict, which could potentially shatter any legitimate hope for a unified jihadi movement. When Azzam arrived in Afghanistan he soon realized that his involvement with the various factions of the Afghan mujahidin needed to be balanced and required a clear understanding of the complex political dynamics which existed within various regions of the country and between these various groups and their leaders involved in this struggle. Failure to do so could not only put his life in potential danger, but could almost certainly shatter the complex yet tenuous trust that existed between these political and religious configurations of Afghan society. Azzam quickly realized that once trusted by these competing groups and their leadership, he would be much better able to use his position and personal stature by which to mediate any existing or emerging difficulties that may occur to this fragile coalition and threaten its existence. However, as his attempts at recruitment of Arab fighters slowly began to see some minor success another problem emerged.

---

[12] The first combat action performed by Arab Mujahidin, which consisted of a force of approximately hundred fighters, occurred at the Battle of Jaji during early days of April 1987. Though this military operation extended over a period of approximately two months, Hegghammer (2020) has observed that the battlefield performance of this group helped to increase the moral of this force, which in turn also helped recruitment to their cause.

Given Azzam's focus on unifying the Afghanistan jihad, he was very interested in managing the arrival of these new Arab recruits in such a way so as not to offend their Afghan hosts. Though this was a call to jihad, it was a call to jihad for Afghanistan and its liberation from the godless Soviet occupation and should, therefore, not be seen exclusively from the specific point of view of the Islamic Brotherhood or Salafist Jihadi perspectives imported from Saudi Arabia, which viewed this process differently. In describing this distinction between Afghan Mujahidin and Afghan Arabs or Fedayeen, the name used by these Arab fighters to describe themselves, Edwards (2017) makes the following observation:

> The terminology is important in that many of the Arabs who came to Afghanistan did so specifically "to sacrifice themselves," which is the root meaning of the Arabic term fedayeen. Their goal was not the liberation of Afghanistan from the Soviet Union or to defeat communism. For many, if not most, it was to die in battle, to go from fedayeen to shahidan: from those willing to sacrifice themselves to those who have succeeded and become martyrs. (Edwards, 2017, p. 94)

The distinction which Edwards observes concerning the differences between these two groups helps to structure the competing phenomenologies, which this difference reveals.

When taken from this perspective, two very different examples of being-in-the-world are revealed: being-in-the-world-as-Mujahidin and being-in-the-world-as-Fedayeen. For the domestic Afghan Muslim resistance, being-in-the-world-as-Mujahidin is structured by a manifestation of the Islamic they-self, which seeks to confront and ultimately repeal the alien nomic order of the invading Soviet Union. However, unlike other configurations of the Islamic they-self, the Afghan example was better able to contain a variety of competing nomic meanings, which if left unaddressed would have almost certainly shattered the existing Islamic coalition of domestic forces, and thwarted their eventual victory over Soviet and government forces. Given its exhaustive focus on the immediate threat posed by the occupying presence of the Soviet military, these sometimes serious examples of disagreement between the competing concerns of these domestic Islamic groups were able to be contained in the name of confronting this greater threat (Anas & Hussein, 2019; Edwards, 2017; Hegghammer, 2020). Though this dynamic did not effectively carry over into the post-war period in Afghanistan, which led to civil war and the ultimate rise to power of the Talban, it did prove to be sufficient in defeating the Soviet occupation of that country.

As Edwards (2017) has observed, this same dynamic was really not witnessed in the same way for those Afghan Arab fighters, who identified themselves as fedayeen. From the perspective of being-in-the-world-as-fedayeen, the project to be pursued was martyrdom and not the liberation of Afghan Muslims from the Soviet occupation, which was simply viewed as an ancillary benefit. When constructed in this way, the Soviet occupation simply provided the rational for jihad, which in turn constructed the military context by which martyrdom could be achieved. Azzam was apparently well aware of these differing intentional relationships to his call to jihad but did his best to keep the topic of martyrdom as the central focus for those individuals traveling to Pakistan to fight in Afghanistan.

It is also important to observe that though Azzam was determined not to challenge or criticize the various Islamic traditions practiced in Afghanistan during his time there that fact did not prevent him from preaching his specific brand of jihad to those Arab fighters who were there to achieve martyrdom. Though the immediate fight was for the liberation of Afghanistan, Azzam was also focused on the goal of creating an army of fedayeen fighters that would take the call to jihad to wherever necessary. Afghanistan became the context from which Azzam's version of the Islamic they-self would become the point from which this new manifestation of being-in-the-world-as-fedayeen would be realized. Our discussion will now move to a brief discussion of the specific texts, where Azzam outlines his understanding of jihad and the call to martyrdom.

In his text, *Join the Caravan*, which would become an important text for the movement, Azzam describes what he calls the reason for jihad:

> Anybody who looks into the state of the Muslims today will find that their greatest misfortune is their abandonment of Jihad (due to love of this world and abhorrence of death). Because of that, the tyrants have gained

dominance over the Muslims in every aspect and in every land. The reason for this is that the Disbelievers only stand in awe of fighting. (Azzam, 2002, p. 7)

Central to Azzam's interpretation of jihad, much like the positions taken by Mawdudi, Qutb, and others, was that jihad is a requirement, a duty of religious faith and practice and not a choice. To abandon jihad is not only to abandon one's religious duty, but to refuse the path of martyrdom as well. The current condition of Muslims to which Azzam was eluding is directly attributed to this failed responsibility.

Though Azzam's interpretation of jihad was certainly consistent with other jihadist theorists, his understanding concerning how this responsibility was to be established does seem to differ from both the other major Salafist theorists of his day and in certain respects to the Qur'an itself (Cook, 2015). For Azzam there was no distinction between the individual circumstances of a given situation and one's individual duty to jihad. The demand for jihad was not predicated upon its specific location (Cook, 2015; Edwards, 2017). Neither was it reserved to only those Muslims, who were directly affected by the immediate attack from an infidel force. Jihad was the required responsibility of all Muslims when a Muslim community was under siege, regardless the actual proximity of the event. Traditionally this responsibility was the exclusive duty of the specific community under siege and not the duty of other Muslims everywhere not directly involved in that event (Cook, 2015; Edwards, 2017). However, for Azzam, any attack on Muslims anywhere was viewed as a legitimate reason for jihad—of which, Afghanistan became his prime example—and as such, was an individual responsibility that could be ignored or abandoned.

It seems reasonable to believe that Azzam's configuration of jihad, as a defensive response to attacks on Muslims specifically and Islam generally, allowed him to remain faithful to both the traditional interpretations of jihad as defensive, while also situating his understanding of this religious construct firmly within the time of the Prophet by which to further legitimize his theological position and perhaps sidestep the charge of innovation. However, such a result may be difficult to achieve. By expanding as he does, both the definitional parameters of defensive jihad along with the way in which this individual phenomenology is to be structured and practiced, Azzam appears to be guilty of the same act of innovation that is often attributed to the opponents of this position. Perhaps none of Azzam's theological rulings has been more controversial than the explicit incorporation of martyrdom into the very structure and practice of jihad.

What becomes most significant to Azzam's understanding of jihad as martyrdom is the way in which the failure to die becomes synonymous with the general failure of jihad. From this perspective the glory of death is to have God accept this sacrifice and allow the martyr to enjoy the rewards awaiting him in heaven. As a result, Azzam believed that the sacrifice of martyrdom became the test for true belief and the only road to paradise (Edwards, 2017). However, this interpretation of jihad and martyrdom was not one that was embraced by the Muslim communities in Afghanistan.

As was the case with much of Azzam's experience in Afghanistan, the influence of his positions was very much predicated upon the make-up of his audience. Though Afghan fighters rejected the demand for martyrdom, in the way discussed by Azzam, such a "rejection" was not predicated on a fear of death; rather, to fight fearlessly and survive showed a willingness to accept death in the name of jihad, making survival admirable (Edwards, 2017). However, for the fedayeen fighters, the proof of one's fearlessness of death could only be established by their martyrdom and any admiration gained would motivate others to follow their example (Edwards, 2017):

> All that mattered to the believer was what God's judgement of him would be, and the judgement was far more likely to be a positive one if the believer's action lead to his death. Such action was not sacrifice by accident or by retrospective certification by some political party but sacrifice by design and through intent (niyat). (Edwards, 2017, p. 105)

Such a phenomenology of jihad re-fabricates Muslim-being-in-a-world in such a way that all aspects of the desubjectified self are redeemed as long as this new fidelity to God is practiced. Taken from this perspective being-in-the-world-as-fedayeen fundamentally transforms the very structure of human being insofar as death is now longer viewed as an

4 Toward a Phenomenology of Jihad: Salifist Jihadi Perspectives

existential finality, but as a reward that must be actively pursued. Those who are able to pursue this "sacrifice by design and through intent" are those that are provided success by this manifestation of the Islamic they-self and those who abandon this duty are not. Azzam's texts become the apparatuses for this sacred transformation, which promises the lofty rewards of eternal life, and reestablishes the Muslim relationship with God.

In closing, the common thread, which can be discerned within the discourse of Mawdudi, Qutb, and Azzam, is the desire to reconstruct the very foundation of the Muslim self. For each of these writers, being-in-the-world-as-Muslim becomes synonymous with being-in-the-world-as-jihadi. The construct of this manifestation of jihad becomes the pivot point from which all other aspects of being-in-the-world-as-Muslim are configured. By focusing on the construct of jihad as they do, they are able, at least from their perspective, to return to the time of the Prophet, while completely distancing themselves from nearly the total corpus of Islamic jurisprudence over the course of its history. Though any number of Islamic scholars have critically discussed the theological legitimacy of their interpretation of jihad and other aspects of religious practice, these critiques have been less than successful with that portion of the ulma that have gravitated toward these more radical readings of the Qur'an and the Prophet's life (Zehr, 2017). In fact, theorists like Mawdudi, Qutb, and Azzam have used these rulings as fodder for their own arguments, particularly as this relates to the current state of Islamic inferiority.

Taken from this version of the Islamic they-self offered by Mawdudi, Qutb, and Azzam, being-in-the-world-as-Muslim becomes empowered and now capable of overcoming the experience of humiliation and inferiority, upon which these writers focus, when describing the current conditions of the ummah. For those who take up this call and become transformed by it, this experience of humiliation and inferiority can now be confronted, even if this struggle results in one's individual death. The phenomenology of this process seems rather straight forward. The call of this specific manifestation of the they-self will resonate for those who feel similarly and are desperate to rebuild the protective canopy of this nomos under siege. The more compelling the call, the more likely that individuals happily join the caravan; this will be particularly powerful for those who have been waiting for such an invitation. However, this potentiality is not the only relationship with the Islamic they-self.

Though Azzam seemed fundamentally focused on the creation of a unified Islamic movement, this hope was predicated upon the peaceful coexistence of competing versions of this process of nomic ordering, which needed to stay focused on the "enemy" and not on the sometimes glaring differences these structures of social meaning provided this emerging Islamic-self. As was stated above, Azzam was keenly aware of the differences between the Afghan Mujahidin and the Afghan Arabs, and perhaps seemed to under-estimate the degree to which his own life may be in danger, as the battle against the Soviets was winding down to its end. This potential fear was realized in Peshawar, Pakistan on November 24, 1989, when Azzam and his two sons were killed by a roadside bomb as they were about to arrive at the Sab' al-Layl mosque for Friday prayers (Anas & Hussein, 2019; Hegghammer, 2020). Though the battle against the Soviets would soon be won, Azzam was unable to see it, as a new confrontation between competing manifestations of the they-self was about to begin.

In the aftermath of the victory in the war against the Soviet Union, a variety of configurations of being-in-the-world-as-Muslim started to emerge. Though disagreements certainly existed between the coalition of Afghan mujahidin and the Afghan Arabs, who by war's end had a considerable presence in Peshawar, Pakistan, these disagreements never really disrupted Azzam's wish for a unified front against the invading Soviet forces. However, with the foreign invader defeated, the necessity for unity seemed to give way to the desire for power in post-war Afghanistan and beyond. As was discussed above, during the war two different versions of the Muslim they-self existed: the one embraced by Afghan Muslims, which was focused on the specific religious traditions of that country and the one imported by the Salafists from Egypt, Saudi Arabia, and elsewhere, who embraced a much more specific version of religious practice, which was actually at odds with many of the beliefs held by their Afghan allies. Though Azzam's assassins have never been identified, it is likely that his death was directly related to the developing phenomenology, which began to unfold at the end of the Afghan conflict.

Azzam's influence and perspective on jihad created a very specific version of being-in-the-world-as-Jihadist that was likely perceived as threating on a variety of levels. As will be discussed in the next chapter, overtime the Afghan Arabs become more determined to create a legitimate force that would be capable of fighting in various countries around the world. Such a capability would certainly be noticed by the various Afghan mujahidin in that country, as well as by Pakistani intelligence, who would likely not want such a force in such close proximity to its own country. Additionally, the fact that these individuals sought to import a much stricter version of Islam, which was not well accepted by the Afghan people, would create further concerns about the stability of region. These competing religious phenomenologies would find it difficult to exist given the very different meaning each provided for being-in-the-world-as-Muslim. Though some of these differences would be incorporated with the emergence of The Taliban some eight years later, it does appear that Azzam's particular construction of Jihad was unwanted and his death was to send a clear message to that effect.

References

Adraoui, M.-A. (2019). Salafism, jihadism and radicalisation: Between a common doctrinal heritage and the logics of empowerment. In S. Pektas & J. Leman (Eds.), *Militant jihadism: Today and tomorrow* (pp. 19–39). Leuven University Press.

Al-Qaradawi, Y. (1991). *Islamic awaking: Between rejection & extremism*. International Institute of Islamic Thought.

Anas, A., & Hussein, T. (2019). *To the mountains: My life in Jihad, from Algeria to Afghanistan*. London, England: Hurst & Company.

Azzam, A. (2002). *Join the caravan*. Retrieved from https://english.religion.info/2020/02/01/document-join-the-caravan/

Barkindo, A. (2013). Join the caravan: The ideology of political authority in Islam from ibn Taymiyya to Boko Haren in north-eastern Nigeria. *Perspectives on Terrorism, 7*, 30–43.

Benjamin, D., & Simon, S. (2002). *The age of sacred Terror: Radical Islam's war against America*. New York: Random House.

Bergesen, A. J. (2008). Qutb's core ideas. In A. Bergesen (Ed.), *The Sayyid Qutb reader: Selected writings on politics, religion, and society* (pp. 14–31). Routledge.

Bori, C. (2010). Ibn Taymiyya wa-Jama'atu-hu: Authority, conflict and consensus in Ibn Taymiyya's circle. In Y. Rapoport & S. Ahmed (Eds.), *Ibn Taymiyya and his times* (pp. 3–20). Oxford University Press.

Calvert, J. (2010). *Sayyid Qutb and the origins of radical Islamism*. Columbia University Press.

Cook, D. (2007). *Martydom in Islam*. Cambridge & New York: Cambridge University Press.

Cook, D. (2015). *Understanding jihad*. University of California Press.

Edwards, D. (2017). *Caravan of martyrs: Sacrifice and suicide bombing in Afghanistan*. University of California Press.

El Fadl, K. A. (2007). *The great theft: Wrestling Islam from the extremists*. HarperOne.

Faraj, M. (2009). The neglected duty. In R. L. Euben & M. Q. Zaman (Eds.), *Princeton readings in Islamist thought: Texts and contexts from al-Banna to bin Laden* (pp. 327–343). Princeton University Press.

Gerges, F. A. (2009). *The far enemy: Why global jihad went global*. Cambridge University Press.

Gerges, F. A. (2018). *Making the Arab world: Nasser, Qutb, and the clash that shaped the Middle East*. Princeton University Press.

Haddad, Y. Y. (1983). Sayyid Qutb: Ideologue of Islamic revival. In J. Esposito (Ed.), *Voices of resurgent Islam* (pp. 67–98). Oxford University Press.

Heck, P. L. (2004). "Jihad" revisited. *The Journal of Religious Ethics, 32*, 95–128.

Hegghammer, T. (2020). *The caravan: Abdallah Azzam and the rise of global jihad*. Cambridge University Press.

Heidegger, M. (2010). *Being and time* (J. Stambaugh, Trans.). SUNY Press.

Hoover, J. (2010). God acts by his will and power: Ibn Taymiyya's theology of a personal God in his treatise on the voluntary attributes. In Y. Rapoport & S. Ahmed (Eds.), *Ibn Taymiyya and his times* (pp. 55–77). Oxford University Press.

Jackson, R. (2013). *Mawlana Mawdudi & political Islam*. Routledge.

Juergensmeyer, M. (2017). *Terror in the mind of God: The global rise of religious violence* (4th ed.). California University Press.

Kafrawi, S. (1998). Methods of interpreting the Qur'an: A comparison of Sayyid Qutb and Bint Al-Shati. *Islamic Studies, 37*, 3–17.

Kepel, G. (1993). *Muslim extremism in Egypt: The prophet and pharaoh*. University of California Press.

Kepel, G. (2005). *The roots of radical Islam*. Saqi.
Khatab, S. (2006). *The political thought of Sayyid Qutb: The theory of jahiliyyah*. Routledge.
Mawdudi, S. A. A. (1980). *Towards understanding Islam*. U.K. Islamic Mission.
Mohammad, N. (1985). The doctrine of jihad: An introduction. *Journal of Law and Religion, 3*, 381–397.
Moniruzzaman, M. (2008). Jihad and terrorism: An alternative explanation. *Journal of Religion & Society, 10*, 1–13.
Moussalli, A. S. (1992). *Radical Islamic fundamentalism: The ideological and political discourse of Sayyid Qutb*. American University of Beirut.
Mitchell, R. A. (1993). *The society of the Muslim Brothers*. Oxford University Press.
Nasr, R. A. (1996). *Mawdudi & the making of Islamic revivalism*. Oxford University Press.
Qutb, S. (2002). *Milestones*. Islamic Book Service.
Rapoport, Y., & Ahmed, S. (2010). Ibn Taymiyya and his times. In Y. Rapoport & S. Ahmed (Eds.), *Ibn Taymiyya and his times* (pp. 3–20). Oxford University Press.
Richardson, J. (2012). *Heidegger*. Routledge.
Wagemakers, J. (2012). *A quietist jihadi: The ideology and influence of Abu Muhammad al-Maqdisi*. Cambridge University Press.
White, J. T., & Siddiqui, N. (2018). Mawlana Mawdudi. In J. Esposito & E. El-Din Shahin (Eds.), *Key Islamic political thinkers* (pp. 44–63). Oxford University Press.
Zehr, N. A. (2017). *The war against al-Qaeda: Religion, policy, and counter-narratives*. Georgetown University Press.

5

Al-Qaeda and the Rise of Global Jihad

The Birth of Global Jihad

If Azzam is the father of global jihad then Osama bin Laden is one of his more famous progeny. Bin Laden initially met Azzam in Jeddah, Saudi Arabia in the late 1970s where he would attend lectures Azzam would give at local mosques and over the Sheikh's time in Saudi Arabia, they became friends (Anas & Hussein, 2019). Their friendship would be furthered during the beginning stages of the jihad waged against the occupying Soviet military in Afghanistan.[1] Azzam sought out bin Laden in the hope that he would be able to provide financial assistance to the newly created Services Bureau, which was focused upon providing a variety of support for the Afghan mujahidin; Azzam also believed that bin Laden could help him to raise money from other wealthy supporters in Saudi Arabia and the Arab world (Anas & Hussein, 2019; Bergen, 2001; Gerges, 2009). Though bin Laden remained close with Azzam during his

---

[1] Scholars such as Hegghammer have pointed out that the call to jihad in Afghanistan was first proclaimed against communist government forces in the mid-seventies, which did not result in the active recruitment of Arab fighters in that struggle. However, with the invasion of the Soviet Union a more legitimate call for a defensive jihad became possible.

extended time in Pakistan and Afghanistan, he also was becoming more frustrated with the lack of involvement of Arab fighters in the actual conflict against Soviet and Afghan government forces. Though the Services Bureau was able to provide certain types of support to both the Afghan mujahidin and the Arab Afghans, none of this support was focused on providing fighters from the Gulf and North Africa any type of quality military training (Anas & Hussein, 2019; Gerges, 2009; Hegghammer, 2020).

As was briefly observed in the previous chapter, the Arab Afghans were viewed by their Afghan mujahidin allies as being highly motivated, but poorly trained for the realities of the battlefield. No one was perhaps more aware of this reputation than was Osama bin Laden, who was very interested in changing this perception. Though Azzam continued to believe that sufficient military training could be gained through the involvement with existing Afghan mujahidin forces (Hegghammer, 2020), bin Laden was concerned with the creation of an exclusive Arab fighting force that would be capable of matching their motivation for jihad, while also exhibiting expertise on the battlefield. To achieve this goal, a more effective system of military training for the Afghan Arabs would be required than was possible under the existing framework of the Services Bureau and it is for this reason that bin Laden ended his direct involvement with that organization (Anas & Hussein, 2019; Hegghammer, 2020).

The problem of the lack of high-level military training was finally addressed with the creation of the al Ma'sada camp near the Pakistan border. Construction of the facility began in the final months of 1986 and was completed in the Spring of 1987 (Hegghammer, 2020). It is also believed that this facility marked the beginning of al-Qaeda (Hegghammer, 2020). However, it is important to note that the construction of the al Ma'sada camp served more than simply fulfilling the need for a high-level military training facility. Perhaps more importantly, it became the location from which bin Laden's vision for being-in-the-world-as-global-jihadi was created. If bin Laden's vision for global jihad was ever to be realized, it required more than highly motivated Fedayeen warriors willing to sacrifice their lives to this fight. As such, al Ma'sada became the crucible from which these well-trained and highly motivated fighters could establish their military legitimacy in Afghanistan, particularly after the defeat of the Soviets, and prove themselves to be worthy of jihad in their pursuit of martyrdom.

Given that this discussion is really more interested in the phenomenology of being-in-the-world-as-al-Qaeda-warrior, and its relationship to the nomic ordering discourse offered by Osama bin Laden and Ayman al-Zawahiri, I will now turn to those texts to more clearly explore this process. The historical development of al-Qaeda as a terrorist organization and its various attacks on both military and civilian targets worldwide since the mid-1990s has been well documented and discussed across the breath of the literature on this topic and therefore will not be dealt with in any detail here. The operational capabilities of al-Qaeda, particularly prior to the emergence of the Islamic State, have been thoroughly studied given the enormity of their impact worldwide and probably do not need to be discussed here. What seems more fruitful from the perspective of this discussion is to explore the phenomenology these texts describe and the manifestation of nomic ordering they impose on those willing to take up this version of being-in-the-world-as-Muslim.

Osama bin Laden

The history of Osama bin Laden is that of a pious young man born into a fabulously wealthy Saudi family, who over time found himself attracted to the war in Afghanistan and the fight to defeat the Soviet invasion of that country (Anas & Hussein, 2019; Hegghammer, 2020; Lawrence, 2005). Initially, he was convinced by his mentor Abdullah Azzam to help provide a variety of financial assistance to the cause that included his financing of the Services Bureau located in Peshawar, Pakistan, which was focused on funding various kind of aid to the Mujahidin and Afghan Arabs in Pakistan and Afghanistan. As his presence in the region increased, so too did his desire to join the fight and enter the battle against Soviet forces in late 1986 and beyond (Anas & Hussein, 2019; Bergen, 2001; Hegghammer, 2020; Lacroix, 2008). Bin Laden returned to his Saudi home in 1990, but with the invasion of Kuwait by Saddam Hussein in 1991, bin Laden went to the Saudi government offering to organize Arab veterans from the war in Afghanistan to defend the kingdom, but was refused by the ruling Saudi royal family (Lawrence, 2005). Instead, the Saudi royal family invited the American lead coalition forces to drive Saddam out of Kuwait, which then led to the first invasion of Iraq. Bin Laden left Saudi Arabia in 1991 and settled briefly in the Sudan where he was joined by Ayman al-Zawahiri (Bergen, 2001).

Bin Laden and his al-Qaeda organization returned to Afghanistan in 1996 and the Taliban came to power in the Fall of the same year. Within the subsequent years bin Laden and al-Qaeda planned a number of terrorist attacks on U.S. targets culminating on with the 9/11 attacks in 2001. On February 23 1998, bin Laden and a group of fellow jihadists issued their famous declaration of Jihad that would be approximately six months before al-Qaeda would launch their car bomb attacks on the U.S. embassies in Nairobi Kenya and Dar es Salamm, Tanzania, which occurred on August 7 1998; in subsequent years al-Qaeda would attack the *USS Cole* in the port of Yemen on October 12 2000, and of course, approximately one year later, the infamous attacks on 9/11. This initial declaration of jihad becomes the initial outline for bin Laden's global Holy war (Gerges, 2009; Lawrence, 2005).

Declaration of Jihad Against the Americans Occupying the Land of the Two Holy Sanctuaries (August 23, 1996)[2]

Bin Laden and his co-writers begin their declaration of Jihad by observing:

> Never since Allah made the Arabian Peninsula flat, created its desert, and encircled it with seas has it been stormed by any force like the Crusader

---

[2] Bin Laden's statement, which was co-written with Ayman al-Zawahiri, Abu-Yasir Rifi'a Ahmed Taha, Shaykh Mir Hamzah, and Fazlur Rahman, proclaiming al-Qaeda's declaration of war against the Jews and Crusaders has appeared in a variety of English translations: *Messages to the World: The Statements of Osama bin Laden*, edited by Lawrence, 2005; *The al-Qaeda Reader: The Essential Texts of Osama bin Laden's Terrorist Organization*, edited and translated by Raymond Ibrahim, 2007; *Al-Qaeda in its Own Words*, edited by Gilles Kepel and Jean-Pierre Milelli, 2008. I will be using the translation offered by Raymond Ibrahim in his text *The al-Qaeda Reader*.

hordes that have spread in it like locusts, consuming its wealth and polluting its fertility. All this is happening at a time in which nations are attacking Muslims in unison—as if fighting over a plate of food! In face of this critical situation and lack of support, we are obliged to discuss current events, as well as reach an agreement on how [best] to settle the matter. (bin Laden et al. as quoted in Ibrahim, 2007, p. 11)

In this brief paragraph, bin Laden and his co-writers identify the basic argument for their call to jihad: (1) Islam is under attack by Crusader armies; (2) Current Arab governments are not respecting their duty to protect the religion; (3) in the face of these failures, al-Qaeda is obliged to protect the religion. Taken from this perspective, the writers identify the problem, those who are deemed responsible for its continuation and a strategy by which the problem can be rectified. It is significant that this initial framing of the problem is contextualized within a narrative of defensive jihad. It will be recalled that defensive jihad is evoked when either Muslims are being attached or the religion itself is under siege and it is often under these circumstances that the waging of jihad becomes theologically legitimate (Gerges, 2009).

Taken from a Heideggerian perspective, al-Qaeda's declaration of jihad reflects a fracturing of the Islamic they-self, in so far it identifies both the attacking Crusader hordes, along with those nations that have been compliant and silent during these assaults. Being-in-the-world-as-Muslim is now challenged with fulfilling their duty to their religion or continue to experience Allah's condemnation and humiliation for not responding to this responsibility. Viewed from the Zealot perspective of the they-self, Islam is under siege and must be defended. As a result of these circumstances, it also seeks to re-fabricate the very identity of being-in-the-world-as-Muslim, which becomes an essential artifact of this process of revitalization.

To strengthen their point concerning these dire circumstances, which now threatens to overwhelm Islam, the writers identify three significant areas of concern, which they claim are widely known by all in the Muslim world: (1) the occupation of the most sacred sites in Islam, and the exploitation of its resources and governments, (2) the continuing occupation of Iraq, and (3) the attempt to destroy the governments of Iraq,

Saudi Arabia, Egypt, and the Sudan and weaken their ability to threaten Israel (bin Laden et al. in Ibrahim, 2007). Bin Laden and his co-writers appear to employ "these well-known facts," as the evidence by which a defensive jihad may be legitimately waged. The difficulty created by this strategy, however, was that the charge of a crusader invasion could not be as easily argued as could the Soviet invasion of Afghanistan. If the U.S. presence in Saudi Arabia constituted an American invasion of that country, then the royal family of Saudi Arabia would need to be complicit in that sin as well, given it was they, who invited the Americans and their allies to defend the Kingdom. It is also important to remember that bin Laden sought permission from the Saudi government to re-form the Arab Afghan fighters to repel the invasion of Saddam's military from Kuwait and was rejected (Gerges, 2009; Lawrence, 2005). Once the evidence is presented, they rest their case and the verdict is clear.

The evidence presented in this declaration reflects for the authors America's desire to wage war against Islam and all Muslims. But more importantly, it is also a reminder that the practice of jihad is an individual duty of all believers to respond to this call when the religion is clearly under siege. To support this verdict, they quote the religious scholar ibn Taymiyya to further attempt to construct the legitimacy of their position:

> As for defensive warfare, this is the greatest way to defend sanctity and religion. This is an obligation consensually agreed to [by the *ulema*]. After faith, there is nothing more scared than repulsing the enemy who attacks religion and life. (ibn Taymiyya as quoted in Ibrahim, 2007, pp. 12–13)

The authors use the well-established criteria for waging a defensive jihad as prescribed by religious tradition and then attempt to apply that logic to the three facts which they identify as the necessary evidence, justifying the obligation to jihad when the religion is under attack. However, as was stated above, though the specific target of this religious indictment is clearly directed at the U.S. and its allies, it also challenges the existing religious authority or ulma as well as Muslims everywhere to recognize this undeniable obligation and act. As such, this obligation becomes the fundamental call to action for being-in-the-world-as-Muslim.

By implicating as they do the existing religious authority of the ulma, they seek to undermine its ability to refuse the evidence they provide concerning the legitimacy of their call to jihad while also attempting to call into question the very legitimacy of one's faith by the refusal to act. Such a strategy becomes essential to the religious phenomenology they are trying to re-create. By focusing on the established tradition of defensive jihad and using the three known facts that they identify as evidence to legitimate such a call, the writers remain for the most part within the more accepted traditional religious understanding of this concept: defensive jihad is compulsory when the religion is under attack as it was in Afghanistan. Though this interpretation was clearly not one accepted by the existing religious authority in Saudi Arabia and elsewhere, it was likely viewed as sufficient enough for those who felt similarly about the circumstances outlined in this declaration.

Validation to this alternative Islamic they-self becomes predicated upon the willingness to kill Americans and their allies wherever they are found. As sinners or hypocrites, and as the enemies of Allah, death becomes the only legitimate conclusion for individuals such as theses (bin Laden et al. in Ibrahim, 2007). Not to follow this edict is to fail to meet one's obligation as a Muslim; but it also becomes proof of one's lack of belief as well. Perhaps more importantly, however, is how the call to kill Americans and their allies "wherever and whenever you find them;" becomes a clear strategy by which this jihad can be cared out. From this perspective, there simply is no requirement for those who respond to this call or to act in ways specifically delineated by the al-Qaeda leadership. Though this declaration reflects a religious call, it also reveals the willingness to inspire a religious insurgency that is not exclusively organized and controlled by the authors of this statement.

Taken phenomenologically, being-in-the-world-as-Muslim is called to action by the dictates of this Islamic they-self and its project is rather simply defined: have faith and pursue jihad. As a result of this specific configuration for being-in-the-world, a specific type of being-with is also constructed. Heidegger (2010) clarifies his construct of being-with by observing that others are not those who are different from me, rather, they are those who are most like me. Heidegger's notion of being-with is an essential underlying phenomenological "structure" which appears to be recognizable within the context of the process described in the Declaration. Through this call to jihad, the ontological quality of being-with becomes manifest within the specific ontic configuration for this type of being-in-the-world-as-Muslim and helps to clarify who is like me and who is not. Though the Declaration is generally speaking a call for all Muslims to take up the duty of jihad, it seems more accurate to observe that its function is relatable to this ontic notion of being-with, which seeks to clarify those who will be valued and those who will not.

Bin Laden and his co-authors appear to lend further legitimacy to this phenomenological perspective when they conclude with this verse from the Qur'an:

> Allah Most High said: "O you who have believed! What is the matter with you? When you asked to go forth in the cause of Allah, you cling so heavily to the earth! Do you prefer the life of this world to the Hereafter? But little is the comfort of this life, in comparison to the Hereafter. Unless You go forth [and fight], He will punish you with a grievous torment, and p u t others in your place. But He you cannot harm in the least; for Allah has power over all things." (The Qur'an as quoted in Ibrahim, 2007, p. 14)[3]

It is probably not surprising that the writers of the Declaration end their case by quoting from the Qur'an. From the perspective of the quoted material, the distinction is rather clear: if you believe you will fight for Allah and if you do not you will be subjected to "grievous torment." "to go forth in the Cause of Allah" is to recognize the duty of jihad and fight to defend Allah's religion, even if this means death. Though it was certainly not the intent of the authors, the Declaration can be situated within Heidegger's construct of concern, which helps to better clarify the phenomenology which appears to be recognizable within this perspective.

Taken from a phenomenological perspective, the Declaration reflects a type of Heideggerian being-with that seeks to address those examples of deficient modes of concern, which become ontically configured within the "three known facts," which the authors identify. Modes of taking-care

---

[3] The above quotation is from Surah 9 At-Tauba 38–39 of the Qur'an.

or solicitude are described by Heidegger as those moments when Dasein fails in this ability (King, 2001). For the purposes of this discussion, these ontic failures of taking-care are reflected in the way in which the authors of Declaration seek to address this lack as exemplified in their view by the Muslim ummah. When viewed within this context, the use of Surah 9 from the Qur'an becomes an example of "leaping-in" by the authors of the Declaration, who are attempting to address the lack of care (faith) they identify within the community of believers.

It will be recalled that Heidegger described two extreme modes of positive concern. The first of these modes is described as leaping-in, which is recognized by its taking-care of the other when he or she cannot. "In so doing, however, it throws the other out of his place by stepping in his stead, so that the other takes over ready-made what he should have taken care of for himself" (King, 2001, p. 77). Taken from the perspective of the Declaration, the authors become an ontic example of "leaping-in," whereby the authors seek to take over the lack of care exemplified by the ummah's failed faith until that faith can be "properly" restored by them. Once faith has been "restored," the second positive mode of care becomes possible, which is identified by a care that "leaps ahead." In this mode of care, the other is able to be herself (King, 2001).

Each of these manifestations of concern do seem apparent within the context of the narrative structure offered in the Declaration. One the one hand, the Declaration seems to identify the urgency for action, the urgency for leaping-in, given that being-in-the-world-as-Muslim is constructed as trapped within various modes of deficient concern related to this dangerous or weakened they-self. This competing manifestation of the Islamic they-self, which the Declaration represents, leaps in, and seeks to take over until being-in-the-world-as-Muslim can "authentically" embrace this concern for itself. For others, this manifestation of the Islamic they-self provides a structure whereby this concern can be reclaimed. With each of these potentialities for being, a different type of phenomenological structure is offered that either re-informs what will be validated and what will not or liberates the possibilities for being in such a way that is alternative view or revitalized view of Islam may be embraced.

Message to the American People (November 24, 2002)[4]

In this speech, bin Laden, directly addresses the American people and provides his specific reasons for waging jihad against the Americans. From this perspective, bin Laden constructs the phenomenology of al-Qaeda within the confines of his understanding of security and freedom. The acts of September 11 and the consequences of war, presumably referring to the conflicts taking place in Afghanistan and Iraq at the time of this writing are not in the service of forfeiting their security but defending it. By implication, as bin Laden observes, Sweden has not been attacked for the simple reason that they present no threat to the Muslims al-Qaeda believes it represents. Bin Laden clarifies this position when he states:

> [W]e fight because we are free men who do not slumber under oppression. We want to restore freedom to our nation, and just as you lay waste to our nation, so shall we lay waste to yours. (bin laden as quoted in Kepel & Milelli, 2008, p. 71)

In the above quote, bin Laden rejects Bush's construction of this version of being-in-the-world-as-Muslim and by so doing situates these experiences within a competing manifestation of the Islamic they-self. As a result, each of these positions serves as an apparatus for the respective they-selves that they represent, and which configure two very different versions of the Muslim subject. Much like the distinction which is observed by bin Laden and his co-authors in the Declaration, here bin Laden evokes his call for defensive jihad and the actions which followed as al-Qaeda's response to the threat posed to those Muslim societies whose freedom and security has been jeopardized by the actions of the U.S. and its allies. Bin Laden then moves from this more general discussion of his rationale for jihad, to the specific effects that these attacks evoked in him personally over a duration of nearly twenty years.

---

[4] Message to the American People appears in the text *Al Qaeda in its own Words* edited by Gilles Kepel and Jean-Pierre Milelli (2008).

He states that he first became personally affected by these events in 1982, when the U.S. "allowed" the Israelis to invade Lebanon. He states:

> I cannot forget those unbearable scenes of blood and severed limbs, the corpses of the women and children strewn everywhere, houses destroyed along with their occupants and high-rise buildings burying their residents, rockets raining down on our land without mercy. (bin Laden as quoted in Kepel & Milelli, 2008, p. 72)

He continues by stating that these actions should be punished in a similar way, and claims that it was the experience of witnessing these deaths, which allowed him to first consider attacking the World Trade Center in New York; bin Laden seems to argue to this speech that by bombing the Twin Towers, the Americans would experience what Muslims had regularly experienced, and perhaps this would stop the murder of women and children (bin Laden, 2008).

The phenomenology, which bin Laden shares in his letter to the Americans, reflects an experience of strain that requires resolution. In virtually every example of perceived nomic threat, the strain which this phenomenology reveals requires a response that is approximate to the threat and one that becomes foundational for all subsequent experiences of the same. When bin Laden observes that he and his followers are both awake and free, he also implies that to slumber is to no longer be free: free men act. However, for freedom to be possible one must respond when the security on which such a possibility is based is continually under siege. For bin Laden, the 9/11 attacks become his response to the injustices he believes have been imposed on the Muslin world by the U.S. and as a result, al-Qaeda was left no other choice but to respond as they did in self-defense (bin Laden in Kepel & Milelli, 2008).

Though one may certainly take exception with the logic employed by bin Laden, which underlies this phenomenology of violence, it provides little insight into the experience which seems to drive this version of being-in-the-world-as-Muslim. How one constructs the experience of being-in-the-world-with-others, regardless its more general ontological structure, will always fall prey to the ontic interpretations, which situate it within a very specific understanding of world. For bin Laden, that point of reference emerges from the Salafist Jihadi perspective, which identifies and validates a very specific potentiality for being-with, and constructs the Muslim experience of victimization from that point of view. However, though bin Laden employs this history of documented victimization as the main rationale for the actions that followed, he seems blissfully unconcerned or perhaps even unaware of the implications these actions will have on the security of free men, who also seek to embrace the more general call to jihad.

Bin Laden's error can be located perhaps in his appraisal of the victory over the Soviet Military by the Afghan mujahidin, which, as was stated above, al-Qaeda played at best a very minor role. He then removes this victory from its historical context and applies it to the jihad that al-Qaeda will now wage against the U.S. and its allies. However, because these superficial comparisons failed to recognize in a more realistic way, some of the more important contributing factors of the mujahidin victory, particularly as this related to the introduction of the Stinger Surface-to-Air missile, the dissimilarities between the Soviet and American economic systems, and the intensity and resolve of the allied American response to the 9/11 attacks, a similar type of victory was hardly guaranteed nor was it very likely. Though a number of critical assessments have been directed at bin Laden and his organization for the subsequent consequences suffered by the jihadi movement in the aftermath of the 9/11 attacks, none is perhaps more revealing than is the one offered by the Egyptian Muslim Brotherhood in the text, *Al Qaeda's Strategy: Flaws and Perils*.[5]

The authors provide an introductory critique of the bombing campaigns employed by al-Qaeda beginning in 1998 and culminating in

---

[5] Though the authors of the text provide a very thorough critic of al-Qaeda's behavior and rationale, for the purposes of this discussion, I will focus on their critic of the fatwa or religious ruling offered in the Jihad Against Jews, and Crusaders (02/23/1998) which in the words of the authors "has been, for all intents and purposes, the manifesto of "The International Front for Jihad Against the Crusaders, the Jews, and the Americans" and has formed the very basis upon which such a front was founded" (Zuhdi et al., 2005, p. 4). However, there does appear to be some confession concerning both the text of this statement as well as the date of its announcement. I have discovered two different dates for this statement 08/23/1996 and 02/23/1998 and two different titles, Jihad against Jews and Crusaders and al-Qaeda's Declaration of War against Americans, in which these titles share some of the same text, albeit without the same dates.

2003.⁶ The writers continue by observing that though these attacks reflect the strategy which al-Qaeda believed would be beneficial in addressing many of the problems facing the "Islamic nation," they have actually contributed to the worsening of that reality (Zuhdi et al., 2005). Regardless the intended goal of al-Qaeda's actions, the only result achieved was the strengthening of the resolve and unity of its enemies and the consequences for the same is ongoing (Zuhdi et al., 2005). Though the writers appear to be more accepting of the basic analysis of the specific realities confronting the Islamic nation offered by al-Qaeda, they seem to strongly reject the misguided violent strategy that has been employed by them to correct these problems. In fact, they argue that such a strategy is a misinterpretation of jihad.

The authors provide their critique of al-Qaeda's interpretation of jihad, by focusing on a statement which appears in the document titled the *International Islamic Front for Jihad against the Jews, the Crusaders, and the Americans*. In that statement bin Laden and his co-authors rationalization that the use of force is the only effective strategy by which to confront America and her allies. Though they do recognize that victory will be difficult to achieve and require significant sacrifice from the total Muslim community, their example of jihad will be the "flame," which will inspire the future generations who follow, and that possibility will be what defines their success (bin Laden, 2005). The Zuhdi et al. (2005) contend that such a model of jihad fundamentally misinterprets the Islamic construct of duty, resulting in a practice that simply becomes an end itself (Zuhdi et al., 2005). Taken from this perspective, such a strategy becomes one that completely ignores the practical capabilities of Muslims and one which also ignores the social benefits and social harms, which may result from such a strategy (Zuhdi et al., 2005).

Taken from a phenomenological perspective, the al-Qaeda proclamation and the critique offered by the authors of the Egyptian Islamic Brotherhood emerge as competing nomic structures or as manifestations of the they-self, which seek to proscribe a specific meaning or validity on

---

⁶ These attacks include the car bomb attacks on U.S. embassies to Kenya and Tanzania in 1996, the 9/11 attacks in 2001, and a variety of bomb attack in Bali, Indonesia, Riyadh, Saudi Arabia, and Casablanca between 2002 through May 2003 (Zuhdi et al., 2005).

what it means to be Muslim. Given that the leadership of al-Qaeda was and is fundamentally forced on recreating or revitalizing being-in-the-world-as-Muslim, their interpretation of jihad becomes perhaps the most powerful apparatus by which to achieve that result. The critique offered by the authors of *Al Qaeda's Strategy: Flaws and Perils* recognizes the central importance which al-Qaeda's interpretation of jihad has played in its justification of violence, as well as how this interpretation has fundamentally misrepresented the religious significance of this practice. As a result, each manifestation of this structure of nomic ordering represents a meaning-generating process, seeking to determine what it means to be Muslim.

One of the central differences between al-Qaeda's understanding of jihad and the Muslim Brotherhood's interpretation of that practice is focused on what this religious action seeks to achieve. Whereas Zuhdi and his colleagues identity the goal of jihad as achieving the promise of the religion, al-Qaeda's interpretation is viewed as being exclusively focused on violence and the slaughter of its enemies (Zuhdi et al., 2005). As can be viewed in these differing constructions of jihad, a very different phenomenology emerges depending upon how this important religious practice is interpreted.

Given that jihad is seen as a means and not an end, it becomes impossible to construct the practice in the way that al-Qaeda does for the simple reason that the practice is not legitimately reducible to an exclusive military meaning (Zuhdi et al., 2005).[7] However, it is also rather clear that for al-Qaeda to achieve its goal of reconstructing being-in-the-world-as-Muslim, it must also reconfigure the interpretation of jihad in the very rigid and misleading way that it does, to make its claim. Whether this strategy is the result of an incomplete understanding of the concept of jihad as presented in the Qur'an, as Zuhdi and his co-authors contend, or as an example of expedient strategizing, the result is still the same: a construction of the meaning of jihad, which seems to blend both the

---

[7] The Islamic scholar Khaled El Fadl has also argued that it is theologically incorrect to attempt to equate jihad with Holy war. In fact, Fadl (2007) observes that "'Holy war' (in Arabic al-harb al-muqaddasa) is not an expression used by the Qur'anic text or Muslim theologians. In Islamic theology, war is never *holy*; it is either justified or not—and if it is justified, those killed in battle are considered martyrs" (p. 222).

offensive and defensive characteristics of this practice, which not only reinterprets the concept, but completely reconfigures the stance for being-in-the-world-as-Muslim.

What the Egyptian Islamic Brotherhood's critique of al-Qaeda provides is a different phenomenological structure for being-in-the-world-as-Muslim that rejects al-Qaeda's illegitimate claims concerning the definition and practice of jihad, along with the strategy of violence which it evokes. Such a stance is significant coming from a group such as the Egyptian Islamic Brotherhood given their long-established presence within the Islamist community. By first offering a critique of al-Qaeda's interpretation of jihad, it then allows Zuhdi and his co-authors to address the strategic consequences of this phenomenology. One of the flaws which becomes the target of their critical review is the Fatwa, justifying the murder of American citizens.

Zuhdi and his co-authors (2005) begin their critique by focusing their attention on the al-Qaeda fatwa that permits the killing of noncombatants. The prohibition against the killing of noncombatants is well established in the Qur'an, but al-Qaeda's interpretation seems to ignore this fact. The authors continue by observing that any fatwa that fails to make the distinction between civilian and military personal is simply in direct opposition to sharia law and is therefore not validated by the Qur'an (Zuhdi et al., 2005). The authors of this critique continue by providing a variety of examples that appear in the Hadiths of both the Prophet and his Companions, which fundamentally prohibits the killing of civilians during war time (Zuhdi et al., 2005).

Given that existing sharia rulings become the specific manifestation of the process of religious nomic ordering, which in turn constructs being-in-the-world-as Muslim, it is not at all surprising that the Islamic Brotherhood becomes fundamentally focused on the phenomenology, which the al-Qaeda fatwa seeks to legitimate. As such, the strategy employed targets both specific misinterpretations of existing sharia law on which the al-Qaeda fatwa seeks to rely, while also delegitimizing the behavior which it encourages and requires. In Chap. 3 of this text, it will be recalled that the construct of nomic fracture was discussed, which becomes exemplified by this clash of competing nomic orders. Though there is certainly no guarantee that critiques like the one offered by the

Egyptian Muslim Brotherhood will have the intended result of reestablishing a process of nomic ordering that is able to construct a different type of being-in-the-world-the-world-as-Muslim, it does help to better clarify the phenomenology each of these perspectives seek to create. We will now move to a brief discussion of some of the ideas offered in the writing of Ayman al-Zawahiri.

Ayman Al-Zawahiri: The Enemy Near and the Enemy Far

Al-Zawahiri was born into a well-placed Egyptian family in 1961, who were well-respected in the fields of medicine and academics. However, unlike those of the westernized Egyptian middle-class of Cairo, al-Zawahiri's family was more conservative and, in some corners, viewed as pious (Kepel, 2005; Lacroix, 2008). Lacroix (2008) observes that it was likely this early quality of piousness, which played such a significant role in his emerging political perspective. Al-Zawahiri was greatly influenced by Qutb's influential texts *Milestones* and *In the Shadow of the Quran* and that influence would intensify after Qutb execution in 1966 (Gerges, 2009; Lacroix, 2008). In the aftermath of Qutb's death, al-Zawahiri, still only fifteen years of age, created his first underground Salifist cell, which he titled the Jihad Group.

With the death of then President Naser and the beginning of the Sadat regime, Islamic militants, who had been incarcerated and often brutally tortured while in custody, were now being released from prison in an attempt by Sadat to offer some degree of reconciliation and relief to the former policies of the Naser regime (Gerges, 2009; Lacroix, 2008). It was during this period, when committed Islamist ideologues sought to actively pursuSadate their version of jihad, which would ultimately lead to the assassination of Anwar Sadat in October 1981. In the aftermath of that assassination, al-Zawahiri along with virtually all of the leaders of the Islamist movement were arrested and many brutally tortured. Once released from prison in the mid-1980s, he would make his way to Peshawar, Pakistan, where he would meet a young Osama bin Laden and were he would become instrumental in creating the structure for the pursuit of global jihad and the battle with the far enemy (Gerges, 2009; Kepel, 2020; Lacroix, 2008).

The constructs of the enemy far and the enemy near represent very different projects for what has been identified as being-in-the-world-as-jihadi. These categorical distinctions become "structural" or perhaps better stated, rhetorical points of reference, which help to not only situate the meaning of being, but also provide it with a specific vantage point by which being finds itself in relation to a very specific social world. More than just clarification of strategic targets for jihadist insurgents, these constructs also help to configure very different "structures" for being-with that effectively transforms the social context from which these phenomenologies emerge. If as argued above, al-Qaeda's fatwa represents a competing manifestation of the Jihadi they-Self, then the constructs of the enemy far and enemy near become artifacts of that process.

The central difference between the constructs of enemy far and enemy near are denoted in their title. The enemy near is generally intended to identify a specific regime or leader that a domestic jihadi group has deemed responsible for those conditions, which now are perceived to be threatening either the faith community or the religion itself. As a result, those countries identified as the enemy near are represented by those Arab regimes that have been charged with failing in their responsibilities to the faith community and the religion and should, therefore, be violently overthrown by the people. Taken from this perspective, the jihad to be waged in response to the conditions of ignorance or jahili regimes was to remove those identified threats to Islam as manifested in traditionally Islamic cultures. Al-Zawahiri, a rigorous proponent of this enemy near strategy (Gerges, 2009) firmly believed that the initial focus of these jihadi insurgences were to pressure Arab regimes into either fulfilling their responsibility to the Qur'an and sharia or be overthrown.

In contrast, the enemy far identifies those non-Arab or non-Muslim regimes that are viewed as being the most responsible for the spilling of Muslim blood and continuing the perceived humiliation and inferiority of Muslim people. They are also seen as using their political and military influence in the region in ways that continues at the detriment of Muslim nations. Osama bin Laden has famously identified a variety of examples, which he used to justify his campaign of religiously driven violence. Whether this was the presence of U.S. troops near the Holy places of Islam, its continued support of Israel, or its ability to pressure Arab countries in the region to capitulate to its economic and political interests, all became in bin Laden's view attacks on the faith community and the religion itself, which in turn justified his call to jihad. He also appeared to argue that the enemy far strategy allowed for the opportunity for Muslims worldwide to regain a sense of dignity in fighting the enemies of Islam; he also seemed to reason pragmatically that their ability to win the hearts and minds of the Muslim community required a strategy that did not wage war in Muslim countries.

Al-Zawahiri's belief in the enemy near strategy of jihad remained through his early presence in Pakistan and Afghanistan but seemed to take a decided turn in the aftermath of the 9/11 attacks. As Hegghammer (2020) has observed, the war in Afghanistan provided for the opportunity for many jihadists coming from the Saudi Arabia, Egypt, North Africa, and elsewhere, the opportunity to wage defensive jihad, albeit in very limited ways, while also providing the environment in the post-war years for the creation of a fighting force that could pursue jihad wherever needed worldwide. Fueling this strategy was the intoxicating influence of the military victory won by the Afghan mujahidin over the Soviet military and the rather humbling history of failed attempts by Arab jihadists to overthrow enemy near regimes in places like Egypt and Alegria and elsewhere. Al-Zawahiri's focus on the enemy far can be clearly viewed in the document titled, "Jihad, Martyrdom, and the Killing of Innocents" prepared by the Council of the Jihad Organization, and supersized by him.

In constructing the context by which jihad and martyrdom become legitimate al-Zawahiri (2007) observed that it is the duty of all Muslims to battle those who reject Allah and his law and to fight until Islam is the only religion. He continues by observing that this fight must be directed toward those rulers, who govern the people without sharia law as their guide and alley themselves with infidels (al-Zawahiri, 2007). Taken from the perspective, al-Zawahiri does not identify the enemy near as the necessary target for jihad, rather, his focus identifies all non-believers of Islam and those societies not governed by sharia, included in this category of non-believer is any Muslim who has abandoned jihad. The "logic" he employs to support this point makes comparative reference to a time when Muslims embraced jihad and were a mighty people, with that of contemporary history, which has witnessed the abandonment of jihad (al-Zawahiri, 2007). The humiliation and inferiority, which currently inflicts the Muslim nation, is directly due to this abonnement of the Muslim nation's duty to God.

From this perspective a vengeful version of the Islamic they-self is evoked that punishes all who fail to adhere to the level of fidelity demanded by al-Zawahiri and his colleagues. Though much of the logic employed by this statement reflects many of the same errors in interpretation critiqued by Zuhdi et al. (2005) above, and much is offered with little context; it does, however, "skillfully" seek to reconfigure the meaning of Muslim "strain" in ways that reconstructs the very foundation related to the phenomenology of Muslim experience. No longer the result of unintended humiliation, the failure of Muslim cultures and the material and psychological consequences which follow ultimately becomes the punishment for the lack of faith in Islam and not due to the actions of those nations bent on dominating these communities.

To love martyrdom is to embrace that which is most valued by this manifestation of the religious they-self: the willingness to pursue jihad and to sacrifice one's life in that cause. As was stated above, this stance is most clearly reflected by the fedayeen fighters in Afghanistan, who were exclusively motivated by the desire for martyrdom as an end in itself. Unlike the Afghan mujahidin, who hoped for martyrdom without intentionally pursuing it, here, the only true criteria of faith is one's death. This configuration of being-in-the-world-as-jihadi is, as Zuhdi et al. (2005) observe, a phenomenological stance that really disconnects itself from the specific goal this jihad is attempting to achieve. Given that the purpose of jihad appears to be directly tied in some way to the ultimate betterment of the religion and the faith community, it is difficult to see how the pursuit of martyrdom as an end itself actually achieves that goal.

When contextualized from this perspective, failed faith, and the abandonment of religious duty, becomes the true cause for this divinely inspired retribution. Being-in-the-world-as-jihadi now becomes more specifically configured as being-in-the-world-as-martyr and all other possible configurations are valued through the success of the same. As such, the averageness which this manifestation of the they-self prescribes now views martyrdom as that which can be venture and all other exceptions are rejected. From al-Zawahiri's perspective, the fact of divine retribution becomes exemplified as the consequence for failing to embrace that which this religious they-self demands. As a result, the Muslim victim becomes transformed into the Muslim sinner and only the pursuit of martyrdom can absolve that "stain;" it is from this new perspective that the phenomenology of martyrdom emerges.

Given that the construct of martyrdom is often situated within the context of suicide bombing or other types of suicide missions, al-Zawahiri is confronted with a difficult task: can one become a martyr if the individual has intentionally, either through some manner of suicide attack or through some type of military operation, lose their life, particularly when the Qur'an specifically prohibits the act of suicide (Cook, 2007; Roy, 2017)? David Cook (2007) has observed:

> The general consensus was that one should not undertake these types of operations except in the direst circumstances and only when there is a clear benefit for Muslims. Otherwise the person who performs a suicide attack is committing suicide. (p. 149)

Cook's observation seems to focus on two important points: circumstances must be dire and the act performed must be beneficial to Muslims. This perspective is one shared by Zuhdi et al. but is still potentially rather vague. How does one determine when these observed consequences become dire and how does one determine a clear benefit? Though various critiques of this position may provide ample evidence by which to evaluate both consequences and benefit, these constructs or qualities are not easily accepted by those following the al-Qaeda line of Qur'anic interpretation. For example, if the current consequences confronting the Muslim community are due to their failure to pursue this version of jihad and the benefit for Muslims becomes realized through the pursuit of martyrdom, then it becomes much more likely that those who feel similarly will embrace this strategy.

Central to this logic of circumstance and benefit is how these two experiences are phenomenologically perceived. Regardless the specific theological evidence that many critiques provide, in their attempt to invalidate this general interpretation of jihad and martyrdom, if, as Berger (1967) has observed, one simply needs to be able to place one's history within the nomic structure being offered, its validity will be difficult to refute. This will be particularly true when this lived-experience is shared within a specific example of being-with. Taken from this perspective, the world, and my place in it, is now transformed. My circumstances are dire and as a result I must fight, which is the only way to end this continued debasement and once again enjoy the glory which only God may provide.

When viewing the version of the they-self constructed by bin Laden and al-Zawahiri, its most significant achievement, if it can be identified in that way, has been its ability to call into question the very foundation of what it means to be Muslim. Though many of its claims and charges can be easily refuted from a specific point of view, that fact has had difficulty in finally stopping the spread of this religious discourse. As Zuhdi and his co-authors have observed, though the various terror attacks culminating with the horrific event of 9/11 have caused almost incalculable damage to the Salafist Jahid movement worldwide, various versions of being-in-the-world-as-Islamic-martyr still retain a powerful resonance; a stubborn fact that will not be bombed out of existence. Al-Qaeda is a perfect example of that resilience.

As a movement or organization, al-Qaeda's history begins in the final years of the Afghan jihad against the Soviet Union and then comes of age in the decade following that war and then announces itself as an adversary to be reckoned with as it spearheads a variety of specular terror attacks ending, of course, on 9/11. However, in the aftermath of 9/11, the U.S. and its allies launch a withering attack on the global jihad movement that destroys much of its structural and organizational capacity, but it still continued, seemingly undaunted by the extent of its defeats. Even with the death of Osama bin Laden, who was killed by Seal Team Six on May 2, 2011 in Abbottabad, Pakistan, their version of being-in-the-world-as-Muslim continues.

What this "resilience" reveals is an almost unshakable fidelity to this version of being-in-the-world-as-Jihadi, that al-Qaeda's Salafist nomos has constructed. Though a number of important inroads have been achieved in Afghanistan, Iraq, and Syria, these are hardly finished victories and a continued threat remain. Al-Qaeda may be in decline, but that fact has not prevented it from threatening to emerge once again. Of greater significance perhaps, is the fact that al-Qaeda simply represents one manifestation of this version of the they-self and its potential defeat has little baring on groups elsewhere. The most obvious example of that fact is the surprising emergence of the Salifist Jihadi group known as al-Qaeda-in-Iraq, ISIL, ISIS, Daesh, the Islamic State.

References

Al-Zawahiri, A. (2007). Jihad, martyrdom, and the killing of innocents. In R. Ibrahim (Ed. & Trans.), *The al-Qaeda reader: The essential texts of Osama bin Laden's terrorist organization* (pp. 141–171). Broadway Books.

Anas, A., & Hussein, T. (2019). *To the Mountains: My life in Jihad, from Algeria to Afghanistan*. London, England: Hurst & Company.

Bergen, P. L. (2001). *Inside the secret world of Osama bin Landen Inc*. Free Press.

Berger, P. (1967). *The sacred canopy: Elements of a sociological theory of religion*. Anchor Books.

bin Laden, O. (2008). Message to the American people. In G. Kepel & J.-P. Milelli (Eds.), P. Ghazaleh (Trans.), *Al Qaeda in its own words* (pp. 71–77). The Belknap Press.

bin Laden, O., Zawahiri, A, Taha, A. R. A., & Hamza, S. M. Rahman, F. (2007). Al-Qaeda's declaration of war against Americans. In R. Ibrahim (Ed. & Trans.), *The al-Qaeda reader: The essential texts of Osama bin Laden's terrorist organization* (pp. 11–14). Broadway Books.

Cook, D. (2007). *Martyrdom in Islam*. Cambridge University Press.

El Fadl, K. A. (2007). *The great theft: Wrestling Islam from the extremists*. HarperOne.

Gerges, F. A. (2009). *The far enemy: Why Jihad went global*. Cambridge University Press.

Hegghammer, T. (2020). *The Caravan: Abdallah Azzam and the rise of global jihad*. Cambridge University Press.

Heidegger, M. (2010). *Being and time* (J. Stambaugh, Trans.). SUNY Press.

ibn Taymiyya. (2007). Al-Qaeda's declaration of war against Americans. In R. Ibrahim (Ed. & Trans.), *The al-Qaeda reader: The essential texts of Osama bin Laden's terrorist organization* (pp. 11–14). Broadway Books.

Kepel, G. (2005). *The roots of radical Islam*. Saqi.

Kepel, G. (2020). *Away from Chaos: The Middle East and the challenge to the West*. Columbia University Press.

King, M. (2001). *A guide to Heidegger's being and time*. J. Llewlyn (Ed.). SUNY Press.

Lacroix, S. (2008). Introduction: Ayman al-Zawahiri, veteran of jihad. In G. Kepel & J.-P. Milelli (Eds.), P. Ghazaleh (Trans.), *Al Qaeda in its own words* (pp. 147–170). The Belknap Press.

Lawrence, B. (2005). Introduction. In B. Lawrence (Ed.), J. Howarth (Trans.), *Messages to the world: The statements of Osama bin Laden*. Verso.

Roy, O. (2017). *Jihad and death: The global appeal of the Islamic State*. Oxford University Press.

Zuhdi, K. M., Abdullah, N. I., AL-Sharif, A. M., Hafiz, U. I., Abdul-'Azim, H. A.-R., Muhammad, A. A.-M., Al-Dawalibi, F. M., & Derbala, M. E. (2005). *Al-Qaeda's strategy: Flaws and perils*. Al-'Obeikan Publications.

6

The Islamic State and the Return of the Caliphate

Al-Baghdadi Announces the Creation of the Islamic State

On July 4, 2014 in the Northern Iraqi city of Mosul, Abu Bakr al-Baghdadi announced from the pulpit of the Great Mosque of al-Nuri the creation of the Caliphate of the Islamic State and that he would be its new caliph. Though al-Baghdadi's announcement caused tremendous concern both in the region, and amongst the U.S. and its allies, it is only a portion of the historical narrative of the Islamic State (Bardaji, 2015; Gerges, 2016; Kepel, 2020). Over a period of approximately twenty years, a variety of iterations of this group has emerged as the circumstances of its reality has required. Beginning around 1999/2000 and continuing in the aftermath of al-Baghdadi's death, which occurred on October 26, 2019 as a result of physical intelligence provided by the Syrian Kurds and executed by American Special Forces troops, parts of this group still remain (Bardaji, 2015; Gerges, 2016). It also seems important to note that this seemingly defeated religious insurgent organization is not unfamiliar with the experience of near total defeat and yet has been

© The Author(s), under exclusive license to Springer Nature Switzerland AG 2021
D. Polizzi, *Toward a Phenomenology of Terrorism*, Critical Criminological Perspectives,
https://doi.org/10.1007/978-3-030-76405-0_6

able to exhibit a tenacious ability to re-organize and re-emerge as a serious threat when the opportunity arises.

What emerges as most significant from this history is not necessarily the shocking operational successes that this group was able to achieve in a relatively short period of time; rather, it is the tenacity by which this version of being-in-the-world-as-Muslim has remained faithful to the specific nomic structure this manifestation of the they-self provides. Though this tenacity of belief is certainly emboldened by the experience of "divinely inspired" victory, it is still predicated upon a structure of faith that is similarly rewarded for its unshakable fidelity. Taken from this perspective, the Salafist view offered by the Islamic State configures a meaning for both individual experience and the social world, which in turn fundamentally structures the projects that are to be pursued.

It should be recalled that regardless the specific theoretical configuration by which phenomenology is employed, a structure of meaning is constructed that to some degree is always co-constituted and always revealing an inseparable intervolvement between individual and world (Polizzi, 2016, 2019). Whether this be situated within the context of a perceiving consciousness and the intentional objects which are revealed from this event, the ways in which being-in-the-world finds itself through its experience of being-with or the way bodies are configured as bearers of behavior, all help to inform not only our understanding of world, but the "structural" realities which make that knowing possible. When applied to the intervolvement witnessed within the phenomenology created by IS, these meanings become clearly apparent.

As was stated above, though the event of the sermon preached at the Great Mosque in Mosul by al-Baghdadi really represents a type of middle ground, as this relates to the overall developmental history of this religious insurgency, its message clearly helps to situate a specific type of religious intervolvement that clearly reflects the type of nomic structure being employed and the type of "selves" it desires to fabricate. Abu Bakr al-Baghdadi begins his sermon by stating:

> So let the world know that we are living today in a new era. Whoever was heedless must now be alert. Whoever was sleeping must now awaken. Whoever was shocked and amazed must comprehend. The Muslims today

6 The Islamic State and the Return of the Caliphate

have a loud, thundering statement, and possess heavy boots. They have a statement that will cause the world to hear and understand the meaning of terrorism, and boots that will trample the idol of nationalism, destroy the idol of democracy and uncover its deviant nature. (al-Baghdadi, 2020a, p. 162)

Though the content of the sermon is familiar with other similarly focused statements by other Salafist Jihadi groups, in both its tone and subject matter, the context of the sermon is decidedly different. For al-Baghdadi, his first public sermon represents the culmination of a series of military victories across Iraq and Syria that not only announced the presence of an emerging Salafist Jihadi threat, but one that had exhibited the initial capability of taking and holding territory and establishing a de facto state (Gerges, 2016; Giglio, 2019). Salafist Jihadi groups such as al-Qaeda have certainly shown the operational capability and the "nomic" reach by which to represent a significant threat to non-Muslim societies, it has not, however, shown the ability to actually take and hold territory in the way that IS was able to do. The Taliban, perhaps, represents the best example of such a capability, but for that group, the victory of its religious insurgency emerges from the ashes of the Afghan civil war that occurred in the aftermath of the defeat of the Soviet invasion of that country.

Al-Baghdadi is certainly aware of these differences, which is clearly exhibited as the sermon continues. He exults his audience to free themselves from their chains of humiliation and confront the tyranny of their enemies (al-Baghdadi, 2020a). For al-Baghdadi success allows confidence, albeit perhaps, as unrealistic as bin Laden's, but a confidence nonetheless. Though many Salafist Jihadi leaders have called for the ummah to rise up and shatter the shackles of their humiliation and weakness, none has been able to do so from the context of such unassailable military success. Even as chilling as the horrific events of 9/11 were, the "success" of that event really does not compare to what al-Baghdadi and his group of religious insurgences were able to achieve. Whereas 9/11 represented the assault on iconic symbols of American economic and military power, the creation of the Islamic State (IS) represented a religious insurgency that rejected the legitimacy of existing international borders, while also exhibiting the "practical" ability to pursue a more traditional military strategy by which to hold and gain more territory in the name of Islam.

The ability of IS to gain territory at the pace that it was able to achieve, likely had a profound psychological effect on those members of the ummah, who were similarly inclined toward the creation of an Islamic State, for the simple reason that this time success was real. As Zuhdi et al. (2005) have observed, the operational successes of al-Qaeda culminating in the attack on 9/11 also resulted in the aftermath of that violence, a devastation of the Salafist Jihadi movement worldwide.[1] Though the territorial gains achieved by IS would be short-lived, that defeat has not prevented its re-emergence in Afghanistan, Pakistan, Northern and Central Africa, and Central and South East Asia (Coll, 2019; Elias, 2020; Jalalzai, 2020). As a result, al-Baghdadi's call for the ummah to rise up does achieve a level of legitimacy given the actual successes achieved prior to this sermon. As a result of that success al-Baghdadi proclaims the world now consists of two competing camps: the camp of the unfaithful and the camp of the unbelievers (al-Baghdadi, 2020a).

For al-Baghdadi, the distinction between that which will be valued and that which will not becomes rather clearly demarcated between those who are believers of the faith and those who are hypocrites or unbelievers. The identification of the camp of hypocrisy is a clear Qur'anic reference to those who claim to be Muslim, but betray that faith when called to protect the religion (Halverson et al., 2013). Salafist Jihadi leaders have regularly evoked the narrative of the hypocrite by which to identify "those that have failed to oppose state regimes that do not implement the Islamist vision of *shari'ah* or the 'Islamic state'" (Halverson et al., 2013, p. 63). Included in this grouping are the members of the ulma, religious

---

[1] Though the differences between al-Qaeda and IS are perhaps more subtle, one difference cannot be ignored: the ability for these religious insurgencies to be successful within the context of a civil war. It is certainly true that al-Qaeda emerged as a legitimate religious insurgency toward the end of the Afghan jihad, and into the decade of the 1990s, it did so as an alien force, and one that simply did not enjoy the same domestic currency as did the Afghan mujahidin. On the other hand, IS emerged as a direct result of the U.S. invasion of Iraq and the civil war which erupted in Syria as a result of the Arab Spring and was largely fought by individuals native to those countries. The military successes achieved by IS prior to al-Baghdadi's sermon were gained by forces indigenous to that country. Though foreign fighters would flock to the Islamic State to join this fight, it happened in the aftermath of these successes (Hegghammer, 2020; Gerges, 2016).

6   The Islamic State and the Return of the Caliphate

clerics who control the interpretative authority within the religion and who these Salafist Jihadi leaders regularly disagree.

Al-Baghdadi's announcement of the caliphate helps to configure a new construction of being-in-the-world-as-Muslim that "must" now accept the fact of this divinely sanctioned event due to its very existence, and which in turn similarly requires that all Muslims recognize him as its ordained caliph. It is probably not by accident that IS refrained from proclaiming the creation of the caliphate until it was successful in conquering those territories in Iraq and Syria, which were traditionally ruled by sharia law. By "ending" the rule of the hypocrites in these areas and reclaiming this territory for Islam, the call to stand and rise up is provided much greater "legitimacy." Again, the proclamation offered by al-Baghdadi is not delivered in some unidentified location or, for example, somewhere in the mountain caves of Bora Bora; rather, it is from the pulpit of the Great Mosque of Mosul.

Al-Baghdadi continues by making the distinction between what he identifies as the secular false slogans of the east and the west and the charge of terrorism. He observes that the accusation of terrorism is the result of their failure to reject the belief in Allah, their refusal to reject their belief in sharia and unwillingness to continue to live in humiliation, and subjugation to non-believers and their hypocrite allies. To fight against such hypocrites and unbelievers is not to be defined as terrorism, but as proof of the ummah and its unwillingness to abandon their religious duty to defend their faith. Taken from this perspective, the accusation of terrorism is deconstructed along with its network of socially constructed meanings; as a result, the master narrative provided by al-Baghdadi evokes a competing hermeneutic structure, which seeks to dismantle these "encrusted" social meanings assigned to Muslim experience by offering an alternative possibly for being-in-the-world-as-Muslim. In so doing, he also offers a different manifestation of Publicness, a different configuration of being-with that rejects the conclusion that non-believers and hypocrites are the sole authors of what Muslim experience ought to mean. However, unlike most of the Salafis Jihadi leaders who preceded him, al-Baghdadi, through his announcement of the creation of the Islamic State, is also able to construct a version of Publicness that becomes predicated upon the specific version of Islam offered in this sermon.

It will be recalled that for Heidegger (2010), Publicness reflects the ontological structure of social reality. As such, the nomic ordering of the Islamic State emerges as an ontic example of this ontological process. By fabricating a manifestation of Publicness that is no longer predicated upon the they-self of non-believers or hypocrites, being-in-the-world-as-Muslim can now take up its projects from the perspective, which this new experience of thrownness provides. No longer does this type of being need to accept its experience of humiliation or subjugation and neither should it continue to equate faith in Islam with terrorism. Once reconfigured in this way, being-in-the-world-as-Muslim becomes transformed in both its faith and capability to resist those who seek to continue to control this process of revitalization.

Though al-Baghdadi (2020a) does not place direct or immediate blame on those who have been forced to suffer humiliation and subjugation at the hands of the non-believers or hypocrites, he does, however, plainly state that the only way out from these "chains of weakness," is to once again surrender to Allah and his laws. If Muslims are to be granted success and delivered from this state of inferiority they must act now, and the creation of the Islamic State is now what makes such a stand possible:

> So if you want the promise of Allah, then fear Allah and obey Him. Obey Allah al-'Adhim [the Almighty] in every matter and in every condition. Adhere to the Truth and hold on to it in matters you like and dislike. (al-Baghdadi, 2020a, p. 167)

The placement of al-Baghdadi's sermon, which he delivered after the fall of Mosul at the Great Mosque of al-Nuri on July 4, 2014, at the beginning of this chapter, is to help better situate the phenomenological progression that began well before the caliphate was established and continues to have influence well after the death of its author. The phenomenology which this sermon evoked is a troubling one given the degree of violence that was "justified" in its name both prior to and after the official announcement of the creation of the Islamic State: a fidelity to violence and death, which still lingers today, even in the years after the caliphate's defeat. This discussion will now turn to that history.

Abu Musab al-Zarqawi and al-Qaeda in Iraq

There is a misconception, even amongst scholars and practitioners, that the Islamic State movement first emerged in 2013–14. In ignoring almost two decades of its history, such a misunderstanding blinkers any attempt to under-stand its nuances. Indeed, even a cursory glance through its early years reveals operational and strategic patterns that emerge time and again even to this day. (Ingram et al., 2020, p. 3)

As the above quote observes, the creation of the caliphate represents the culmination of that history, which required the "acquisition" of actual territory by which to legitimize their claim to Islamic authority. Beginning approximately 12 months prior to the 9/11 attacks, the various iterations of this religious insurgency have been continually focused on conquering territory that could then be claimed in the name of an Islamic state. Though this vision came to an end with the return of control of those areas of Iraq and Syria formerly claimed by this group, these defeats have not ended this pursuit. The IS story begins with its original founder Abu Musab al-Zarqawi.

Ahmad Fadeel al-Nazal al-Khalayleh better known as Abu Musab al-Zarqawi was born in Jordan in 1966, but did not enjoy some of the same pedigree as those involved in the leadership of al-Qaeda. However, after the death of his father in 1984, al-Zarqawi quickly turned to street crime and soon after found himself in a Jordanian prison (Gerges, 2016). Upon his release from prison, he discovered Islam and ultimately made his way to Afghanistan in 1989 to pursue jihad. However, his arrival was ill-timed. With the defeat of the Soviet invasion coinciding with his journey to Afghanistan, his desire to participate in that jihad was denied and by 1993, he made his way back to Jordan (Bardaji, 2015; Gerges, 2016). Soon after his return, al-Zarqawi became involved with a Salifist Jihadi group in that country where he met the Jihadi scholar Abu Mohammad Taher al-Maqdisi, who also helped to influence his understanding of jihad (Gerges, 2016). During his involvement with al-Maqdisi, al-Zarqawi further developed his perspective on jihad which was very much focused on the concept of the "enemy near."

It will be recalled that the construct of the "enemy near" is employed by Salafist Jihadi groups to identify those Arab regimes that have failed to allow the institution of sharia law in those societies and has failed in their duty to protect the ummah. Within this context, the focus on the enemy near becomes fundamentally concerned with regime change, which will be led by these local jihadi groups, with the assistance and support of the local faith community, who will be liberated in this process. However, though this point of view had been embraced by a variety of Salafist Jihadi groups in the region, this strategy has really never been effective and has often resulted in widespread incarceration, torture, and execution as has been witnessed in countries such as Algeria, Egypt, Saudi Arabia, and Yemen. Al-Zarqawi's plans resulted in a similar fate.

In 1994, al-Zarqawi and al-Maqdisi were arrested and ultimately convicted and sentenced to fifteen years for their offenses (al-Zarqawi, 2020). During the sentencing phase of the trial, al-Zarqawi gave his first public speech to the Jordanian court. Though al-Zarqawi and al-Maqdisi are arrested for possessing weapons of war, he claims his real intention is to issue the call for a return to Islam. As a result, his trial, and the trial of others, is for their attempt to achieve this goal (al-Zarqawi, 2020). Zarqawi continues by equating the violent behavior of the Jordanian security forces as the price paid by those brothers who have honorably taken up this call of the prophets.

Ingram, Whiteside, and Winter (2020) contend that this initial speech helps to perhaps deconstruct the understanding of al-Zarqawi as merely drug dealer or street thug; here, we are witness to a narrative style that is similar to many of the Salafist Jihadi leaders already discussed and one which identifies many of the same charges these other Salafist thinkers have directed toward the religious circumstances of their day. It is also interesting to recognize how al-Zarqawi's focus on the Jordanian government and what he sees as the hypocrisy of democracy is similar to the way al-Baghdadi explores the construct of terrorism. For Zarqawi, democracy is the process that seeks to silence violently, the voices of Islam. For al-Baghdadi, the term terrorism is applied to those Muslim who stand up for the perceived attacks on their religion.

Gerges (2016) contends that it was during this experience of incarceration and bouts of torture where al-Zarqawi's psychopathic characteristics

6 The Islamic State and the Return of the Caliphate

of a cold-blooded killer start to emerge. It is also not at all surprising that clinically these experiences would also help to greatly strengthen an already configured animosity toward those identified as the enemy near. Having now directly experienced regime-sanctioned violence for his views on Islam, he becomes the example of the very process he desires to overthrow. Interestingly enough, bin Laden, though apparently personally traumatized by the vicarious strain imposed by his witnessing of Muslim deaths at the hands of non-Muslim aggressors, never seemed to stray too far from his strategic position of focusing on the enemy far:

> The viciousness of the Zarqawi generations is organically linked to its social status in the hierarchy of the global jihadist movement. In a way, Zarqawi was representative of a new wave of jihadists who came from deeply disadvantaged and marginalized backgrounds. (Gerges, 2016, p. 57)

Taken from this perspective, the experience of social marginalization endured by those of Zarqawi's generation unfolds as a twofold phenomenological structure. As members of the socially disadvantaged class, they are marginalized by the existing economic and political structures and left without a voice relative to the circumstances of their existence. However, upon their entry into the hierarchy of the global jihadi movement, they were once again marginalized, and once again silenced by the existing elite who were reluctant to share power (Gerges, 2016). This phenomenological dynamic was specifically present within Zarqawi's relationship with Osama bin Laden and is likely in part related to his decision to leave Afghanistan and pursue his own strategy of jihad. Gerges' (2016) observation concerning Zarqawi's significance to the existing strategic concerns of the global jihadi movement as well as the initial role he played in the process, which ultimately led to the creation of the Islamic State, is an important one. His initial creation of al-Qaeda-in-Iraq, not only reflects his desire to create a movement in that country, but also reveals his clear disagreement with the strategy for global jihad of his day.

Though Gerges is historically correct in his position that Zarqawi did not play a key role in the construction of the Islamic State, he similarly seems to undervalue his role relative to the phenomenological structure he evoked and developed until his death. After his return from Afghanistan in 1999, where he failed to ingratiate himself with the top al-Qaeda leadership, in part over his aggressive disagreement over their strategies for waging jihad, he begins to slowly construct his own organization. Zarqawi, unwilling to accept the generational process, which bin Laden and others in al-Qaeda seemed to envision, was ready to strike now at both the enemy of the United States and at those Arab regimes that refused to support the religion. In the aftermath of the 9/11 attacks and the U.S./allied invasion of Iraq, Zarqawi was able to take advantage of the opportunities the situation offered, which allowed for his reign of terror to effectively begin. If Gerges (2016) is correct in his analysis of the processes of marginalization that were in play for individuals like Zarqawi, then the phenomenology which underlies this manifestation of being-in-the-world can also be explored.

What seems most prominent within the phenomenology of jihad pursued by Zarqawi and others within this movement is the unshaken belief in the correctness of their faith and the legitimacy of their claim. Zarqawi's view of the world is simplified by an "us or them" dynamic that leaves no room for compromise or caution. As a result, it can similarly focus on the causes of Sunni Muslim humiliation regardless whether its perpetrator is the enemy near or enemy far; while also confidently challenging the general strategy and leadership of the global jihadi movement. When taken from this more "simplified" understanding of the social world, such distinctions become unnecessary. Within the context of this "revised" manifestation of the Salafist Jihadi they-self, being-in-the-world-as-Sunni-jihadist is "disburdened" of the complexities of the meaning for such existence when reduced to such black and white certainties. This is not to downplay the unspeakable viciousness, which was witnessed in the emerging years of this movement and throughout its history; rather, it is simply intended to show how this change in phenomenological perspective fundamentally transformed the various ways in which this type of being-in-the-world would take up its own existence.

However, what this beginning history reveals is that by 2004, al-Zarqawi realizes that his call for jihad has not been sufficiently taken up by his Iraqi brothers and American forces and their allies are becoming emboldened by this fact. His concern over the situation at this time must have been sufficient enough to reach out to potential fighters, given that this was his first public speech in approximately a decade. Al-Zarqawi attempts to evoke the empathy of those like-minded individuals, who will perhaps heed his call at this time when the need and situation was becoming more desperate. It is also interesting that though he can recognize the current plight of his movement, there is no hint or loss of purpose that this fact will deter him, even if his depleted ranks must act alone.

It is also important to note that in the previous year Zarqawi actively called for attacks on the Shi'a population in Iraq, who had formerly fought against the U.S. and its allies. These seemingly indiscriminate attacks, which targeted weddings, funerals, mosques, and other public spaces, were exclusively directed at areas under Shi'a control and likely greatly undermined any real ability to broaden his base of support; in fact, his network went so far as to charge that Shi'a support of the American invasion was similar to the Mongol invasion of the Muslim world in the thirteenth century (Gerges, 2016). One of his most infamous attacks and one which would leave no confusion concerning his intentions was the attack on the Iman Ali Mosque, viewed as one of the most sacred sites in Shia Islam along with the murder of the spiritual leader of that community Ayatollah al-Hakim (Bardaji, 2015; Gerges, 2016; Kepel, 2020).

It is likely because of this strategy of indiscriminate violence that Zarqawi's call was more often heard by foreign fighters and not individual Iraqis. To some degree, the jihad in Iraq had some of the general distinguishing characters with that of the war in Afghanistan, except for perhaps the most essential one: the lack of a cohesive coalition of domestic fighters who were capable of bracketing their differences, while focusing on a shared identified goal. Once Zarqawi's strategy of total jihad was launched, the possibility for domestic coalition building was likely lost as well.

Once Al-Zarqawi (2020) announces his plans for total jihad, he also comes to the realization that the numbers in his movement have drastically decreased. Faced with this reality, a reality that was likely tied to his break with al-Qaeda and the strategies he employed in Iraq, al-Zarqawi begins to question the faith of those who continue to refuse to join his movement. He argues that if we share the same belief, what is your excuse for not joining this jihad (al-Zarqawi, 2020)? What of course Zarqawi is unable to even to contemplate is the possibility that his audience understands the pursuit of jihad differently and is one that is not as pathologically committed to violence as he most certainly was. This distinction again has some comparative similarities with the Afghan jihad and to some degree validates the position taken by Abdullah Azzam upon his arrival to Afghanistan.

It seems reasonable to argue that the Iraqi jihad became the very example of that religious practice, which Azzam worked very hard to avoid. He quickly recognized upon his arrival in Pakistan and Afghanistan that for the Afghan jihad to be successful, it had to be led by the coalition of Afghan mujahidin, whose specific religious traditions and practices should not be critiqued or in any way disrespected. Fighters from the coalition of Arab Afghans coming from Saudi Arabia, Egypt, and elsewhere were immediately informed on their arrival in Pakistan that they must be seen as supporting the Afghan jihad and not attempting to stamp it with their specific brand of Salafist theology and interpretation (Anas & Hussein, 2019; Hegghammer, 2020). Zarqawi apparently had no such concerns.

It is reasonable to observe that Zarqawi's failure was also doomed by his inability to recognize that his call to jihad and the brutal violence, which that call evoked, particularly when directed toward other Muslims, would almost certainly evoke the ire of all those other domestic groups still fighting the American invasion, while anxiously awaiting the post-Saddam era to begin (Kepel, 2020). So brutal was the violence directed toward Shiites in Iraq that al-Qaeda leaders wrote Zarqawi and ordered him to end these killings and focus his efforts on defeating the American and allied forces still occupying Iraq. "More important still, Al Zawahiri showed his displeasure with the massacres of Shiites and reminded the emir of Al Qaeda in Iraq that such actions would fail to gain the popular support needed by the cause of the Caliphate" (Bardaji, 2015, p. 7).

However, Zarqawi was left unconvinced and his reign of violence was now directed at various Sunni tribal leaders, which greatly troubled the al-Qaeda leadership, given that such a strategy would most likely deprive him of the needed support of this group. Though Bardaji (2015) claims that evidence does exist concerning his willingness to take these criticisms seriously, it did not result in an effective change of strategy. In fact, he

6 The Islamic State and the Return of the Caliphate

argues, it was at this point that Zarqawi started to actively contemplate distancing himself from al-Qaeda and announce the creation of the Islamic emirate in Iraq (Bardaji, 2015; McCants, 2015). Though bin Laden[2] continued to argue for the need for patience, lest the Iraq jihad meet the same fate of the Taliban in Afghanistan, Zarqawi seemed uninterested in such a strategy. Al-Zarqawi continued to pursue his strategy for jihad, but saw those plans cut suddenly short, when on June 7, 2006 he was killed by a laser-guided bomb fired by an American F16 jet.

However, as Zarqawi's religious insurgency has proven, you may kill the leader, but you cannot so easily kill the idea. Shortly after the death of its creator, Abu Ayyub al-Masri was chosen as the new leader of al-Qaeda in Iraq. Though the insurgency continued under the al-Qaeda "brand," it was clearly still fundamentally driven by the vision Zarqawi initiated. However, this continuity in "branding" was effectively ended when al-Masri formally announced the creation of the Islamic State of Iraq a few months after assuming leadership of this religious insurgency. Included in this announcement was the naming of the new leader of the Islamic State Abu Omar al-Baghdadi (Bardaji, 2015; Gerges, 2016; Kepel, 2020). During this announcement of the Islamic State in Iraq and its new leader Abu Omar al-Baghdadi, the group also announced its plan moving forward. Included in this strategy was the elimination of the State of Israel along with the reclaiming of the other states in the Levant: Syria, Lebanon, and Jordan, ending with the "liberation" of the Arabian Peninsula (Kepel, 2020).

What this period in the development of the Islamic State reveals is a consistent fidelity to a process of nomic ordering that has remained intact, even in the face of the near annihilation of this religious insurgency. So steadfast is this belief and fidelity to this specific manifestation of a zealot they-self that not even the possibility of death can weaken this relationship. As Berger (1967) observes, "Anomy is unbearable to the point where the individual may seek death in preference to it" (p. 22). As a result no level of sacrifice or experience of suffering will be deemed as too much if it viewed as serving this nomic order.

---

[2] It is ironic that bin Laden would make such an observation, given it was his decision to launch the 9/11 attack, which is most responsible for quickly ending the reign of the Taliban in Afghanistan.

The dynamic, which Berger describes, is central to the phenomenological structure that is configured by the process of nomic ordering, unleashed by al-Zarqawi. At the very core of this nomic narrative is the call to embrace sacrifice and suffering and even death in the pursuit of re-establishing a true Islamic state, which will be ruled by God's law. By deconstructing the more traditional understanding of "legitimate" martyrdom, death becomes an end in itself and provides being-in-the-world-as-Muslim a "divinely inspired" path to heavenly reward. Sacrifice, suffering, and death are "removed" from their more existential context and re-configured from the exclusive purview of religious faith. Fail to successfully satisfy this religious litmus test is to be deemed an unbeliever and worthy of death.

On December 22, 2006, approximately six months after the death of al-Zarqawi and a few months after the announcement of the formation of the Islamic State of Iraq, the religious insurgency's new leader, Abu Umar al-Baghdadi, issued his second speech titled, "Truth Has Arrived and the Falsehood Perished" (Ingram et al., 2020). He begins by stating that the establishment of the Islamic State was made possible by those who sacrificed by blood and money in the name of Islam (al-Baghdadi, 2020b).

The phenomenology which Abu Umar al-Baghdadi describes is one that openly and without apology places the pursuit of martyrdom at the center of this "project." There is simply no manipulation or attempt to conceal what is actually being offered to those who may choose to join the caravan. It is also psychologically significant that the possibility of victory is also included, which seems to disrupt the fedayeen pursuit of death as an end itself, as has been discussed previously. If victory is achieved, the Islamic State is established and sharia law will be enforced; one the other hand, if martyred in the cause of Islam, one receives a divinely sanctioned reward. It also probably does not matter very much that such an interpretation seems to contradict the more traditional understanding of this process, for the simple reason that groups like ISIS were and are fighting the existing religious authority, who they view as innovators or as imposing manmade law rather than enforcing the Qur'an. To further make the point that this call to martyrdom is straightforwardly requested Abu Umar al-Baghdadi (2020b) continues by affirming that there is no need for tears or slogans, only those whose deeds reflect their faith.

The manifestation of the they-self offered by Abu Umar al-Baghdadi is one that values sacrifice as well as the need for one to prove their fidelity to God and his law. Superficial examples of sadness or support are insufficient and only action can affirm the question. Taken from this context, what belongs to this manifestation of the they-self becomes exemplified by Abu Umar al-Baghdadi's (2020b) requirement for the proof of faith, which can only be legitimated by sacrifice and martyrdom. When the author states that what is most needed belief and deeds and not tears and slogans; he is prescribing that which may be ventured and that which may not. Those soldiers who have come before are now representative of the type of sacrifice that this new nomic order will value and require to be emulated by those that will follow. What will be watched over is any "exception" that fails to heed what this they-self now stipulates.

The example of averageness, or what Heidegger (2010) has also identified as leveling down, is clearly recognized by the Islamic they-self of al-Baghdadi concerning what will be permitted. This process of leveling down by this manifestation of the they-self seeks to invalidate any interpretation of jihad, martyrdom, or the Qur'an itself as something already known and therefore indisputable within the claim offered by al-Baghdadi. The desire for the creation or return of a monic world is a world where everything is leveled down and becomes predicated upon the dictates of this rigid configuration of the they-self. As the title of this speech announces, the Truth has arrived and all falsehoods must perish.

The Islamic State of Iraq After the Death of Abu Musab al-Zarqawi

The period directly following the death of al-Zarqawi in June 2006 up to the deaths of Abu Umar al-Baghdadi and Abu Ayyub al-Masri in April 2010 represents the most difficult period for the religious insurgency of the Islamic State in Iraq, leading many to believe that perhaps the group was finished. Not only did this four-year stretch of time include the deaths of its founder and his replacement successor, but also witnessed a variety of major military defeats in part related to what has been termed the American Surge and the Sunni Awakening. It will be recalled that in response to the escalating insurgent violence, which threatened to spiral out of control, then President George W. Bush, against the advice of those calling for an end to the war in Iraq, introduced over 20,000 combat troops by which to address the deteriorating situation in Baghdad and in various parts of the country (Biddle et al., 2007; Simon, 2008). However, though this counterterrorism strategy was able to reduce in a significant way the levels of violence it was addressed to curb, this became possible in large part due to the various types of cooperation, which it received from domestic groups who had previously been the victims of the horrific actions perpetrated by the Islamic State of Iraq (Gerges, 2016, Simon, 2008). But as Simon observed, this was only a short-term solution to a more long-term problem.

Though the military success of the Surge cannot be argued given the significant decreases in the general dangerousness of Baghdad and the significant decreases in American causalities, it was unable to address the underlying political dynamics that overtime would once again escalate and provide a reemerging Islamic State, the opportunity to take advantage of the situation (Simon, 2008). It is certainly undeniable that the circumstances leading up to the launching of the Surge helped to legitimate the participation of those domestic Iraqi Islamic groups who for a variety of different economic, political, and religious reasons saw it in their interests to cooperate with this American counterinsurgency strategy. As violence escalated between al-Zarqawi's group and the various domestic factions within Iraq, the initial rationale of focusing on the American invasion started to unravel (Gerges, 2016); add to this, the fact that ISIS was also targeting various Sunni Tribal leaders, who were now resisting the push by the Islamic State of Iraq to take over those areas traditionally under the influence of tribal control, it becomes clearer, why these groups would join with the U.S. to fight their most immediate threat (Gerges, 2016).

However, Gerges (2016) observes that the likely driving force behind the actions of al-Zarqawi and the leaders that followed were focused on the idea of evoking a war between Sunni and Shi'a Muslims with the

6 The Islamic State and the Return of the Caliphate

American invasion being an ancillary benefit that would help this group achieve that goal. "Zarqawi belonged to a new wave of Salifist-Jihadists who are obsessed with identity politics and the struggle to purify Islam and Islamic lands of apostasy. The Shias top the list of real and imagined enemies" (Gerges, 2016, p. 82). This focus on the purity of identity becomes central to this phenomenological structure and seems to also speak to the intensity of belief that allows it to continue even when its realization appears to be the most unlikely. Even in the aftermath of al-Zarqawi's death, and in the face of the diminishing returns that this Islamic scorched earth strategy realized, the insurgency continued its pursuit of purifying both the religion and the state from what they perceived as the apostasy all around them and did so unconcerned of its potential consequences.

The phenomenology which emerges from this anti-Shi'a manifestation of the they-self reveals that which will be most valued and that which will not. Taken from this perspective, the purification of Islam requires the elimination of the Shia as an apostate manifestation of Islam along with those Sunni tribal leaders who refuse to recognize the single religious authority of the Islamic State (Gerges, 2016). If a religiously pure Islamic state is to be created, it is first necessary to eliminate all those hypocrites and non-believers, who stand in the way of this goal. It is likely for this reason that the warnings offered by Osama bin Laden and Ayman al-Zawahiri were constantly ignored by al-Zarqawi and the various iterations of the ISIS leadership that followed.[3] Though the creation of an Islamic state was certainly a goal for al-Qaeda, it was not one that was being immediately sought. ISIS on the other hand was fundamentally focused on that goal and therefore needed to confront those groups within Iraq that could prove to be a barrier to that result.

---

[3] It is also necessary to remember that al-Zarqawi and bin Laden disagreed on this point as far back as 1999 while both were in Afghanistan.

The Rise of the Islamic State and Its New Leader Abu Bakr al-Baghdadi

In the aftermath of the deaths of Abu Umar al-Baghdadi and Abu Ayyub al-Masri in 2010, it appeared that the defeat of the insurgency started by al-Zarqawi had been finally realized. The Surge proved to be successful in drastically decreasing the escalating cycle of violence and Sunni tribal leaders were able to find a "suitable" compromise in joining with American forces to stop the growing influence of the Islamic State of Iraq, particularly in those areas traditionally controlled by Sunni tribal communities. However, the sudden "calm" which emerged in the aftermath of these successes would be short-lived and would prove to be the gestational stage for yet another iteration of the religious insurgency started by al-Zarqawi approximately fourteen years earlier (Gerges, 2016; Giglio, 2019).

As Iraq moved further into its post-Saddam, "post-war" development, a number of lingering political and ideological factors once again came to the fore (Gerges, 2016). With the establishment of the Shi'a lead government of Nuri al-Maliki, ethnic and religious tensions once again started to emerge (Giglio, 2019). The policies initiated by al-Maliki evoked a great deal of suspicion within the Sunni community, who were now growing more concerned over the potential of an increasing Iranian influence in their country (Gerges, 2016). As the animosities between the Shi'a government and the Sunni committees grew, so too did the opportunity for ISIS to reemerge and yet again take advantage of the situation.

In 2004, Ibrahim ibn Awwad Ibrahim Ali al-Badri al-Samarrai, along with other suspected insurgent fighters, was arrested by U.S. security forces and ultimately sent to the American-run detention facility Camp Bucca, where he officially joined the ranks of the Islamic State of Iraq. The prison population of this facility housed approximately "[t]wenty-four thousand men, many of whom were Baathist officers and nationalist fighters who worked for the Saddam Hussein's regime" (Gerges, 2016, p. 133). For al-Samarrai, soon to be known by his more infamous nom de guerre, Abu Bakr al-Baghdadi, this experience would prove to provide him the unprecedented opportunity to meet and learn from the most senior jihadists in the country and to do so in the relatively secure

6 The Islamic State and the Return of the Caliphate

environment of his prison setting. This is not to imply that the prison experience at facilities like Camp Bucca was either comfortable or pleasant, only that it offered the jihadist community the opportunity to meet without the fear of surprise counterterrorist operations that would almost always end in death. And, as a result, al-Baghdadi took full advantage of this opportunity and quickly rose through the ranks of the ISI (Gerges, 2016).

Though al-Baghdadi's prison experience at Camp Bucca provided him access to an unprecedented network of jihadi leaders and fighters from all over Iraq, it also exposed him to the various forms of physical abuse and torture, which fundamentally transformed him. During his time at Camp Bucca, Baghdadi became known as the "fixer" by U.S. prison authorities, which he used to solidify his position with captors and fellow inmates alike. Though he lacked many of the skills of the more well-known jihadist leaders, he was still able to use certain personality traits that allowed him to gain the trust of those around him (Gerges, 2016). Gerges observes that this ability was particularly event with his relationship with then ISI leader Abu Umar al-Baghdadi.

Abu Bakr al-Baghdadi served approximately two years with the then leader of ISI, Abu Umar al-Baghdadi and became his "closest aide" (Gerges, 2016), which ultimately resulted in him assuming the leadership of ISI, when Abu Umar al-Baghdadi was killed in a joint U.S./Iraqi military operation. Given the closeness of Baghdadi's relationship with the now deceased leader of ISL, his transition to leader of that organization seemed to make sense:

> In this sense, Baghdadi's ascendancy to the top post did not signal a dramatic change in ISI's predicament. Survival was the name of the game for ISI in 2010, though its commander never lost sight of their strategic goal: to dominate the Sunni areas of Iraq and to consolidate and transform their fragile existence into an Islamic state. (Gerges, 2016, p. 137)

As Gerges explains, in 2010, ISI was almost completely defeated, yet this fact seemed to have little effect on al-Baghdadi's plans moving forward. The relationship between this structure of nomic ordering and the identities, which it helped to create, remained undaunted by the immediate circumstances of the situation and allowed al-Baghdadi to remain focused on his goal of the establishment of an Islamic state.

> According to Baghdadi and his cohorts, the Islamic revival is contingent on rekindling a fervor for jihad in the hearts and minds of Muslims and building an ideological army willing and ready to battle the enemies of Islam near and then far. (Gerges, 2016, p. 140)

However, the rekindling of jihadi fervor and the creation of an army willing to fight the enemy both near and far, at least as this pertained to the project of al-Baghdadi, required one more important variable: the "acquisition" of territory.

Perhaps the single most important difference between the Islamic State of Iraq and all other Salafist Jihadi groups was the need to conquer land, which could then legitimate al-Baghdadi's claim that the caliphate had been recreated. Once the caliphate had been established, and al-Baghdadi named as its caliph, sharia law could be legitimately mandated and the pursuit of offensive jihad legitimately required. Without the establishment of the caliphate, there could be no legitimate naming of a caliph or the legitimate application of sharia law. In an interview with Graeme Wood of the Atlantic, British Islamic State supporter Anjem Choudary clarifies this important distinction:

> Before the caliphate, "maybe 85 percent of Sharia was absent from our lives," Choudary told me. "These laws are in abeyance until we have khilafah—a Caliphate—and now we have one." Without a caliphate, for example, individual vigilantes are not obliged to amputate the hands of thieves they catch in the act. But create a caliphate, and this law, along with a huge body of other jurisprudence, suddenly awakens. (Wood, 2015, p. 17)

It is also necessary to add that with the establishment of an Islamic state, and the naming of its new caliph, Muslims in theory would be obligated to immigrate to this territory, given it was now being ruled by sharia law (Gerges, 2016). Included would be the legitimation of al-Baghdadi's call for offensive jihad, given that once the caliphate had been established, it would become incumbent upon its caliph to expand the

6 The Islamic State and the Return of the Caliphate 165

territory now governed by the Qur'an. Such an obligation would be somewhat easier to pursue as a result of the unresolved circumstances in Iraq, particularly in the north of that country and the deteriorating conditions in neighboring Syria that was now involved in a violent civil war as a consequence of the Arab Soring and the brutally violent repression of the Assad regime, which stubbornly attempted to remain in power (Gerges, 2016; Phillips, 2016). As Phillips (2016) observed, the unfolding civil war in Syria allowed for the introduction of ISIS forces, many of whom were formerly members of Saddam's military, which resulted in the acquisition of both large areas of Syrian territory and supporters. Included in this process was the capture of Raqqa in 2013, the city that would become the capital of the Islamic State (Phillips, 2016).

The Islamic State's capture of parts of Eastern Syria, the naming of Raqqa as its capital, along with the capture of Mosul in Northern Iraq, represents arguably the most significant set of achievements ever realized by this type of religious insurgency. It is particularly "impressive" given that within a span of less than four short years, this group went from near total defeat to the triumphant establishment of the Islamic State. One of the main contributing factors of this success was reflected in their ability to recruit from the ranks of the former Iraqi army, as well as various jihadi groups in Syria, which in turn allowed them to use these victories to reach out to individuals worldwide. As these successes continued to multiply so did the numbers of individuals willing to join this cause. The question which remains is why?

It is probably not by accident that much of the Islamic State's growth in both Iraq and Syria occurred at very significant historical moments, when the attraction to such an ideology would most loudly resonate for those seeking some respite from their difficult existence. In the years leading up to al-Zarqawi's killing in 2006, al-Qaeda in Iraq was almost finished due in large part to the tactics practiced by that group. However, as the domestic situation in Iraq changed due to the attitude and policies pursued by the Shiite lead government, the narrative offered by al-Baghdadi provided a recognizable nomic structure by which to revitalize the shattered Sunni identity, which was now under siege by the new ruling order of the country. Additionally, it provided the opportunity for many of the displaced Baathist military, to reenter the fight, but this time under the banner of Salafist Jihadi Islam. As a result, all manner of enemies could be identified and confronted, and honor restored.

Likely related to the above fact, is the simple psychological benefit provided by the intoxicating effect of the groups' swift and convincing military victories over seemingly superior military forces. Though a great deal of "excitement" was generated by al-Qaeda's devastating attack on the United States on 9/11 that victory proved to be rather short-lived and dealt a powerful setback to the Jihadi movement worldwide, the announcement of the creation of the Islamic State was qualitatively different. Not only was IS able to exhibit impressive military prowess in their territory capturing operations, but were then able to use those successes to establish an Islamic state.

Al-Baghdadi was certainly aware of this effect when he begins his sermon from the Great Mosque of Mosul by stating that the way to freedom is through the confrontation of the tyranny and nonbelief. Al-Baghdadi's command to rise up also includes the duty to annihilate all of the nonbelievers and hypocrites that remain obstacles for this long-awaited moment to come to fruition. Al-Baghdadi eludes to this when he states that this new Muslim nation will have its voice heard worldwide and its boots "will trample the idol of nationalism, destroy the idol of democracy and uncover its deviant nature" (al-Baghdadi, 2020a, p. 162). Taken from this perspective, to rise up becomes the call for a type of moral retribution that will cleanse the Muslim nation from both its sense of inferiority and the humiliation that such an experience has placed upon it. This sense of moral retribution closely mirrors what Jack Katz has described as moralistic rage or righteous slaughter.

In his important text, *Seductions of Crime: Moral and Sensual Attractions in Doing Evil*, Katz (1988) explores the phenomenology of homicidal violence. Central to his discussion are questions concerning how the killer understands himself, his victim, and the context in which this interaction will occur. Taken from this perspective, moralistic rage emerges as the artifact of a specific type of social experience or relationality that can no longer be tolerated by the individual. However, though the initial context offered by Katz concerning this phenomenological structure is situated within individual experience, its application to the moral rage often witnessed in various examples of political and religiously motivated violence becomes similarly recognizable (Polizzi, 2016, 2020).

For Katz (1988), the construct of righteous slaughter is phenomenologically predicated on the affective components of humiliation and rage. As has been discussed in numerous examples above, the phenomenology of humiliation and the rage that this experience evokes has been continually identified and employed by those Salafist Jihadist leaders and theorists, who have called for the Muslim nation to rise up and wage jihad. However, Katz does not imply that the experience of humiliation is covered over by this emergent rage; rather, it is viewed as a co-constituting aspect of this phenomenology. "As a lived experience, rage is livid with the awareness of humiliation" (Katz, 1988, p. 23). Katz (1988) continues by observing:

> In both humiliation and rage, the individual experiences himself as an object compelled by forces beyond his control. That is, his control of his identity is lost when he is humiliated. (p. 24)

The loss of control related to identity formation and the experience of humiliation which follows is an essential aspect of this phenomenology.

Within the above context, the loss of identity becomes manifest within individual and group experience from two different aspects of relationality. On the one hand, the inability to control one's identity becomes situated within the experience of those, who are either not permitted to practice their faith in the ways they perceive the religion requires or when they do so are almost reflexively identified as terrorists and prevented from engaging in religious practice. As a result of this meaning-generating process, individuals will likely confront a sense of humiliation due to the degree of control this structure imposes upon lived-experience, which in turn will further accentuate the levels of powerlessness that constructs and defines their existence. However, this is not the only aspect of identity control that is present in this context.

Al-Baghdadi also focuses on the type of characteristics that a true Muslim should exhibit. From this perspective, Muslim identity is constructed from a specific point of view of the Islamic they-self, which offers a way out of the experience of humiliation, if it is willing to embrace what is being offered. When situated in this way, Muslim "living being" is asked to choose between two competing apparatuses, each attempting to fabricate a different manifestation of the subject: one which will continue the desubjectification of the Muslim subject and one which will provide its liberation from a continual experience of individual and group humiliation. It is from this recreated version of the Islamic subject that the use of righteous slaughter becomes validated.

Katz (1988) observes that "Humiliation becomes rage when a person senses that the way to resolve the problem of humiliation is to turn the structure on its head" (p. 27). This is preciously what al-Baghdadi is able to accomplish. If humiliation is the recognition of a future that will remain more or less the same, rage is that which emerges in the moment unconcerned about what the future may bring (Katz, 1988).

> And righteousness, concerned only with what always has been and will always be right, is justly indifferent to the historical moment. In this way, the Good serves as the springboard for the leap into blind rage. (Katz, 1988, p. 31)

Katz's observation of the indifference of righteousness is clearly witnessed in the blind rage of the Islamic State and its well-documented practices of barbaric violence and ethnic cleansing over the course of its brief existence as a quasi-nation. Tragically, its practices of public beheadings, crucifixions, summary executions by firing squad, and other horrific genocidal practices by which to execute capital religious offenders all become subsumed under this new configuration of the Good. Once so confirmed there is simply no longer any question concerning how the individual understands who they are, or who their victim is or the meaning of this moment in which these actions are taking place. The individual becomes divinely sanctioned to eliminate all those deemed to be "responsible" for the humiliation, which drives this righteously inspired rage. Violence in all of its various forms now simply becomes the tool by which this divinely sanctioned retribution may be visited upon those deemed unworthy of any moral recognition due to their lack of belief, religious affiliation, or innovate practices.

6 The Islamic State and the Return of the Caliphate

Such a process also has a profound transformational influence upon those who use this righteous rage as the mechanism by which personal humiliation and inferiority may be overcome. It has been anecdotally reported that recent converts to the IS brand Salafist Jihadi practices often follow directly from a life of crime or drug use and often with little actual knowledge of Islam. However, what these observations normally miss is the transformative impact that such a narrative of liberation may offer to those, who have become lapsed in their religious identification with Islam or trapped within a life of psychological marginalization that offers few legitimate avenues of escape. It becomes or can become what Roger Griffin (2012) has described as the process of heroic doubling.

Taken from this perspective, the phenomenology of heroic doubling transforms the individual and their specific experience from a place of psychological marginalization to that of psychological relevance. Perfected by this newfound faith or by the return to a set of beliefs formerly left behind, the shortcomings of the self are overcome and those acts that were formally viewed as criminal or shameful now become part of this larger mission to vanquish evil and the humiliation it evokes (Griffin, 2012):

> The feeling of having been born to serve a higher will or destiny, of being "sent" to fulfill a suprapersonal historical, or even supranatural divine purpose crystallizes in the mission. This locates the individual life within a powerful living drama in which the "enemy", the source of decadence and evil, is unmasked and identified, enabling the solution to be visualized in a heroic struggle to establish, or to re-establish, purity and good. (Griffin, 2012, pp. 93–94)

When configured in this way, the experience of righteous rage described by Katz becomes recognized within the phenomenology of heroic doubling and becomes the vehicle by which evil will be confronted and defeated. Once the "source of decadence" has been identified within this narrative process, the means employed by which to achieve the purity of the good almost become irrelevant. In fact, by some accounts, any admission of self-doubt concerning the moral or religious legitimacy of these actions becomes evidence of one's lack of faith, which now makes them eligible to the same fate (Giglio, 2019; Speckhard & Yayla, 2016; Wood, 2017). Such a transformation becomes so psychologically intoxicating that such lapses of faith simply cannot be tolerated.

Though the reign of the Islamic State has officially come to an end and all of the former conquered territories have been regained by the former governing authorities, the idea of the Islamic State and the zealot narrative which it offers to potential recruits remains alive and well, albeit in a far less visible way. The near capture and death of the former caliph of the Islamic State, Abu Bakr al-Baghdadi[4] in Syria on October 26, 2019, simply resulted in the naming of an al-Baghdadi deputy Amir Mohammad Sa'id Abdul-Rahman al-Mawla as the new leader of this religious insurgency. However, it is important to note that al-Mawla did not assume the title of caliph, most likely due to the fact that the caliphate no longer exists, rendering such a claim illegitimate. In the absence of a caliphate, there can be no caliph, which in turn would also imply that sharia is once again placed in abeyance.

Given that the "legitimacy" of the Islamic State was fundamentally predicated on the capture and control of territory stretching from Mosul in Northern Iraq to Raqqa in Eastern Syria, it remains to be seen how the lingering pockets of this group will reemerge. The loss of this territory seems particularly significant to their nomic structure and the behavior it evokes, due to its Islamic "end-of-days" implications. Will the loss of captured territory be perceived by its believers as the proof of God's displeasure or simply a burden that must be endured until the Mahdi returns (McCants, 2015)? How this phenomenology unfolds will likely be predicated upon what the fall of the caliphate means for those who fought for its creation and how its believers will continue in the aftermath of its defeat.

---

[4] Abu Bakr al-Baghdadi was able to claim legitimacy to the title of caliph, given his contested claim that he is a descendant of the Prophet's tribe, "which many Muslims consider a prerequisite for the caliph… Abu Umar even claimed descent from one of the Prophet's grandsons, Husayn, in an attempt to appeal to those who would confine leadership of the Muslim world to descendants from Muhammad's family, just as medieval caliphs had done" (McCants, 2015, p. 14).

References

al-Baghdadi, A. B. (2020a). 'Message to the mujahidin and the Muslim ummah in the month of Ramadan', 1 July 2014. In H. Ingram, C. Whiteside, & C. Winter (Eds.), *The ISIS reader: Milestone texts of the Islamic State movement* (pp. 162–167). Oxford University Press.

al-Baghdadi, A. U. (2020b). 'Truth has arrived, and falsehood perished' 22 December 2006. In H. Ingram, C. Whiteside, & C. Winter (Eds.), *The ISIS reader Milestone texts of the Islamic State movement* (pp. 65–67). Oxford University Press.

al-Zarqawi, A. M. (2020). Untitled speech, 4 January 2004. In H. Ingram, C. Whiteside, & C. Winter (Eds.), *The ISIS reader Milestone texts of the Islamic State movement* (pp. 21–31). Oxford University Press.

Anas, A., & Hussein, T. (2019). *To the Mountains: My life in Jihad, from Algeria to Afghanistan*. London, England: Hurst & Company.

Bardaji, R. (2015, November 27). *Roots of the Islamic State* (No. 182). Foundation for Social Studies and Analysis.

Berger, P. (1967). *The sacred canopy: Elements of a sociological theory of religion*. Anchor Books.

Biddle, S., Friedman, J. A., & Shapiro, J. N. (2007). Testing the Surge: Why did violence decline in 2007? *International Security, 37*, 7–40.

Coll, S. (2019). *Directorate S: The C.I.A. and America's secret wars in Afghanistan and Pakistan*. Penguin Books.

Elias, B. (2020). Directorate S: The CIA and America's secret wars in Afghanistan and Pakistan. In M. K. Jalalzai (Ed.), *Pakistan's spy agencies: Challenges of civil control over intelligence agencies bureaucratic and military stakeholderism, dematerialization of civilian intelligence, and war of strength* (pp. 135–141). Vij Books India Pvt Ltd.

Gerges, F. (2016). *ISIS: A history*. Princeton University Press.

Giglio, M. (2019). *Shatter the nations: ISIS and the war for the Caliphate*. Public Affairs.

Griffin, R. (2012). *Terrorist's creed: Fanatical violence and the human need for meaning*. London & New York: Palgrave Macmillan.

Halverson, H. L., Goodall, J., & Corman, S. R. (2013). *Master narratives of Islamist extremism*. Palgrave Macmillan.

Hegghammer, T. (2020). *The caravan: Abdallah Azzam and the rise of global jihad*. Cambridge University Press.

Heidegger, M. (2010). *Being and time* (J. Stambaugh, Trans.). SUNY Press.

Ingram, H., Whiteside, C., & Winter, C. (2020). Introduction. In H. Ingram, C. Whiteside, & C. Winter (Eds.), *The ISIS reader Milestone texts of the Islamic State movement* (pp. 1–11). Oxford University Press.

Jalalzai, M. K. (2020). The political and military involvement of Inter Services Intelligence in Afghanistan. In M. K. Jalalzai (Ed.), *Pakistan's spy agencies: Challenges of civil control over intelligence agencies bureaucratic and military stakeholderism, dematerialization of civilian intelligence, and war of strength* (pp. 142–159). Vij Books India Pvt Ltd.

Katz, J. (1988). *Seductions of crime: Moral and sensual attractions in doing evil.* New York: Basic Books.

Kepel, G. (2020). *Away from Chaos: The Middle East and the challenge to the West.* Columbia University Press.

McCants, W. (2015). *The ISIS apocalypse: The history, strategy, and doomsday vision of the Islamic State.* Picador.

Phillips, C. (2016). *The battle for Syria: International rivalry in the new Middle East.* Yale University Press.

Polizzi, D. (2016). *A philosophy of the social construction of crime.* Policy Press.

Polizzi, D. (2019). The aesthetics of violence. In R. Lippens & E. Murray (Eds.), *Representing the experience of war and atrocity* (pp. 45–71). Palgrave Macmillan.

Polizzi, D. (2020). Righteous slaughter and the phenomenology of the assailed self. In D. Polizzi (Ed.), *Jack Katz: Seduction, the street and emotion* (pp. 57–72). Emerald Publishing.

Simon, S. (2008). The price of the surge: How strategy is hastening Iraq's demise. *Foreign Affairs, 87*, 57–72.

Speckhard, A., & Yayla, A. S. (2016). *ISS defectors: Inside stories of the terrorist caliphate.* Advances Press.

Wood, G. (2015, March). What ISIS really wants. *The Atlantic.* Retrieved from theatlantic.com/magazine/archive/2015/03/what-isis-really-wants/384980/

Wood, G. (2017). *The way of the strangers: Encounters with the Islamic State.* Random House.

Zuhdi, K. M., Abdullah, N. I., AL-Sharif, A. M., Hafiz, U. I., Abdul-'Azim, H. A.-R., Muhammad, A. A.-M., Al-Dawalibi, F. M., & Derbala, M. E. (2005). *Al-Qaeda's strategy: Flaws and perils.* Al-'Obeikan Publications.

7

The Taliban and Hezbollah: Political Parties or Terror Organizations

The Political or Terror

The rise of insurgency-based religious organizations is a relatively new phenomena and is one that has been most visible over the last forty years. Since the early 1980s,[1] a variety of religious insurgency groups have made their way to power via the "rifle" or the election ballot. It will be recalled that the long-banned Muslim Brotherhood of Egypt under the auspices of the Freedom & Justice Party was successful in seeing their candidate Mohamad Morsi ascend to the office of the presidency in Egypt on June 30, 2012, albeit only briefly until that regime was brought to a quick end by the Egyptian military approximately one year later. Hamas, a Palestinian group that has been described as a fundamentalist Sunni religious organization, a religious insurgency that has been fighting the Israeli government for nearly thirty-five years and a terror organization,

---

[1] The Iranian Revolution, which was led by the Grand Ayatollah Khomeini removed Western ally Shah Mohammad Reza Pahlavi from power in 1979 and established the Islamic Republic of Iran. The victory of this Shi'a lead revolution has had lasting economic, military and political effects in the region since its inception and was actively involved in the support of Shia fighters battling the Soviet invasion of Afghanistan as well as highly influential in their support of various groups in Southern Lebanon and Syria.

has still been able to garner popular political support, which has allowed it to remain a competitive alternative to the Palestinian Authority on the Gaza Strip. Each of these groups, much like the Taliban and Hezbollah, which will be discussed below, all represent a specific definitional challenge, similar to those confronted in attempting to define the construct of terrorism: are these terror organizations as designated by the West and its allies; are they examples of religious insurgencies attempting to gain power within their given countries; or are they proxy forces involved in the pursuit of domestic interests, while also involved in some manner of patron-client relationship with a larger regional actor? If on the other hand, these groups are all these things, must we then use an another means of analysis by which to better understand this highly complex phenomenological dynamic?

The phenomenology which is revealed or co-constituted within the relationship between political party and its members becomes a process of social construction that in some way re-configures the personal identity of the individuals, who will make up that organization. The degree to which this process is successful will likely be determined by the degree to which its narrative reflects the cultural reality of those individuals or groups it is trying to attract or convert to its cause. Once this relationship has been established, personal identity and the various types of discrete behaviors which follow will generally coincide with the narrative requirements of this type of nomic ordering (Berger & Luckmann, 1966). This phenomenological process has been identified by Berger & Luckmann as institutionalization.

For Berger and Luckmann (1966) the phenomenology of institutionalization reflects a set of habituated activities performed by various types of social actors. From this perspective, certain types of discrete behavior emerge as a result of the specific value provided to them by this process of nomic ordering. The receptivity of these habituated sets of "valued" social experience become predicated upon the degree to which they resonate with the cultural and historic structure of nomic meaning they seek to employee. Berger and Luckmann (1966) observe that "Institutions always have a history, of which they are the products. It is impossible to understand an institution adequately without an understanding of the historical process in which it was produced" (p. 55).

Given that any process of nomic ordering is fundamentally tied to the historical context from which it takes its phenomenological import, the narratives which are employed become the "structural" foundations for the institutions which it creates. Taken from this perspective, the discursive process involved in identity creation becomes situated within the nomic narrative(s), which provides this structure its cultural significance. As such, these discursive structures mirror a specific image or interpretation of cultural history, which allows for individuals to recognize their own biography with this narrative structure. If I can recognize my own sense of being-in-the-world from the perspective of the "institutional" narrative being offered, I will likely be more receptive to the normative structure it provides. Such a phenomenological process can be clearly witnessed within the institutional structure provided by the Salafist Jihadi narrative embraced by the Taliban in Afghanistan and the Shite Islamic perspective offered by religious organization and proxy religious insurgency of Hezbollah in Lebanon.

The Rise of the Taliban

In chronicling what he describes as the genealogies of the Afghan jihad, Edwards (2002) makes an important distinction between the historical development of jihad in Afghanistan and the structure of jihad which emerged between 1975 and 1980 in that country. Prior to the mid-1970s there was little disagreement concerning the meaning of Islam, which in turn allowed for the creation of various religious alliances based on this agreement (Edwards, 2002). However, the period of jihad, which began in the mid-1970s, saw the creation of "ten separate parties in Peshawar, all claiming to represent Islam, all claiming to represent the best interests of Islam, all working to advance their own interests and to undermine the interests of their rivals" (Edwards, 2002, p. 227). Rashid (2010) in his text on the Taliban supports this position by explaining that the Salafist Jihadi perspective embraced by this religious insurgency was generally viewed as being incompatible with more traditional views regarding the meaning and practice of Islam in that country. Rashid (2010) observes:

> Traditionally Islam in Afghanistan has been immensely tolerant—to other Muslim sects, other religions and modern lifestyles. Afghan mullahs were never known to push Islam down people's throats and sectarianism was not a political issue until recently. (p. 82)

However, for the Taliban, there was only one legitimate interpretation of Islam, their own and very little interest in accommodating views different from their very rigid understanding of the religion.

The religious perspective embraced by the Taliban was for the most part exclusively located in the southern Afghanistan city of Kandahar, which shares a border with a region of Pakistan that also shares a similar Salafist Jihadi view of Islam. When Islamist groups waged their failed uprising against the then President of Afghanistan, Mouhammad Daud in 1975, the members of this insurgency fled to Pakistan where they received support from the government there, which in turn was used by Pakistan to apply political pressure on the future governments to take power in Afghanistan (Jalalzai, 2020; Rashid, 2010). Pakistan initially supported Islamist leaders such as Gulbuddin Hekmatyar and Ahmad Shah Masud, but they would later shift that support to the Taliban which remains to this day. Though this patron-client relationship strongly existed during the period of the war against the Russian invasion of Afghanistan, it took on considerable importance in the aftermath of that conflict. Pakistan has employed the Taliban as a proxy force within that country as well as a training ground for fighters destined for military action in Kashmir fighting against insurgency forces supported by India.

The emerging story of the Taliban is first and foremost tied to its Salafist Jihadi understanding of Islam, which will be described below; however, this history is also related to the larger context of competing regional and international interests, which have intermingled with the more immediate concerns of a domestic civil war, which has greatly complicated this equation. The U.S./Pakistani/Saudi partnership as this relates to the fight against the Soviet invasion of Afghanistan has been so-well documented that it will not be repeated here (Jalalzai, 2020). Probably the most important detail of that history is attributed to the introduction of U.S. supplied Stringer missiles, which fundamentally turned the course of that war that ultimately resulted in the defeat and retreat of Soviet forces from that country. If the Soviet defeat in Afghanistan was one of the defining moments in the collapse of that government and the beginning of the end of the Cold War, the victory by the mujahidin signaled the start of a new type of international and regional competition that has yet to firmly coalesce.

The emergence of the Taliban regime in 1994 represented the first time in recent history that a Sunni jihadist religious insurgency removed an existing regime from power and assumed the position of governmental control of a given country. Upon assuming power, a number of powerful contradictions would emerge, greatly complicating the situation. The defeat of the Soviet Union energized the Salafist Jihadi movement believing that the defeat of one Superpower could now be used to confront the other (Rashid, 2010). Though the Taliban was not directly involved in the terrorist attacks planned and launched by al-Qaeda, its willingness to harbor this organization also made it easy for the U.S. and its allies to identity it as a terrorist organization and seek to isolate it internationally. Such a strategy, however, was greatly complicated by the fact that regional actors viewed the Taliban as an extension of their own national security interests and therefore had a much different option of how to address the "problem" of the Taliban.

Though Pakistan was clearly a strategic regional partner with the U.S., and still remains one to this day that relationship became riddled with numerous contradictions and incongruent security concerns as this related to the existence of the Taliban regime. These contradictions became immediately apparent in the aftermath of the 9/11 attacks, when Pakistan continued its support of the Taliban even as they continued to refuse to turn over Osama bin Laden to U.S. authorities. It is also likely why U.S. authorities failed to inform the Pakistani government of its plans to capture or kill bin Laden in the raid on his Abbottabad compound on May 2, 2011. Pakistan has also contributed men and resources to the current conflict in Afghanistan, who are currently trying to regain power and are now directing their fight against U.S. forces in that region. "In fact, encountering ISI operatives fighting alongside the Taliban in Afghanistan has become a common occurrence that no longer surprises Afghan or U.S. forces" (Jalalzai, 2020, p. 147).

The briefly stated reasons of concern and contradiction stated above are those that continue to threaten the U.S./Pakistan relationship, but the more important concern is probably more directly related to the type of regime Pakistan will tolerate on its border (Elias, 2020; Jalalzai, 2020). Most importantly, what type of Islamist regime is likely to come to power, and which of these groups can be best "managed" by its regional patron. Given that Pakistan has been deeply involved in the Afghan jihadist movement since 1975 and has heavily supported the Taliban for nearly the totality of that religious insurgency's existence, it is reasonable to observe that its support of that relationship will likely continue (Riedel, 2010); perhaps one of the reasons for this result is due to its shared understanding of Islam and a shared ethnic identification[2] (Yadav, 2010).

One of the more intriguing aspects of the nomic structure of the Talban is that it embraces a Salifist Jihadi perspective that is not traditionally practiced in Afghanistan except in the areas around Kandahar. Rashid (2010) observes:

> The Taliban interpretation of Islam, jihad and social transformation was an anomaly in Afghanistan because the movement's rise echoed none of the leading Islamist trends that had emerged through the anti-Soviet war. The Taliban were neither radical Islamicists inspired by the Ikhwan, or mystical Sufis, nor traditionalists. They fitted nowhere in the Islamic spectrum of ideas and movements that had emerged in Afghanistan between 1979 and 1994. (p. 87)

Rashid (2010) continues by observing: "The Taliban represented nobody but themselves and they recognized no Islam except their own" (p. 88). However, he also observes that this stance should not be viewed as the total lack of any theological foundation for their interpretative understanding of Islam; rather, it reflects an extreme version of a branch of Sunni Hanafi Islam known as the Deobandis, but "the Taliban's

---

[2] Yadav (2010) observes as does Rashid (2010) that some of the top Taliban leaders studied at a madaris run by Jammat-e-Ullema-e-Islami (JUI) in Karachi, Pakistan and as a result, these individuals had more in common with the Deobandis version of Islam practiced by JUI, then were the other leaders of the Afghan mujahedeen. "A possible reason is that the curriculum of the JUI madaris was substantively different from the one taught in madaris run by Afghans" (Yadav, 2010, p. 140).

interpretation of the creed has no parallel anywhere in the Muslim world" (Rashid, 2010, p. 88). However, it is also important to note that this version of the Deobandis is well rooted in those areas of Pakistan, which are adjunct to Kandahar and was the religious perspective being used "by Pakistani Islamic parties in Afghan refugee camps in Pakistan" (Rashid, 2010, p. 88).

What Rashid's description invokes is a type of hybrid Zealotry, which is reminiscent of the construct offered by Roger Griffin (2012), except that in this configuration, the newly created nomic structure reaches back into histories of a variety of Islamic traditions by which to construct this version of being-in-the-world-as-Muslim. Taken from this perspective, the emerging process of identity formation, which this process of nomic ordering facilitated, created a version of Islam and religious practice that was incompatible with the Islamic traditions of the country. As a result, the more tolerant acceptance of different versions of Islam, which was witnessed during the jihad waged against the Soviet Union, was no longer viable after 1994. With the luxury of a common enemy no longer present, Afghanistan was once again thrown into the chaos of civil war, allowing the Taliban to employ its emerging strength to claim to all of that country and with it, create an Islamic emirate under its control. However, the identity formation witnessed within the Taliban is not exclusively related to this idiosyncratic version of Islam.

Though the version of Islam practiced by the Taliban is for the most part exclusive to this religious group in Afghanistan, its Pashtun ethnic identity is not. In fact, some scholars have attempted to view the Taliban as a nationalist political/religious movement that would once again, secure Pashtun rule over that country (Ahmed, 2014). However, Ahmed (2014) makes a convincing argument for the emergence of a hybrid Pashtun identity that emerged from the predominantly rural regions of Southern Afghanistan in populations, who still identified as Pashtun, but did so from the religious point of view that they were taught in madrasas run by the Deobandis in Pakistan. It also provides a reasonable description of the phenomenology, which emerged through the Taliban's close relationship to its Pakistani supporters and groups like al-Qaeda, and their specific understanding of Islam. It also helps in clarifying that Pashtun identity would not be a sufficient ethnic commonality concerning peaceful relations with these other Pashtun groups, who refused to accept this interpretation of Islam as their own.

What this version of Islam also represents is a similar manifestation of Salafist Jihadi exceptionalism that can be witnessed in virtually every example of this larger global movement (Hamid, 2016; Moghadam, 2019). As a result of this exceptionalist nomic structure, the need for the type of religious accommodation, which was witnessed during the war with the Soviet Union, is rendered moot in the face of such absolutist certainty. In virtually any example of exceptionalist ideology—be that political or religious—ontic constructions of processes of nomic ordering, become transformed into "ontological" structures of absolute religious "truths" which become unassailable. The phenomenology that this type of being-in-the-world reveals is the pursuit of a specific configuration of Islamic purity that only the Taliban can fulfill. When taken from this point of view, any group or individual who fails to interpret Islam from the rigid manifestation of the Islamic they-self employed by the Taliban simply becomes the target of this process of religious purification. Such a phenomenological structure, driven by the sole desire to purify religious belief and practice, has been fundamental to the Taliban's process of nomic ordering from its very inception.

The "mythic" beginnings of the Taliban and its leader, Mullah Omar[3] emerge from the conflict which ensued due to the inability of competing mujahedin groups to settle their differences and the lawless environment which it helped to create. In an attempt to "purify" these corrupt parties and establish a true Islamic government, Omar called for another jihad to be waged by which law and order could be restored (Riedel, 2010). The identifying moment of this newly emerging Islamic party concerns the attempted rape or actual rape[4] of two young boys by a mujahedin leader, which resulted in Omar organizing a group of individuals to apprehend and hang those individuals deemed to be involved in this crime. The

---

[3] Mullah Omar died on April 23, 2013, but his death was not officially confirmed until two years later; he was placed by Mullah Akhtar Mansour, who was killed in a U.S. drone strike on May 21, 2016. Mansour was replaced by Mullah Haibatullah Akhundzada, who apparently is still the leader of the Taliban, but there does appear to be some question whether or not he is still alive.

[4] Different versions of this event seem to exist, but it remains uncontested that this was the organic moment when the Taliban was created.

individuals were killed and hung from the barrel of a tank and the Taliban was born (Riedel, 2010).

The narrative account which defines the nomic structure of the Taliban closely resembles the rigidly absolutist interpretations of the Qur'an preferred by ISIS, al-Qaeda, and certain segments of the Islamic Brotherhood. Like all Salafist groups, the Taliban sought an interpretation of Islam, which attempts to justify its specific application of sharia law, its understanding of the concept of jihad, and its symbolic connection to the earliest days of the Prophet and his companions. To further accentuate the relationship to this sacred past, Omar donned the Prophet Muhammad's cloak, which had been housed for centuries in a mosque in Kandahar, and wrapped it around his shoulders when he "proclaimed himself the leader of the ummah, 'Commander of the Faithful,' in effect making himself known as the Prophet's heir" (Riedel, 2010).

Regardless how one constructs the legitimacy of the Taliban and its interpretation of Islam, it cannot be denied that it has been successful in its ability to manifest a specific brand of nomic ordering, which in turn has allowed for the "fabrication" of a specific version of the Muslim self. The strength of this type of being-in-the-world-as-Muslim has benefited from the lack of cohesion between traditional Islamic groups inside Afghanistan, its strong ethnic connection to Pashtun Deobandi zealots in Pakistan, and its initial influence of al-Qaeda leadership in the late 1990s, all of which have allowed for it to exert a great deal of influence in various parts of the country.

Johnson (2017), in his text, *Taliban Narratives*, explores the various ways in which storytelling has been employed by the Taliban to gain and keep power among certain segments of the civilian population. Johnson (2017) observes:

> The Taliban seem to be well aware that the center of gravity of their insurgency, wrapped in the narrative of mandatory jihad, is the rural hinterland of Afghanistan, and they target their informational messages and propaganda accordingly. (p. 35)

The central themes of these narratives focus on the various grievances related to the existing government and since 2002, toward the presence of occupying U.S. and Coalition forces (Johnson, 2017). Though generally directed toward rural Pashtun audiences, from which most of its support has traditionally derived, these are not the only targets of this style of messaging.

Johnson (2017) contends that the Taliban's narrative strategy is focused on three different target audiences: those segments of the local population who support the Taliban; those individuals who are undecided or neutral to their agenda; and those who are in opposition to Taliban. Taken from a Heideggerian perspective, this narrative strategy reflects how a specific manifestation of they-self structures or attempts to structure the types of discrete behavior which will be valued and that which will not. As a result, the various targeted audiences are constructed as specific manifestations of being-in-the-world-as-Muslim and become identified by the types of discrete behavior these variations of being-with represent. The signifying descriptors of support, neutrality, and opposition help to configure the potentiality for being-in-the-world-as-Muslim, which is either validated or prohibited from this version of the they-self.

Central to this process of identity construction is how various possibilities of being-with become infused with those attitudes and beliefs identified by the they-self that helps to re-affirm a specific understanding of the shared social world. The possibility of offering support, neutrality, or opposition are predicated on the phenomenology this co-constituted understanding of world reveals (Polizzi, 2019). If these narratives reflect an understanding of individual existence and social world, which is sufficiently recognizable and validating, it becomes more likely that this view of social experience will be embraced by those who can see themselves in these stories. The stance of neutrality reflects a level of ambivalence, which is neither willing to embrace the narrative structure which the they-self represents, but neither is it willing to confront directly those aspects of the story it is unwilling to accept; while those who oppose this narrative account, remain connected to a competing version of the they-self that offers an alternative understanding of self and world. What this account of storytelling reveals is the layered aspects of the they-self, which can exist as potentially co-validating nomic structures or alternative points of identity construction, which can often clash in this struggle for the authorship of social meaning and lived-experience. The notion of a layered they-self is clearly witnessed in the narrative strategy employed by the Taliban.

The notion of the layered[5] they-self reflects a view of this Heideggerian structure that cannot be convincingly reduced to a singular process of identity construction (Polizzi, 2019; Polizzi et al., 2014). If it is the they-self that determines what will be valued and what will not, then it must presuppose that those possibilities for the meaning of being will have no recourse then to accept such a conclusion. Obviously, such a position is simply not true. The process by which being-in-the-world finds itself and takes up its projects must certainly take into account such configurations for the meaning of being, but it is not totally subservient to them. In such moments of nomic disconnection, a variety of structures of meaning may be cobbled together in a "good enough" way that will allow being-in-the-world, perhaps for the first time, to recognize their existence from this alternative point of view. The narrative process employed by the Taliban becomes such an example.

When taken from this perspective, the narrative structure of the Taliban relies on a specific configuration of Pashtun identity that is both rural and for the most part uneducated, along with an interpretation of Islam that is only recognized within very specific areas of the country. As a result, this nomic process rejects both the more urbanized variations of Pashtun identity, along with the other prominent ethnic identities that also exist in this multi-ethnic culture (Johnson, 2017; Rashid, 2010). The resulting configuration of this version of being-in-the-world-as-Muslim is able to legitimize its cultural credibility through its continued identification with its rural Pashtun roots, while also embracing a version of Islam that is specifically domestic, and which provides it a broader international appeal to those who are attracted to its Salafist sensibilities (Ahmed, 2014). Such a strategy was capable of retaining a clear connection to its Pashtun identity, while introducing an alternative version of Islam intended to displace and delegitimize the traditional interpretative framework of Islam traditionally practiced in Afghanistan and, by so doing, provided a "clear" structure for what would be valued and what

---

[5] I have discussed my configuration of the layered they-self in by text, *A Phenomenological Hermeneutic of Antiblack Racism in the Autobiography of Malcolm X*.

would not. The signifiers of support, ambivalence, and opposition becomes the artifacts of such a storytelling strategy.

The Rise of Hezbollah: Religious Surgency and Regional Proxy

Unlike the examples of religious insurgency practiced by those groups identified by their Sunni Salafist Jihadi orientation, Hezbollah or The Party of God represents a more complex target for theoretical analysis, particularly as this relates to its identification as a terrorist organization. Not only are there decided differences between Hezbollah's Shi's interpretation and practice of Islam, but included here are also a variety of domestic and regional historical and political concerns, which are not simply reducible to the conclusion that Hezbollah is exclusively a religious proxy force for Iranian regional political interests and one that has ignored any identification with its Lebanese national identity (Daher, 2019; Farha, 2019; Kawtharani, 2016; Saouli, 2019). Though such conclusions may be convenient, they really are too restricted in scope, and tend to oversimplify what is a far more complex phenomenological process. If a more fluid understanding is required, how does that help in providing greater clarity toward a more accurate understanding of Hezbollah?

What seems to be most important to this discussion concerns a couple of organizing observations, which help to better contextualize the question. First, how is the construct of the political understood when coming from a social context that is not reliant upon the separation of church and state; and secondly, how then are we to understand an organization or political party like Hezbollah, which seems to mingle both of these social concepts within a singular conceptualization or ideological point of view. It seems reasonable to argue that without answering the first more general question, the answer to the second becomes almost irrelevant given that it will almost certainly be constructed in such a way so as to satisfy an existing point of view and will be reduced to that singular purpose. What then does the political imply when situated within this context?

Generally speaking, when the "political" becomes introduced into the discussion of Islamic religious insurgency, it is usually employed as the mechanism by which the more traditional duties of the secular state are separated from the religious responsibilities of sacred authority. Within these specific constellations of cultural meaning and practice, the political and the religious are configured in ways that best reflect Westerner philosophy's belief in the separation of church and state: a conclusion which often results in the diminishing role of religious practice relative to liberal democratic pursuits. Such a conclusion for the given discussion is simply untenable or completely incorrect. Part of the logic for such an observation is located in the fact that almost any religious insurgency one can name, particularly those located in the Middle East, North Africa, and the Near East have emerged in the aftermath of the failure of some manifestation of the secular state. For some of these cultures, the lingering nomic power of the religious they-self is often perceived as a legitimate choice by which to end the never ending reality of secular decline. Hezbollah reflects such a phenomenological process.

Aurelie Daher (2019) in her text, *Hezbollah: Mobilisation and Power*, offers an important view of Hezbollah, which challenges much of the existing understanding related to the belief that Hezbollah is an Islamist organization. This position does not imply that Hezbollah is not an Islamic organization, only that it is not Islamist in its religious orientation. However, given the context of this observation, the distinction is indeed significant:

> Yet it appears that while the Hezbollah ego is not lacking the religious dimension, this dimension did not assume meaning, and to this day has had no effect other than as a vector for a different original value: that of resistance. (Daher, 2019, p. 8)

Daher continues by observing that "If we define Islamism as an effort directed towards Islamizing a political system, we need to note that Hezbollah's political practice has never aimed at such outcome, even a partial one" (p. 8). Her observation also recognizes that the religious affiliation of a given group does not immediately confer the designation of terror organization simply because its uses "religious referents" within its public discourse (Daher, 2019). For Daher, if any meaning-generating process is to be employed by which to understand Hezbollah, it is from the original value of resistance.

Hezbollah or AMAL[6] al-Islamiyya as it was initially known emerged in the early 1980s as a result of the inadequate response from existing Shiite groups to the Israeli invasion, which occurred in 1982. The initial goal of the Israel Defense Forces (IDF) was to secure a small section of Lebanese territory directly adjacent to the Israeli border, for the purpose of establishing a security zone from which it could confront the threat posed from PLO forces launching guerilla operations from Lebanon[7] (Daher, 2019; Saouli, 2019). The PLO arrived in greater numbers to Southern Lebanon after the group was military expelled from Jordan in June of 1970, which has come to be known as Black September (Bonsen, 2020; Daher, 2019; Saouli, 2019). Upon establishing their presence in Southern Lebanon, the PLO increased the level of military operations directed toward Israel, which in turn evoked a similar response from that country, resulting in the victimization of the majority Shite community living in Southern Lebanon. As the PLO's military operations continued to intensify, so too did the scope of the Israeli military response, which ultimately resulted in extending their occupation all the way to Beirut. In 1982, a contingent of Iranian Revolutionary Guards or Pasdaran sent to Lebanon by the Imam Khomeini to assist in the Lebanese resistance recognized that the isolated strategies and tactics of individual groups or political parties were simply insufficient in addressing the issues posed by the Israeli military (Daher, 2019). As a result of this unorganized resistance, it was suggested that a more structured organization be created, which would be Islamic in disposition and identity but focused on ending the Israeli occupation of Lebanon; it was from this perceived need that Hezbollah was born

---

[6] AMAL is a political movement started in Lebanon in 1974 by Musa al-Sadr; its members were almost exclusively Shiite, and the organization was secular in scope. AMAL al-Islamyyia an Islamic religious movement emerges in the aftermath of the disappearance of al-Sadr and as a result of the disagreement between secular and religious members of that organization. (Bonsen, 2020).

[7] In 1969, the Lebanese government signed what has become known as the Cairo accords, which outlined the level of guerilla activities that would be allowed the PLO in that country. The signing of these accords and the PLO's forced removal from Jordan in 1970 motivated the migration of the PLO from Jordan to Lebanon, which ultimately resulted in the Israeli invasion of that country (Daher, 2019).

(Nasrallah, 2007). Though the Israeli occupation of Lebanon certainly played a significant role in the creation of Hezbollah, this was not the only issue of concern at the time of its appearance in Lebanon.

The notion of Shi'a Islamic resistance emerges as early as 1298/1305 in Lebanese history and has continued to manifest itself up to and beyond the Lebanese Civil War, which erupted in 1975 and continued on for approximately fifteen years (Daher, 2019; Saouli, 2019). However, the construct of a Shiite-Lebanese identity is also deeply related to the social experience of the Shiite community in that country (Bonsen, 2020; Daher, 2019; Farha, 2019). Daher (2019) and Farha (2019) have observed that the Shiite community has been traditionally viewed by Christians and Sunni Muslims in Lebanon as socially inferior and were the last of the three Muslim communities to be given the right to control the activities in their own communities (Daher, 2019; Farha, 2019). All this changed with the work of Sayyid Musa al-Sadr, a Shiite reformer, who was able to enact fundamental changes within the Shiite community that helped to address this long-felt experience of social isolation and marginalization (Bonsen, 2020; Daher, 2019; Farha, 2019; Saouli, 2019).

Al-Sadr was perceived as a charismatic personality who was able to improve the conditions in Shiite communities through his abilities to embrace the existing political structure of Lebanese society and work across ethno-religious lines to achieve this goal (Daher, 2019. Farha, 2019; Saouli, 2019). However, as the Palestinian presence in the South of the country took on a more prominent role, his initial support for the PLO soured, placing him in conflict with this organization. As the political environment in Lebanon turned increasingly violent, al-Sadr created the Harakat al-Mahrumin, which was made up of various militants from existing religious and secular Shiite groups to provide protection for that community (Daher, 2019). Al-Sadr's popularity was further weakened when he supported then President Sleiman Frangieh's decision to seek military aid from Syria in the hope of preventing a victory by Muslim progressive forces over Christian militias (Daher, 2019). It was also proven that al-Sadr had taken a position against Palestinian forces in the country, which further fractured his movement. All of this came to an end when al-Sadr traveled to Libya in August of 1978 and was never seen again (Daher, 2019). The sudden absence of al-Sadr provided the opportunity for less charismatic individuals to seek to fill the void his disappearance created, and it was from the aftermath of this void that AMAL al-Islamiyya would eventually emerge (Daher, 2019).

With al-Sadr no longer in the picture, AMAL began to experience strife within the Movement between secular and religious factions, which in the past its former leader was able to contain (Daher, 2019). The religious membership hoped that AMAL would embrace the example of the Iranian Revolution and take up an explicitly Islamic perspective, whereas the secular wing of the party, while willing to accept some level of Islamic identification, was unwilling to turn over the decision-making authority to religious clerics, per Daher's (2019) observation. As a result of this continuing deterioration of the Movement from within, the formal creation of AMAL al-Islamyyia was announced, which was to be a new organization and one which intended to return the Movement to its original Islamic perspective:

> Its charter reiterated that AMAL was originally set up as an "Islamic Movement." AMAL al-Islamyyia represented a return to this original path, presenting itself as "an Islamic ideological movement that adopts Islam as dogma, as principle, as perspective, and as criterion." (Daher, 2019, p. 44)

One of the more significant strategies which emerged from the introduction of Iranian Revolutionary Guards or Pasdaran in the Bekaa Valley was the establishment of the paramilitary structure known as the Islamic Resistance in Lebanon (IRL) and it is form this initial network of relationships, which attracted members from all of the existing Shiite religious groups that Hezbollah was created (Daher, 2019). Central to this new structure of resistance was the recognition that such a relationship must be culturally reciprocal. What this implied was simply that support for the resistance must also include the resistance's support for the community, particularly when the Lebanese government found itself incapable of doing the same (Daher, 2016, 2019). As a result of this cultural reciprocity, a very different type of phenomenological structure can be witnessed within this emerging form of Shiite relationality.

What is perhaps most interesting about the development of Hezbollah is how its phenomenological process greatly differs from those other

Salafist Jihadi or Islamist groups formerly discussed. From the very beginning, Hezbollah, though certainly unapologetic of its Shi'a religious roots, has been most focused on Israeli's past occupation of Lebanon, which in turn has continued to feed its ongoing antagonism and obsession with that country, than it has with the creation of an Islamic state similar to that of Iran. The group's leader Sayyed Hassan Nasrallah has contended as much when he observed that *"we wanted a Resistance, we did not come to form a political party*, for we had no choice but resistance for putting an end to the occupation" (Nasrallah as quoted in Daher, 2019, p. 51). However, it is important to reiterate that resistance is simply not synonymous with the pursuit of an Islamic state in Lebanon.

The name Hezbollah was first used in a communique in what is known as The Open Letter of 1985, which also included its logo or flag. It also helped to describe how this name symbolized the type of resistance it intended to pursue:

> The party leadership acknowledges that it adopted the name Hezbollah in reference to two suras of the Qur'an: the sura *al-Mujadala*, which states that "it is the party of God that will know bliss" and the *al-Maida* sura, which proclaims "it is the party of God that will be the victor." (Daher, 2019, p. 52)

The logo also concludes the slogan the Islamic Resistance of Lebanon, which Daher (2019) insists was to remove Hezbollah from the belief that it was merely an Iranian proxy and not the Lebanese resistance movement it saw itself to be.[8]

The emerging phenomenology, which the new nomic structure of Hezbollah constructs is an identity that is focused on the fight against the Israeli occupation of that country along with a version of "Islamic nationalism" that does not seem focused on the necessity for the creation of the Islamic State of Lebanon. Though leaders of Hezbollah such as Muhammad Husayn Fadlallah openly admit to their desire for an Islamic state, they also observe that such a result must not be imposed on the

---

[8] This is not to imply that there was no connection between Hezbollah and Iran, only that the mission of the movement was to fight the Lebanese occupation and to reestablish the sovereignty of Lebanon.

country and can only be possible when a majority of the population agrees on such a result (Speidl, 2017). Included in the 1985 communique was the promise that it held no ill will toward other religious groups in the country and would never seek to impose Islam on individuals of other faiths, which would be a strategy rejected by the Qur'an (Daher, 2019).

What complicates this phenomenology even further is the role that Hezbollah has played and continues to play in the region. Though it is reasonable to view the quality of an organization by its actions, such logic fails, when the conclusions that this type of analysis reaches, returns us to the "Who is killing Whom" understanding of the topic under study. Hezbollah emerges in the aftermath of the Israeli military operation of Lebanon to neutralize the PLO military presence in the southern regions of that country, which ultimately extends to Beirut. More importantly, it seeks to address the specific victimization of Shite Muslims living in the south of Lebanon as a result of the Israeli/Palestinian conflict. As is often the result when competing nomic structures clash, a variety of socially constructed meanings emerge that become foundational to the phenomenology that follows. As was briefly discussed in Chap. 2, the Hezbollah fighter and his captive Terry Anderson have two very different constructions of their immediate situation and the larger context from which this set of experiences emerge.

Whether these competing socially constructed meanings are fabricated by the continuing experience or sudden presence of unmitigated social strain or as a result of the process of mutual radicalization, some understanding of these differing examples of social experience must be understood from the perspective they provide. For example, Hezbollah, unlike the Taliban, has remained focused on its main goal of Lebanese independence along with its identification as the party of God. Though it has been for the most part faithful to its understanding of Lebanon as a multi-ethic/religious culture, its historical behavior toward Israel and the region has raised concerns of its actual intentions. However, are these concerns sufficient to label Hezbollah as a terrorist organization?

As Daher observes (2019), Hezbollah has evolved in a variety of ways from its initial beginning briefly discussed above; this phenomenological process has developed from resistance movement to a political party significantly involved in the social dynamics of Lebanon. Central to her argument is that Hezbollah has evolved in response to the contextual realities it has faced over the course of its history. These realities have included various challenges from external foes and patron-client alliances, which at times have worked hand-in-hand and at other times have reflected the presence of substantial disagreement and threat to its specific interests. The history this phenomenology of resistance has constructed, has helped to tie the identity of Hezbollah to both Islam and Lebanon, and has helped to configure an image for being-in-the-world-as-Muslim that is capable of embracing both its nationalistic and religious characteristics.

The question concerning whether or not Hezbollah should be viewed exclusively as a terrorist organization, as a proxy for Iranian and at times Syria interests, or as a Lebanese resistance movement will need to be left to the discretion of the individual reader. Like any co-constituted structure of social relationality, the existing evidence can be configured in such a way to lend credence to a variety of conclusions. How one situates such evidence will undoubtedly be in the service of a desired conclusion. As was eluded to at the beginning of this chapter and discussed in Chap. 2 of this text, the difficulties in defining terrorism are equally present in the attempt to definitively construct a legitimate conceptualization of this group.

References

Ahmed, R. (2014). Transformation from Pashtun nationalism to religious nationalism. *Pakistan Horizon, 67*, 83–100.
Berger, P., & Luckmann, T. (1966). *The social construction of reality: A treatise in the sociology of knowledge*. Anchor Books.
Bonsen, S. (2020). *Martyr cults and political identities in Lebanon*. Springer VS.
Daher, A. (2019). *Hezbollah: Mobilisation and power*. Oxford University Press.
Daher, J. (2016). *Hezbollah: The political economy of Lebanon's Party of God*. Pluto Press.
Edwards, D. (2002). *Before the Taliban: Genealogies of the afghan jihad*. University of California Press.
Elias, B. (2020). Directorate S: The CIA and America's secret wars in Afghanistan and Pakistan. In M. K. Jalalzai (Ed.), *Pakistan's spy agencies: Challenges of civil control over intelligence agencies bureaucratic and military stakeholderism,*

dematerialization of civilian intelligence, and war of strength (pp. 135–141). Vij Books India Pvt Ltd.

Farha, M. (2019). *Lebanon: The rise and fall of a secular state under siege*. Cambridge University Press.

Griffin, R. (2012). *Terrorist's creed: Fanatical violence and the human search for meaning*. London & New York: Palgrave Macmillan.

Hamid, S. (2016). *Islamic exceptionalism: How the struggle over Islam is reshaping the world*. St. Martin's Press.

Jalalzai, M. K. (2020). The political and military involvement of Inter-Services Intelligence in Afghanistan. In M. K. Jalalzai (Ed.), *Pakistan's spy agencies: Challenges of civil control over intelligence agencies bureaucratic and military stakeholderism, dematerialization of civilian intelligence, and war of strength* (pp. 142–159). Vij Books India Pvt Ltd.

Johnson, T. H. (2017). *Taliban narratives: The use and power of stories in the Afghanistan conflict*. Oxford University Press.

Kawtharani, F. (2016). Integrating Shi'a in the modern nation-state: Shaykh Muhammad Mahdi Shams al-Din, Hizbullah, and engagement in Lebanese politics. *Middle East Journal, 70*, 419–438.

Moghadam, A. (2019). *Nexus of global jihad: Understanding cooperation among terrorist actors*. Columbia University Press.

Nasrallah, S. H. (2007). *Voice of Hezbollah: The statements of Sayyed Hassan Nasrallah*. Verso.

Polizzi, D. (2019). *A phenomenological hermeneutic of antiblack racism in the autobiography of Malcolm X*. Lexington Books.

Polizzi, D., Draper, M., Andersen, M. (2014). Fabricated selves and the rehabilitative machine: Toward a phenomenology of the social construction of offender treatment. In B. Arrigo & H. Bersot (Eds.), *The Routledge Handbook of International Crime and Justice Studies* (pp. 233–255). Routledge.

Rashid, A. (2010). *Taliban: Militant Islam oil and fundamentalism in Central Asia* (2nd ed.). Yale University Press.

Riedel, B. (2010). *The search for al-Qaeda: Its leadership, ideology, and future*. Brookings Institution Press.

Saouli, A. (2019). *Hezbollah: Socialisation and its tragic ironies*. Edinburgh University Press.

Speidl, B. (2017). The rhetoric of power in Muhammad Husayn Fadlallah's al-Islam wa-mantiq al-quwwa. In H. Shadi (Ed.), *Islamic peace ethics: Legitimate and illegitimate violence in contemporary Islamic thought*. Nomos Verlagsgesellschaft mbH.

Yadav, V. (2010). The myth of the moderate Taliban. *Asian Affairs: An American Review, 37*, 133–145.

8

White Supremacy and the Digital World: The Social Construction of White Identity

The Rise of the Digital They-Self

In a recent policy brief provided by the International Centre for Counter Terrorism at the Hague the authors make the following opening observation. "It is widely acknowledged that the increasing prevalence of computer-mediated communication technologies has compounded the devasting effects that extreme-right ideologies can have on communities across the world" (Bliuc et al., 2020, p. 1). Though the process of online radicalization is similar to the phenomenology witnessed by individuals attracted to Salafist Jihadi or Islamist websites, it differs in a variety of ways related to cultural applicability and cultural familiarity with the identity construction it seeks to achieve. Whereas Islamic versions of this process are almost always incorporated within the existing structure of various manifestations of religious insurgency groups, the far-right versions of the same are really not as culturally visible in quite the same way: and, it would be the contention of this discussion that they would be even less effective or visible if the opportunities offered by the internet were not available to them.

Atwan (2015) claims in his text *Islamic State: The Digital Caliphate* that IS could not have achieved its goal of gaining territory by which to establish their caliphate without the use of the internet. However, this statement seems to ignore the fact that a large number of Iraqi military personal, who were purged from that institution due to their Baathist party affiliation in the aftermath of the U.S. occupation, joined ISIL/ISIS and were instrumental in the rapid succession of military victories that the group achieved, particularly as this relates in the capture of the Northern Iraqi city of Mosul (Gerges, 2016). Syria offers a similar equation insofar as a variety of Salafist Jihadi groups were actively involved in the attempt to remove the Assad regime from power, which in turn resulted in the clash between competing domestic, regional, and international actors, pursuing a variety of interests as a result of the civil war, which emerged following consequences of the Arab Spring (Phillips, 2016). It is certainly, true that in the aftermath of these successes, a number of foreign fighters and supporters flocked to take part in the newly formed Islamic State but did so after the "proof of success" and not before. However, this type of relationship does not currently exist for far-right groups and its phenomenology, as a result, is quite different.

When one thinks of fanatical violence emerging from the far-right, it is most likely seen as the behavior of a lone actor or the actions of a small group of like-minded individuals, whose actions are not "specifically" and "directly" authorized by a functioning organization. With the advent of the digital age, the need for a direct face-to-face relationship with a specific organizational authority becomes much less necessary and provides various strategic advantages that were simply not available to other groups of this kind in the past. In fact, it could be argued that the availability and accessibility of the net have made such traditional relationships almost obsolete. As was witnessed in the cases of Dylann Roof, the individual, who systematically murdered nine parishioners at the Emanuel AME Church in Charlestown, South Carolina and Robert Bowers, who murdered eleven individuals attending Saturday services at the Tree of Life Synagogue in Pittsburgh, Pennsylvania, no direct face-to-face interaction was necessary for each of these individuals to become sufficiently radicalized to kill.

However, though no evidence seems to exist that would tie either Roof or Bowers to any face-to-face far-right involvement, they were still radicalized all the same. Such a result is not at all surprising. What often fails to get sufficient emphasis is the specific nomic ordering process, which one encounters through these interactions with far-right "social media" sites. The net does not function simply as a vehicle which may be utilized in a variety of ways from connecting friends and family to degrading various private and public digital infrastructures, though this is certainly one of its functions. More importantly, or at least most important to the current discussion, is the way in which these digital sites serve as a manifestation of the they-self, which in turn provides a type of nomic structure that allows some of these individuals to not only recognize their own biography, but recognize it in such a way that helps to validate a phenomenology of violence.

As a digital manifestation of the they-self, this process of nomic ordering reveals a structure(s) of social meaning and identity formation that no longer requires the presence of a face-to-face event. In fact, if a face-to-face relationship is necessary, then the images and written text one encounters on these social media sites becomes the "other" in this interaction (Miller-Idriss, 2020). Just like any traditional manifestation of the they-self or process of nomic ordering, this digital version of the same both "informs" and "imposes" upon individual identity a sense of social meaning and purpose, which reconstructs the marginalized self, allowing it to once again become recognizable within the current context of subjective experience. This phenomenology of marginalization emerges in response to the shifting structure of cultural meaning, which can overtake the self, leaving it in a social world that is no longer recognizable and no longer firmly rooted within personal identity. It is in the aftermath of this changing social world that the digital they-self may be embraced.

What the digital experience provides in these moments of perceived nomic collapse or threat is a "safe haven" where one's personal identity may once again be informed by a nomic structure that resonates with a "familiar" understanding of self and world (Wong et al., 2015). As Berger (1967) contends, nomic structures continually evolve and change, but in so doing, also tend to marginalize those who are unable or unwilling to evolve as well or may see such change as the evidence of nomic collapse or failure. The advent of the internet has provided the possibility for individual identity to reconnect with those aspects of the nomic order that no longer enjoy the same social currency which they once did. As a result, the very ability to discuss such ideas are no longer welcome and tend to remain unspoken attitudes or beliefs or shared only with those individuals who are similarly inclined.

What is often reflected on many of these far-right internet sites are the same "socially" marginalized attitudes and beliefs that are not only discussed and shared between member discussants, but openly praised and valued (Wong et al., 2015). However, as Miller-Idriss (2020) observes the process or phenomenology of radicalization is not the exclusive artifact of the online experience. How could it be? If this were true, the number of radicalized individuals willing to act per the dictates of this manifestation of this digitized Far-Right they-self would likely be larger and their acts of violence more pronounced. But this is apparently not the case. What then is the function of the internet and what role does it actually play in the phenomenology of white supremacist radicalization?

As was stated above, the internet constructs a locality(s) where direct interaction with this version of the they-self becomes possible. But the selves which are created from this process are the artifacts of a specific profile of being-in-the-world-as-white-supremacist that is finished or completed by involvement with these nomic structures and not exclusively created by them. What this implies is the presence of an existing type of being-in-the-world that has already structured a set of social meanings that reflect a certain context of social experience and relationality. Miller-Idriss (2020) observes that what this relationship reveals is what she describes as the weaponizing of online spaces, which ties off-line communities with online localities by which these extremist ideologies may finish the work of the fabrication of the far-right self.

Taken from the perspective of the phenomenology of the nomos, these weaponized spaces function as the apparatus of this process of nomic ordering, which introduces individuals to a shared space of nomic agreement, which in turn helps to further strengthen or better organize the specific contours of this type of being-in-the-world. As such, these spaces become foundational to the nomic relationship they seek to construct. But, unlike their "brick and mortar" equivalents, these virtual spaces

8 White Supremacy and the Digital World: The Social Construction...

allow for both the validation of these shared social views of the world, while also providing a space that is safe and likely free from the types of social ostracization that these same ideas may attract if freely discussed within the context of more traditionally configured social spaces. Miller-Idriss observes that the internet provides two specific benefits for these far-right groups.

> First, online spaces broaden exposure to and amplify extreme content and far-right ideas. Second, they help those on the far right communicate with one another, broadening networks; building resources that support activism, violence, and movement growth; and bridging online connections with off-line engagements and networks. (Miller-Idriss, 2020, p. 144)

Central to the benefits made available by the internet that Miller-Idriss identities is the process of nomic ordering, which helps to solidify and strengthen this type of relationality. Though I would certainly agree that the influencing aspects of online radicalization are fundamentally related to the phenomenology which exists prior to any active involvement with these types of social media sites, these pre-existing attitudes and beliefs are not sufficient in describing the transformative power of this version of the they-self (Miller-Idriss, 2020).

What seems most phenomenologically essential to the benefits which Miller-Idris describes is the way in which individual identity becomes recognized and reflected through this co-constituting process of social meaning: Individuals bring with them a preconceived sense of self, derived from the socially constructed meaning(s) of subjective experience and then have that experience validated by individuals, who have a similar understanding of self and world. Though these networks of support are certainly strengthened by online involvement, the more significant psychological or phenomenological benefit appears to be achieved by the way in which this experience ties the individual to a larger context of social meaning that far transcends the purview of individual experience and identity. If this experience was equally available or accessible in day-to-day, face-to-face experience, the power of this embrace with the far-right they-self would likely be less complete.

Heidegger observed that *being-with* is fundamentally predicated upon an understanding of "other" that is understood as the type of being that is *most* like me. As a result, these recognizable examples of being-in-the-world reflect a similar type of thrownness, which in turn reveals a similar place from which the world is encountered. When situated within a digital environment, this experience of *being-with* evokes a similar type of relationality. As such, to find one's self thrown in such a way reveals a type of *being-with* that is likely quite different from one's normal lived-experience. Taken from this perspective, being-in-the-world finds itself within a shared world of meaning that values what I value and rejects what I reject. This is not to argue that the world of off-line experience is somehow subordinate to this digitized type of being; rather this digitized experience of *being-with* provides a degree of near complete validation, which is simply not likely to be available in the same way or to the same degree that these digital encounters provide. The power which this experience of relationality provides is exemplified in Miller-Idriss' discussion of the strategies employed by far-right groups when internet access is denied.

Miller-Idriss (2020) observes that though white supremacist groups immediately recognized the opportunity the digital world provided as early as the 1980s, this new technology offered little in the way of actual growth in popularity of their far-right agenda; all of this changed, she argues with the advent of social media platforms. Unlike dial-up forums or digital message boards, these new platforms provided easy access and dissemination of these far-right materials and as a result played a positive role in the growth of that community (Conway et al., 2019; Miller-Idriss, 2020; Wong et al., 2015). Though a variety of browsers like Google have attempted to reconfigure its algorithm search process, the issue of easy accessibility remains. And perhaps more significantly, these same groups have been able to thwart certain attempts at blocking such sites, by simply going elsewhere or deeper into the web. The structure which Miller-Idriss (2020) describes reflects a number of similarities, which make some metaphorical connections to the dynamics of conscious/unconscious processes recognized in the psychodynamic constructs of repression and suppression.

In its most general sense, the psychodynamic construct of repression serves as a defense mechanism, which is employed to keep unpleasant thoughts or feelings from entering conscious awareness. Taken from this perspective, the place or locality created by social media sites reflects a manifestation of a social unconscious or they-self—either work equally as well—which contains various configurations of social meaning or discredited nomic structures, which in turn may be accessed by individuals, who retain a strong psychological connection to these ideas. Attempts at de-platforming or banning, when viewed from this context, reflect a type of psychological strategy similarly employed when unconscious material is no longer containable within the current structure of conscious/unconscious defenses. When this occurs, the client or analysand must either address the implications this formerly unconscious material portends or develop a sturdier defensive structure capable of returning this material to its previous unconscious abode. However, certain unconscious material can at times be difficult to contain and will find any employable avenue by which to make itself explicitly known to waking consciousnesses; a process which is similarly observed in the various attempts by right-wing or any extremist group for that matter, to develop various responses to those attempts to remove their voice from the web.

What becomes most troubling about this digitized configuration of social experience is that not only do these dangerously radical and violent views continue to remain, but they continue to resonate in very powerful ways within the lived-experience of many individuals. One possible psychological benefit can be recognized by the fact that not every individual who interacts with this digitized they-self has taken up violence as a way to evidence their fidelity to this nomic structure of meaning. Such a result could be attributed to a type of psychological process known within psychodynamic circles as suppression. Taken from this perspective, the phenomenology of suppression involves the conscious recognition of certain desires, but these urges are not embraced or pursued. Though there may be a degree of agreement with what is being viewed, this agreement does not require that specific action be taken against those who have been identified as a threat to this nomic structure.

The Return of the Repressed

When traditionally described, the return of the repressed represents a return to consciousness of formerly repressed material that is fundamentally perceived as being incapable with one's conscious sense of self. The sudden appearance or reappearance of these uncomfortable attitudes, beliefs, and desires can evoke varying degrees of anxiety that at their most intense can become so debilitating that a therapeutic intervention is required. As a result, two general strategies are often pursued, (1) the direct examination of this material by the individual to gain a better comprehension of its current significance within the context of ongoing psychotherapy or (2) the attempt to construct a sturdier psychological perimeter of defense to return this material to the confines of unconscious. Within the context of the current discussion, the dynamic of the return of the repressed can be applied to the presencing of extreme attitudes and beliefs assumed to have been appropriately consigned to the social unconscious of the body politic.

When situated within the dynamic of nomic ordering, a different type of phenomenological "structure" seems to appear. From this perspective, repression becomes reconfigured theoretically as that which is generally repressed or marginalized by the existing or changing nomic structure, which has moved away from those attitudes and beliefs that are no longer compatible with this changing manifestation of social meaning. As the nomic structure changes, as too does the relationship between identity formation and the discrete experience(s), which are now recognized by this process (Polizzi, 2020). However, for some, as has been discussed within various contexts throughout this discussion, these changes may be viewed as a direct assault on those aspects of nomic ordering, which still retain a degree of social currency within certain segments of a given society, and their devaluation will not be accepted. The degree to which this nomic "devaluation" is challenged will likely determine the degree of social unarrest these changes will evoke. Perhaps further clarification of this point will be helpful to this discussion.

When taken from this perspective, the construct of the return of the repressed represents a type of social psychological process that is reflected within this dynamic of nomic change. As a result, certain attitudes and beliefs are no longer viewed as legitimate and are relegated to the margins of social experience. However, this process of nomic devaluation is not capable of completely eliminating these social meanings from the public imagination and can reemerge on the scene in very explosive and unexpected ways. This result is likely due to the fact that repressed material never goes away, it is simply repressed, and remains so, until something occurs within the defensive psychological structure of an individual or society that once again allows it to make its way back into consciousness awareness. The return and perhaps normalization of the far-right is an example of such a process.

Such a return of the repressed was on vivid display on January 6, 2021 when a mob of domestic terrorists and "protesters" stormed the Capitol Building with the purpose of disrupting the debate and vote that was taking place in both chambers of Congress to certify the results of the Electoral College and officially confirm that Joe Biden would be the next President of the U.S. on January 20, 2021. During the siege on the U.S. Capitol Building, the grounds, offices, and chambers of the U.S. Senate and House of Representatives were both illegally occupied, ransacked, and vandalized by a horde of seditious domestic terrorists. Though the initial assault on the Capitol Building did result in the suspension of the Electoral College certification process and required the evacuation of both chambers of Congress, the legislators, determined not to be intimidated by this act of sedition and terrorism, returned to their chambers later that night and authorized the Electoral College results and affirmed that Joe Biden would in fact be the next President of the U.S. However, these details, shocking as they are, cannot be viewed as all that surprising given Trump's continual seditious rhetoric and the open planning for this assault, which took place on various social media sites.

Though the events, which unfolded at the Capitol Building were incited by Donald Trump and others, earlier that day at a rally numbering approximately 30 thousand of his supporters, the resulting chaos and violence which followed was not the "spontaneous" result of that seditious gathering. The subsequent assault on the U.S. Congress was apparently openly discussed on a number of public social media sites in the weeks leading up to January 6; this tragic event is really the culminating moment of the last four years of Trump's relentless authoritarian assaults on many of America's most cherished institutions. Central to Trump's strategy of sedition could be witnessed in his unrelenting attempts to widen the already dangerous fissures within the American body politic, which in turn allowed him to take personal advantage of the cultural weakness these continual attacks helped to exasperate. However, it is also essential to recognize that Trump did not create these problems; rather, he simply used them in a variety of very dangerous and seditious ways to accentuate his own political power.

During the unfolding of these events a variety of troubling realizations emerged that are fundamental to this discussion of the return of the repressed. Perhaps the most salient of these was the continual need for commentators and reporters to state that "These events are unacceptable;" "This is not supposed to happen in America," "This is not who we are," but what if it is? Many of these same commenters made the uncomfortable comparison between the way Black Lives Matter protesters in the aftermath of the George Floyd killing, where treated by federal law enforcement authorities in Washington D.C. with that of the near total lack of response by federal law enforcement, who remained invisible as the Capitol Building was under siege for nearly three hours. Unfortunately, the inconvenient truth, then, is that this is exactly who we are.

The fact of white supremacy is the manifestation of the return of the repressed as witnessed by the terrorist attack on the U.S. Congress. Though various iterations of white supremacy has been part of the American psyche well before the official creation of the nation, at various moments in the history of the country, it has made itself known with varying degrees of violent intensity. The attack on the U.S. Capitol Building has now become one of those moments. Add to this uncomfortable fact that it is now seemingly more likely that certain elements within the Capitol police force may have aided terrorists by directing them to specific congressional offices of Democratic legislatures, which were then ransacked or vandalized. Additionally, Vice President Mike Pence was also a target of the seditious mob, who were recorded chanting "Hang Mike Pence, Hang Mike Pence." It has been subsequently reported by a variety news media sources that Trump actually tweeted that Mike Pence had betrayed them (Samuels, 2021). His alleged crime, apparently, was "evidenced" by his refusal to decertify the results of the Electoral College Vote of certain states, a power which the Vice President does not have, per the specific language offered in the U.S. Constitution under article II, Section 1 of that document.[1] With the functioning defensive structures of the Capitol Building completely compromised and subsequently overwhelmed, all of this formerly "contained" affective rage could now be clearly witnessed in the clear light of day.

What is most metaphorically significant to this discussion are the psychological consequences one must confront when these psychological defenses are breeched and subsequently overwhelmed by the release of this formerly repressed material. As the perimeter defenses of the Capitol Building compound gave way to this swarm of insurrectionist rage and was quickly overwhelmed, the repressed material of the American psyche was placed on full display. As was mentioned above, the return of the repressed is usually confronted by two general strategies of defense: (1) confront and in some way integrate those aspects of this repressed material, which can be included and redirected and much better contained by waking consciousness or (2) continue to employ a defensively enhanced structure of psychological repression that returns this material to the unconscious, predicated upon an "out of sight, out of mind" sensibility. However, given that repressed material cannot really be removed from the psyche without actually confronting the psychological implications this material "suddenly" imposes on waking consciousness, the later strategy is unwise.

If we conclude with what the material and psychological facts of this siege seem to articulate, then the traditional American body politic embrace of a process of psychological repression is no longer a viable therapeutic strategy. We can longer simply insist that this is not who we are because our history has revealed time and time again that this inconvenient truth cannot any longer be denied. All one needs to do is go through the historical record and view those videos or print accounts of various protests that have taken place where the individuals involved were

---

[1] The U.S. Constitution describes the role of the Vice President, the President of the Senate, in the following way. "The President of the Senate shall, in the presence of the Senate and House of Representatives, open all the Certificates, and the Votes shall then be counted" (Founding Fathers, 2019, p. 22). *The Declaration of Independence and The Constitution of the United States of America.*

either predominately black or predominating white and see how differently these groups of individuals were treated by law enforcement authorities. One retired Capitol police officer stated on the cable news show "The Beat" anchored by Ari Melber of MSNBC on Wednesday January 7 that "if they (terrorists) were black they would have not gotten on the steps." He continued by observing, "Where were the horses, where were the dogs?" He added that it was also strange that so few police were on hand for such an event that many believed could be potentially explosive.

When repressed material makes its way back into conscious awareness, it is quite often met with denial or disbelief: Such rationalizations as "That's not me; that's not really who I am," etc., etc., are quite common. A similar level of shocked disbelief was also on display during and in the aftermath of this literal assault on American democracy. However, unlike the more common struggle that can occur for an individual in their attempt to confront the sudden appearance of unwanted thoughts or behaviors, these "formerly" repressed "unconscious" thoughts were on full display via the avenues provided by mainstream media outlets and social media sites, where this "unconscious" content could be both accessed and lived.

Taken from this point of view, those social media platforms, which allow for the dissemination of various types of hate speech, or which allow for the planning of outright treason or sedition, becomes a type of unconscious process, which is no longer containable within the psyche of American society and explodes into conscious awareness and must be directly confronted. As a result, what was believed to be finished or resolved, or relegated to the darkest corners of the societal unconscious reemerge with a vengeance for the simple reason that this dynamic now represents, through its existence on the web, the unconscious desires of the total society. The sudden reappearance of these various manifestations of white supremacy and the myriad of cultural implications they reveal speaks to the degree to which these conflicting ideas have actually been resolved.

White Supremacy and the Threat to the Nomic Order

The reemergence or normalization of the far-right is often situated within the context of white supremacy, providing those drawn to this set of beliefs, a structure of nomic ordering that validates those aspects of personal identity that have become alienated by the process of social change. Central to this perceived nomic threat is the belief that "whiteness" itself is now under siege and the very foundation of social meaning, at least as it is constituted from this perspective, is called into question. As the name suggests, white supremacy seeks to reverse those aspects of nomic change that have threated the hegemonic power historically enjoyed by whites in various cultures.

> The groups that are part of the white supremacy social movement industry are interested in preserving or restoring what they perceive as the natural racial or ethical hierarchy by enforcing social and political superiority over minority groups such as African Americans, Jews, and members of various immigrant communities. (Perliger, 2020, pp. 18–19)

As Perliger (2020) observes one of the central components of the far-right/white supremacist nomos is a structure of ethnic homogeneity, which embraces the superiority of "whiteness" relative to all other ethnic configurations and demands a hierarchal social structure, which accentuates the "fact" of this socially constructed reality. Any cultural strategy that seeks to attain a degree of cultural diversity or recognition that places "whiteness" as simply another potentiality for social identity and visibility is viewed as a threat to this demand for superiority. Such a conclusion is supported by the numerous examples of violence directed toward minority populations by white perpetrators driven by this belief (Conway et al., 2019; Hamm & Spaaij, 2017; Hutchinson, 2019; Perliger, 2020; Weinberg, 2013). Once so configured, social presence itself becomes criminalized within the imaging of the body, which now becomes hermeneutically constructed as the carrier of that crime or sin.

It will be recalled that Merleau-Ponty (2012) in his seminal text, *Phenomenology of Perception*, observes that, "The very first cultural object, and the one by which they all exist, is the other's body as the bearer of behavior" (p. 364). He continues by observing,

> Nevertheless, the analysis of the perception of others encounters the essential difficulty raised by the cultural world because it must resolve the paradox of a consciousness seen from the outside, the paradox of a thought that resides in the exterior and that, when compared to my own, is already without a subject and is anonymous. (Merleau-Ponty, 2012, p. 364)

However, this essential difficulty is resolved, albeit tragically when the body before me is reduced and objectified to that of the anonymous ontological manifestation of inferiority and threat. Once so configured, subjectivity is rendered invisible and no comparison is possible or even necessary. What is seen is not a consciousness, but a type of objectified social visibility that becomes hermeneutically sealed within the surfaces of the presencing body, and all behavior is interpreted by that fact and that fact alone: taken from this point of view, criminality and sinfulness precede existence and construct the body of this non-white other as a perpetual existential threat that must be eliminated or at the very least controlled and contained (Polizzi, 2012, 2016, 2019a, 2020).

This perspective concerning the body as a bearer of behavior should not be underestimated given that it is a central component of the ontological structure that becomes the driving force of the epistemological "strategies" which follow this meaning-generating process. When situated within the "ontological" perspective offered by far-right white supremacists, the presencing of the non-white body becomes all that is required for this bearer of behavior to be constructed as a social threat. Given that appearance and behavior now become conflated as a singular configuration of the presencing social body, no other factor is required by which to arrive at that conclusion. If this bearer of behavior is defined as social threat, even before any actual direct interaction occurs, the actual performative value of any of the specific behaviors performed will have already been socially constructed within this fanatical frame of reference.

> There is no room, then, for others and for a plurality of consciousnesses within objective thought. If I constitute the world, then I cannot conceive

of another consciousness, for it too would have to have constituted the world and so, at least with regard to this other view upon the world, I would not be constituting. Even if I succeeded in conceiving of this other consciousness as constituting the world, it is again I who would constitute it as such, and once again I would be the only constituting consciousness. (Merleau-Ponty, 2012, p. 365)

Though Merleau-Ponty's critique was originally offered in 1945 as a response to the existing biological and philosophical theorizing about the body and consciousness of his day, this observation becomes particularly poignant for the current discussion. When applied to our discussion, the relevance of this quote is obvious: when situated within the ontological frame of reference of white supremacy there is no room for others, no room for those who are not like me. What is fundamentally absent from such a process is any possibility of the legitimate recognition of another consciousness, whose view upon the world could somehow be as valid or significant as my own. Such a rationale is exemplified within the examples of Dylann Roof, Robert Bowers, and Brenton Tarrant.

Dylann Roof and the Radicalized Self

On June 17, 2015, Dylann Roof entered the historic Emanuel African Methodist Episcopal Church located in Charleston, South Carolina with the intent of murdering all those attending a weekly Bible study group with the intent of starting a race war within the U.S.. His choice of target also reflected this goal, given that this church, also known as Mother Emanuel, is famously known as one of the oldest black churches in the U.S. Upon entering the church, he immediately made his way downstairs where he was met by Church Pastor and South Carolina state senator, Clementa Pinkney, and some of his congregation, who were regular participants in this weekly Bible study group (Polizzi, 2020). By his own account, Roof stated that he was genuinely surprised by the warm welcome he received from group members, who encouraged him to join their discussion. He also admitted that his initial experience with these individuals actually had him briefly rethink the murderous mission he was about to unleash (Horwitz et al., 2015; Morris, 2017). However, the narrative account provided to Roof from a variety of white supremacist social media sites, which led him to Mother Emanuel Church, provided to be more resilient than the fact of his actual experience.

In recounting his experience during his shooting spree, he admitted that he told his victims prior to shooting them that "[y]ou all are taking over our country. Y'all want something to pray about. I'll give you something to pray about" (Horwitz et al., 2015). After this "charge" he began firing. It was later determined by police investigators that of the 77 pistol rounds, which Roof fired, 50 of those actually hit found its target (Morlin, 2016). Roof was subsequently arrested, tried, and convicted for the murder of nine members of the Mother Emanuel congregation along with other charges and is currently on death row awaiting execution for his actions.

The case of Dylann Roof reveals an example of white supremacist radicalization, which was completed through his involvement with far-right social media sites, which in turn helped to clarify those attitudes and belief that were likely already present prior to this initial interaction. In what has been identified as Dylann Roof's jail journal, which was written after his arrest for the Mother Emanuel Church murders and confiscated on August 3, 2015 during a search of his jail cell, Roof provides some interesting commentary concerning his attitude and motives. He begins this journal by stating:

> My name is Dylan Storm Roof. I was born on the third of April 1994 in Columbia, South Carolina. I was not raised in a racist home or environment. Living in the South, almost every white person has a small amount of racial awareness, simply because of the numbers of negroes in this part of the country. But it is a superficial awareness. Growing up, in school, the White and black Kids would make racial jokes toward each other, but that's all it was, jokes. Me and my White friends would sometimes watch American History X, or some videos online of black nationalists talking about killing White people, but there was no real understanding behind it.

8 White Supremacy and the Digital World: The Social Construction…

(Retrieved from https://age-of-treason.com/2017/01/09/dylann-roofs-jail-journal)[2]

Roof's opening introduction seems to reveal some lingering "suspicions" concerning the true nature of African-Americans living in Columbia and elsewhere. The racial awareness, which he claims every white person has, as the result of their proximity to the African-Americans living in their community is superficial, is an awareness which does not really understand or even recognize the real truth of the issue. He includes himself in this grouping and then states that it was not until George Zimmerman killed Trayvon Martin that he "truly awakened" to the truth. He stated that he could not understand why this event appeared to be such a big deal. "It was obvious that Zimmerman was right. But more importantly this prompted me to type the words 'Black on White crime into Google and I was never the same since'" (Retrieved from https://age-of-treason.com/2017/01/09/dylann-roofs-jail-journal).

By his own admission, Roof visited certain white supremacy sites, such as The Council of Conservative Citizens, and lastrhodesian.com[3] where he states he was exposed to the real truth:

> There were pages upon pages of these brutal, disgusting black on white murders. I was in disbelief. At this moment I realized that something was very wrong. How could the news be blowing up this Trayvon Martin case while hundreds of these black on white murders got no airtime? (Retrieved from https://age-of-treason.com/2017/01/09/dylann-roofs-jail-journal)

He continues by stating that this initial "research" led him to "go deeper" to determine if a similar "pattern" was occurring in Europe as well. He states that he was similarly shocked by the results of this search. "As an American, you are taught to accept living in the melting pot, and that blacks and other minorities have just as much right to be here, since we

---

[2] This address will not actually take you to Roof's Jail Journal page; I tried and was unable to access the journal. The journal can be accessed by going to the Age of Treason website and search Dylann Roof. His journal will be the first link that appears.

[3] Lastrhodesian.com has been identified as the site where Roof discussed some of the ideas later discovered within the jail journal, explaining both his process of radicalization as well as his attack on The Mother Emanuel Church in Charlestown, SC (Robles, 2015; Wren & Pardue, 2015).

are all immigrants" (Retrieved from https://age-of-treason.com/2017/01/09/dylann-roofs-jail-journal). After completing this "research," he concludes, "I can say with confidence that I am completely Racially aware" (Retrieved from https://age-of-treason.com/2017/01/09/dylann-roofs-jail-journal).

Though no real evidence exists that would substantiate any of the claims, which Roof attributes to his radicalization, it does appear that he easily and quickly embraces these conspiratorial "facts" by which to justify what follows. It also greatly damages any claim that he is not racist, regardless his denials to the contrary. In fact, during his interview with the FBI investigators Michael Stansbury and Craig Januchowski on June 18, 2015, Roof admits that the reason why he chose Mother Emanuel Church as his target was because he was certain that black people would be present. "I wasn't going to go to another church because there could have been white people there. I didn't want to kill white people." In attempting to clarify Roof's response, one of the FBI investigators asks, "So you didn't want to kill white people, or shoot them." Roof quickly responds with a slight giggle, "No." So, you only wanted to shoot black people and Roof responds, "Right."

It also raises the possibility that even though he did not apparently openly share these ideas with those in his immediate circle, those thoughts were still "present" to some degree, as suppressed or repressed thoughts and feelings. As a result when he goes to these white supremacist websites, he quickly realizes that there is no prohibition against these beliefs and realizes that he is experiencing a "place" of kindred spirits. Once firmly situated within a co-constituted intervolvement with the white supremacist they-self, a "new" nomic order is embraced, which in turn begins to fabricate a new reversion of the self.

Once this new version of the self had been finished or completed, Roof was no ready to act. In his "manifesto" and reaffirmed in his videotaped interview with the FBI conducted on 06/18/2015, Roof maintains that he could no longer continue to do nothing concerning his belief perpetrated by black people on innocent whites:

> I couldn't go another day without doing something, I couldn't live with myself seeing these things happen to my people and do nothing about it.

Sometimes sitting in my cell, I think about how nice it would be to be able to watch a movie, or eat some good food, or drive my car somewhere, but when I remember how I when I did these things, and how I had to do something. And then I realize it was worth it. (Dylann Roof quoted in Swartz, 2017)

Roof's perceived need to do something, reflects the phenomenology of murder described by Katz (1988) in his text *Seductions of Crime*. In that text, he describes what he identifies as righteous rage, which becomes the moral justification for the violence which follows. Much like the construct of strain as described by Agnew, righteous rage reflects the phenomenology of moral indignation, which is tied to both the experience of humiliation and the violence this process unfolds:

As Katz (1988) observes, "killers develop a righteous passion against the background of taking a last stand in the defense of respectability" (p. 19). However, unlike the killers studied by Katz, who seem to act for personal Reasons intended to resolve personal experiences of humiliation, killers Like Roof are motivated by a sense of what he perceives as a group Humiliation, even when that experience is more general and vicarious in nature. (Polizzi, 2020, p. 61)

For Roof, the experience of humiliation emerges from his sense of personal "responsibility" for having not acted sooner to avenge the daily violence believed to be directed at innocent white people by black perpetrators. However, because all blacks are guilty due to the fact of their ethnicity, and nothing else, any black will do because all are guilty. He admits as much during his interview with the FBI when he observes that he realizes that these church going people are not criminals and are in fact innocent, but that fact is not sufficient to spare them from his rage. His rationalization of this fact is resolved by simply observing that innocent white people are killed or raped every day by blacks, making his act of murder far less significant than what occurs to white folk on a daily basis. To substantiate this point, Roof states the following in his jailhouse manifesto:

> I would like to make it crystal clear; I do not regret what I did. I am not sorry. I have not shed a tear for the innocent people I killed. I do feel sorry for the innocent white people killed daily at the hands of the lower races. I have shed a tear of pity for myself. I feel pity that I had to give up my life because of a situation that should never have existed. (Dylann Roof quoted in Swartz, 2017)

Taken from the perspective offered by Roof, the nomic ordering of white supremacy constructs being-in-the-world-as-white-nationalist as that which is being both threated and called to war. When he states that he has shed no tear for the innocent lives lost, this becomes due to the conclusion that there is no innocence for blacks because all are guilty (Polizzi, 2020). However, this guilt is ontologically configured, making it unnecessary for anything other accompanying performance of criminal behavior to be present. Even church going blacks, who are clearly not criminals, still remain a "legitimate" target. The cultural object of the black body in any of its possible manifestations can be nothing other than criminal and must be eliminated.

In Roof's distinction concerning the construction of innocence, Sontag's "who is killing whom" dynamic is clearly articulated. For Roof, innocence in all of its various manifestations is reserved exclusively for whiteness. The murdered whites that he witnesses on the pages of the Council of Conservative Citizens website become similar to the images of murdered Jewish or Palestinian children or the various photos from U.S. detention facilities in Iraq or Guantanamo Bay, which evoked such rage by Muslim viewers. For Roof, there is no consideration concerning the reality or truth for what he is viewing; rather, there is only the consideration concerning how this threat should be met. As a result of this unshakeable certainty of guilt, any possible recognition of the innocence of his black victims, an innocence that he readily identities, is overwritten by the facticity of their blackness. Though he seems initially to struggle with this conclusion prior to his act of violence, his uncertainty is quickly brushed aside as he reminds himself why he is there. With his "certainty" restored, his retribution can begin without further "moral" distraction.

It is also important to note that Roof admitted to FBI investigators[4] the next day that he firmly believed that he would die in that attack. One of the reasons he had so much ammunition with him was to be sure he would be able to take his own life when confronted by the police, who he expected to find waiting in the parking lot of Mother Emanuel Church as he exited that building. In his interview with FBI investigators, Stansbury and Januchowski, Roof also states that he had no intention in "killing cops;" if a confrontation occurred, he planned to kill himself. He made this admission when one of the investigators asked what he did after the shooting:

> Well … To be honest, I was in absolute awe that there was nobody out after I shot that many bullets. I was like, Oh my God, what are these cops doing. They're not really doing their job. I don't know how many shots there were, 7 × 11, and there wasn't a single cop outside. (Roldan & Monk, 2016: FBI interview with Dylann Roof 06, 18, 2015)

He continued by saying,

> Obviously, I walk out that door. I peeked out the door. I thought there was Going to be somebody there ready to shoot me. You know what I mean? That's why I had the last magazine; it wasn't to shoot cops, it was to shoot myself … When I saw a cop. I wasn't ever going to shoot at a cop; I was going to shoot myself. (Roldan & Monk, 2016: FBI interview with Dylann Roof 06, 18, 2015)[5]

It is interesting that though he stated that he fully intended to die at the scene, either by police fire or suicide, he had no intention of killing himself in the absence of police presence at the scene. His stance is most consistent with Afghan mujahidin fighters, who were certainly ready and willing to die for their beliefs, but were not interested in dying simply for the sake of dying. If death was to be the way his mission was to end on

---

[4] Roof made this admission to FBI investigators during their 06/18/2015 interview with Roof. In that interview, Roof refused a lawyer and openly admitted to his involvement in the church murders.

[5] The above transcription of the FBI interview occurred 25:25/26:23 of counter of that recorded interview.

that night, so be it; but absent that he was apparently unwilling to take his own life outside of that context. There is a sense of disappointment when he realizes that he will not be confronted by police, and is almost disturbed that the police are actually failing to do their job. However, this does not mean that he was unwilling to give up his life for this cause.

During the first fifteen to twenty minutes of his interview with FBI investigators, Roof waives all of his Miranda Rights and then proceeds to describe in some detail both his level of premeditation prior to the crimes, as well as a description of his actions during the murders. Given his clear and forthright description of his involvement in these crimes, he seems almost determined to ensure that this time the authorities will not fail in taking his life. What does become surprising is that there is very little sense of grandiosity shown by Roof when he is asked about what he believed his crimes would accomplish; rather, he matter-of-factly responds by saying, "I'm not delusional; I don't think what I did will start a race war." One of the FBI investigators asked if he would like to see a race war occur. Roof responds by saying, "No a race war would be terrible" (Roldan & Monk, 2016). Though he seems to understand that his former life is over, that fact is simply not sufficient to evoke a lasting sense of remorse or the belief that his act of "martyrdom" was in anyway meaningless.

What Roof's phenomenology reveals is a manifestation of being-in-the-world-as-white-supremacist that is shamed by the "truth" he is provided by this digital process of nomic ordering and becomes determined to respond. Though he openly admitted to FBI investigators that he was never a member of any white supremacist group and never discussed or received any help from anyone in executing his act of terror, he was still fundamentally radicalized by a structure of nomic ordering that is quite consistent with the general construction of white supremacy/white nationalism:

> I would rather live imprisoned knowing I took action for my race than to live with the torture of sitting idle. It isn't up to me anymore. I did what I could do, I've done all I can do. I did what I thought would make the biggest wave. And now the fate of our race sits in the hands of my brothers who continue to live freely. (Hawes, 2017, pp. 18–19)

Regardless the absence of any official affiliation with an existing white supremacist group, Roof still shares a sense of connection and shared vision with those who "continue to live freely" (Hawes, 2017, p. 19). His becomes a personal act of insurrection, a personal attempt to assuage the guilt for having not acted sooner. Though there does appear to be some question whether he actually believed that his action would be the wave that would motivate others, who shared his beliefs to act similarly, or that his act was motivated by a personal need to "make right," the intent was still the same. What can be said is that Roof's actions were intended to symbolize the exact responsibility this "awakening" revealed and the exact strategies by which to achieve its goal.

The Case of Robert Bowers

On October 27, 2018, Robert Bowers entered the Tree of Life Synagogue, located in the prominently Jewish neighborhood of Squirrel Hill in Pittsburgh, PA, with the intent on killing members of that congregation who had gathered there for Shabbat morning services. Much like Dylann Roof's choice of Mother Emanuel Church, Bowers came to this place of worship to kill Jews attending morning services. A few hours before his attack, Bowers posted on his Gab social media page that "HIAS (Hebrews Immigrant Aid Society) likes to bring invaders in that kill our people. I can't sit by and watch my people get slaughtered. Screw your optics, I'm going in" (Katz, 2018).

HIAS is a refugee-aid organization that is connected to the Tree of Life Synagogue. As a result of that relationship with HIAS, Bowers apparently believed that this made Tree of Life Synagogue an appropriate target, given their association with that organization. HIAS was created in 1881 for the purpose of helping Jewish refugees receive legal and financial aid which would allow them to go to the U.S. or other nations who would provide them some degree of a haven. More recently, HIAS has been charged with partnering with organizations that associated with anti-Semitic or anti-Zionist views (Sobel, 2020). In an attempt to answer this charge, HIAS CEO Mark Hetfield told the Jewish Journal that "At HIAS, we used to help refugees because they were Jewish; today, we help refugees because we are Jewish" (Sobel, 2020, p. 2). For Bowers, the HIAS involvement with refugees and asylum seekers coming from Central America, which in his mind, was to "kill our people," was proof enough that the congregants of Tree of Life Synagogue were equally guilty and needed to be punished, given their association with that organization.

Bowers' rationale, similar to the "logic" employed by Roof, seemingly concluded that those involved in providing aid to the so-called caravan of Central American refugees fleeing the political and criminal violence in their own countries, made them complicit in the crime of killing white folk in America. Though Bowers certainly believed in the far-right rhetoric of talk radio, far-right social media, and the vitriolic rhetoric of Donald Trump, as this pertained to individuals seeking asylum from Central America, but these White Supremacist attitudes simply became the pretext by which to strike out at those who Bowers perceived as the real enemy: Jews.

By most accounts of those who knew and worked with Bowers, he never espoused publicly any of the vitriolic hatred toward Jews or immigrants that would lead him to his violent assault on Tree of Life Synagogue (Lord, 2018). Bowers begins as an anti-government conservative in the early 1990s, who directed most of his anger toward the United Nations; however, over the thirty years since, his involvement with white nationalist and white supremacist websites helped to pave the way toward this murderous conclusion. It is important to recognize that Bowers' slow and steady transformation reflects a co-constituted phenomenology of radicalization that simply cannot be reduced to the sum of independent parts. His involvement from the early beginnings of the internet, over time allowed him to create websites[6] housing various conspiracy theories related to the Blue Hats of the United Nations bent on disarming Americans for the purpose of creating a global government (Lord, 2018). As this co-constituted relationality with the expanding web increased, his ability to reach out to like-minded individuals expanded as well. As a result of this fact, the need to discuss his ideas openly no longer becomes

---

[6] Bowers built his own computers and per Lord's reporting was using encrypted communications as early as 1998 (Lord, 2018).

necessary. The grievances which he identifies and the solutions which are offered and shared reflect a much more powerful phenomenological impact given the affirmation they provide.

Bowers' phenomenology of radicalization emerges from a context of nomic ordering, which validates certain aspects of "discrete behaviors" that may then be pursed. As a result, the content located on these various far-right social media sites becomes the nomic structure that in turn co-constitutes the process of identity formation and transformation. Once Bowers has been transformed by his fidelity to this white nationalist nomic they, he can then proudly proclaim, "screw your optics I'm going in." Bowers now no longer satisfied with the chatter of conspiracy apparently felt that the time to act was now. His cries of "All Jews must die" becomes the battle cry for this nomos of hate, which he shares with others similarly afflicted.[7]

The Case of Brenton Tarrant

Dylann Roof and Robert Bowers exemplify two specific configurations of American White Supremacy & White Nationalism. In each of these examples, these individuals bring to their encounters with this digital nomic structure a set of preconceived beliefs and grievances that are both affirmed and validated by this co-constituted phenomenological structure, resulting in a reconfigured manifestation of the self now willing to act. Though these events were rigorously investigated by media and legal authorities, they were after the fact accounts of what occurred, which relied on either the recollections of perpetrators, eyewitnesses, or the story told by physical evidence at the scene. All of that changed, however, when Brenton Tarrant, a white supremacist or self-identified ethno-nationalist from Australia, who entered two Mosques located in Christchurch, New Zealand with the intent of not only killing as many individuals as possible, but also, to provide livestreamed chronicling of this horrific event:

---

[7] Some of the responses to Bowers' violence can be accessed at age-of-treason.com/2018/10/27/robert-bowers/

Unlike the attacks performed by Roof and Bowers, Tarrant took two years to plan his attack and three months prior to executing his plan to decide on his targets. Part of his preparation included writing a manifesto, which he uploaded to Twitter, Facebook, and 8chan (Hutchinson, 2019). Hutchinson (2019) observed that "The manifesto represented Tarrant's desire to gain maximum attention, communicate an ideological position and validate the online far-right extremist community where he perceived himself a member" (p. 20). Though the written text provided by Tarrant may have achieved its intended result, the visceral intensity of the live streaming of Muslim congregants being murdered in their place of worship in the name of far-right "retribution" is far more powerful.

Tarrant's use of livestreaming to capture the horrific nature of these events recalls a similar aesthetic strategy employed by the producers of the ISIS snuff films, particularly those stylized images of Western captives kneeling in their orange prison jumpsuits in front of the all black-clad Jihadi John as he readies for their executions (Polizzi, 2019b). However, Tarrant's production is far less stylized than ISIS, whereas the ISIS executions were quite often composed with specific consideration to foreground/background "staging" and other aesthetic effects, the Christchurch murders are filmed as they are happening in real time, so as to better chronicle the horror and terror being inflicted upon the victims; and, it is from this point of view that Tarrant seeks to solidify his far-right "credibility" and identity.

Whatever "credibility" Tarrant gained by making his manifesto accessible to like-minded members of the far-right "community," likely pales in comparison to how he was perceived by these same individuals, as they watched this episode of mass murder unfold in real time on various social media platforms. When Sontag (2004) observed, "To the militant, identity is everything" (p. 10), the astuteness of her claim should not be underestimated. Tarrant does what he does, precisely because identity is everything and as such, his chronicled acts of terror provide the proof to substantiate that connection.

> However, livestreaming the event was significant because it also created a direct connection to the online audience and provided personal content for online viewers. This connection cultivated a sense of propinquity between

offline actors and online viewers, which may propel popular perceptions of the assailant as acting on the behalf of the far-right online community. This grant of recognition and affinity for the assailant can motivate other members of the online community to commit similar acts. (Hutchinson, 2019, p. 21)

References

Atwan, A. B. (2015). *Islamic State: The digital caliphate*. University of California Press.

Berger, P. (1967). *The scared canopy: Elements of a sociological theory of religion*. Anchor Books.

Bliuc, A.-M., Betts, J., Vergani, M., Iqbal, M., & Dunn, K. (2020, April). *The growing power of online communities of the extreme-right: deriving strength, meaning, and direction from significant socio-political events 'in real life'* (ICCT Policy brief). International Centre of Counter Terrorism-The Hague.

Conway, M., Scrivens, R., & Macnair, L. (2019, October). *Right-wing extremists' persistent online presence: History and contemporary trends* (ICCT policy brief). International Centre for Counter-Terrorism-The Hague.

Gerges, F. (2016). *ISIS: A history*. Princeton University Press.

Gordon, L. (2013). The irreplaceability of continued struggle. In G. Yancy & J. Jones (Eds.), *Pursuing Trayvon Martin: Historical contexts and contemporary manifestations of racial dynamics* (pp. 85-90). Lanham, MD: Lexington Books.

Hamm, M. S., & Spaaij, R. (2017). *The age of lone wolf terrorism*. Columbia University Press.

Hawes, J. B. (2017, January 05 Updated January 06). Dylann Roof Jailhouse Journal. *The Post and Courier*. Retrieved from https://www.postandcourier.com/dylann-roof-jailhouse-journal/pdf_da3e19b8-d3b3-11e6-b040-03089263e67c.html.

Heidegger, M. (2010). *Being and time* (J. Stambaugh, Trans.). SUNY Press.

Horwitz, S, Harlan, C., Holley, P., & Wan, W. (2015, June 20). What we know so far about Charleston church shooting suspect Dylann Roof. *The Washington Post*. Retrieved from www.washingtonpost.com/2015/06/20/what-we-know-so-far-about-charleston-church-shooting-suspect-dylann-roof

Hutchinson, J. (2019). Far-right terrorism. *Counter Terrorist Trends and Analyses, 11*, 19–28.

Katz, J. (1988). *The seductions of crime: Moral and sensual attractions in doing evil*. New York: Basic Books.

Katz, R. (2018, October 29). Inside the online cesspool of Anti-Semitism that housed Robert Bowers. *Politico*. Retrieved from www.politico.com/magazine/story/2018/10/29/inside-the-online-cesspool-of-anti-semitism-that-housed-robert-bowers-221949

Lord, R. (2018, November 10). How Robert Bowers went from conservative to white nationalist. *Pittsburgh Post-Gazette*. Retrieved from post-gazette.com/news/crime-courts/2018/11/10/Robert-Bowers-extremism-Tree-of-Life-Massacre-shooting-pittsburgh-Gab-Warroom/stories/201811080165

Merleau-Ponty, M. (2012). *Phenomenology of perception*. Routledge.

Miller-Idriss, C. (2020). *Hate in the Homeland: The new global far right*. Princeton University Press.

Morlin, B. (2016, December 19). Unrepentant and radicalized online: A look at the Trial of Dylann Roof. *Southern Poverty Law Center*. Retrieved from www.splcenter.org/hatewatch/2016/12/19/unrepentant-and-radicalized-look-trial-dylann-roof.

Morris, T. (2017). *Dark ideas: How neo-Nazi and violent jihadi ideologues shaped modern terrorism*. Lexington Books.

Perliger, A. (2020). *American zealots: Inside right-wing domestic terrorism*. Columbia University Press.

Phillips, C. (2016). *The battle for Syria: International rivalry in the new Middle East*. Yale University Press.

Polizzi, D. (2012). Social presence, visibility and the eye of the beholder: A phenomenology of social embodiment. In G. Yancy & J. Jones (Eds.), *Pursuing Trayvon Martin: Historical contexts and contemporary manifestations of racial dynamics* (pp. 173–183). Lexington Books.

Polizzi, D. (2016). *A philosophy of the social construction of crime*. Policy Press.

Polizzi, D. (2019a). *A phenomenological hermeneutic of antiblack racism in the autobiography of Malcolm X*. Lexington Books.

Polizzi, D. (2019b). The aesthetics of violence. In R. Lippens & E. Murray (Eds.), *Representing the experience of war and atrocity* (pp. 45–71). Palgrave Macmillan.

Polizzi, D. (2020). Righteous slaughter and the phenomenology of the assailed self. In D. Polizzi (Ed.), *Jack Katz: Seduction, The street and emotion*. Emerald Publishing.

Polizzi, D. (in press). The negation of innocence: Terrorism and the state of exception. In B. Arrigo & B. Brian Sellers (Eds.), *The pre-crime society: Crime, culture and control in the ultramodern age*. Bristol University Press.

Robles, F. (2015, June 20). Dylann Roof photos and a manifesto are posted on website. *New York Times*. Retrieved from www.nytimes.com/2015/06/21/us/dylann-storm-roof-photos-website-charleston-church-shooting.html.

Roldan, C., & Monk, M. (2016, December 9). Roof talks of the how and why of his hate in taped confession. *The State*. Retrieved from thestate.com/news/local/crime/article120075733.html

Samuels, B. (2021, January 11). Pence's relationship with Trump fractures in final days. *The Hill*. Retrieved from thehill.com/homenews/administration/533723/pences-relationship-with-trump-trump-fractures-in-final-days

Sobel, A. (2020, May 7). The conspiracy theories around HIAS, debunked. *Jewish Journal*. Retrieved from. jewishjournal.com/commentary/analysis/315444/hias-refugee-resettlement-nonprofit-anti-israel-groups-debunked/

Sontag, S. (2004). *Regarding the pain of others*. Picador.

Swartz, A. (2017, January 6). The most disturbing revelation from Dylann Roof's jailhouse manifesto. *Mic*. Retrieved from www.mic.com/articles/164586/the-most-disturbing-revelation-from-dylann-roof-s-jailhouse-manifesto

Weinberg, L. (2013). Violence by the far right: The American experience. In M. Taylor, P. M. Currie, & D. Holbrook (Eds.), *Extreme right-wing political violence and terrorism* (pp. 15–30). Bloomsbury.

Wong, M., Frank, R., & Allsup, R. (2015). The supremacy of online white supremists—An analysis of online discussions by white supremacists. *Information & Communications Technology Law, 24*, 1–33.

Wren, D. & Pardue, D. (2015, June 19 Updated 2016, December 12). Dylann Roof had outlined racist views online prior to chuch shooting. *The Post and Courier*. Retrieved from https://www.postandcourier.com/archives/dylann-roof-had-outlined-racist-views-on-website-prior-to-church-shooting/article_f4c732e5-9bee-5e99-830a-780176f4a0e7.html.

9

The Reemergence of the Far-Right

The General Structure of White Supremacy and White Nationalism

The reemergence of the far-right almost seems like a misnomer for the obvious reason that it really has never gone away. Though it has shown an ebb and flow of political currency in various degrees for centuries within the American body politic, the contradictions which it reveals have rarely been sufficiently addressed, in such a way to quiet its sometimes insatiable voice. In fact, that voice has been at its loudest and most disagreeable, when attempts at resolution seemed to be gaining a degree of political and social momentum. These moments of potential transformation, these moments of nomic expansion, though necessary and at times essential, also can evoke considerable backlash when this phenomenology of social existence is perceived to have gone too far.

The reemergence of these far-right attitudes and beliefs is almost always most pronounced whenever the nomos of white supremacy, and white nationalism is threatened or in fear of collapse (Belew, 2018; Jackson, 2020; Perliger, 2020; Weinberg, 2013). The specific manifestation of these various nomic structures or nomic adumbrations, whether situated within the context of Christian Identity movements, White Supremacy, or White Nationalism, all share a sufficient degree of nomic agreement that allows them to be grouped within a similar phenomenological structure of social meaning (Belew, 2018; Jackson, 2020; Ong, 2020; Perliger, 2020). For Belew (2018), this structuring of far-right nomic ideation becomes defined within her more general rubric of white power. Taken from this perspective, the construct of white power employs the definitional capability of incorporating a variety of groups under this evolving nomic canopy. Though there exist differing theoretical and religious considerations across groups situated within this nomic structure, there is much more shared nomic agreement with and fidelity to the white they-self or nomos which is perceived to be under siege (Belew, 2018; Weinberg, 2013).

As such this shared nomic structure reflects what Lipset and Rabb (1970) termed monism:

> By "monism" they have in mind the belief that there is only one correct answer to any problem and that the powers that be ought to prevent competing views from being expressed. If the powers do not act accordingly, there is a reason: a conspiracy has taken charge. (Weinberg, 2013, p. 15)

Lipset and Rabb's construct of monism informs the type of phenomenological process, which one would expect to encounter within more extreme manifestations of Berger (1967) and Griffin's (2012) application of the nomos, Heidegger's construct of the they-self, and Agamben's configuration of the apparatus. With each of these examples, the process of nomic ordering takes on a very rigid and specific configuration of social meaning, which in turn creates a very specific fabrication of the subject or being-in-the-world.

Regardless the specific manifestation of this monic process, the core constitutive "element" is the embrace of white power. As such, this manifestation of the they-self provides to being-in-the-world as-White Supremacist, White Nationalist, KKK member, Christian Identity, or Neo-Nazi, a structure for social meaning that not only informs and constructs individual identity, but provides a very clear distinction between what will be valued and what will not. Taken from this perspective the they-self, which represents the various manifestations of white power, "disburdens the meaning of being" from those who embrace this nomic structure by demanding that any validation of difference be viewed as an example of treason. As was witnessed within the rationale of individuals such as Dylann Roof, Robert Bowers, and Brenton Tarrant or more recently with groups such as the Oath Keepers, The Proud Boys, or the various iterations of the same, the main focus has in some way been motivated by this embrace of white power.

Belew (2018) centers the current trajectory of the nomos of white power within the context of the Viet Nam War and its aftermath. However, she observes the racial animus which was clearly visible during the conflict in Southeast Asia simply represented one example of the articulation of white power that has been with us since the end of the Civil War. Just as former Confederate veterans would form the first iteration of the Ku Klux Klan after the defeat of South and terrorize black citizens during the Reconstruction, a similar dynamic was in play in the aftermath of World War I, World War II, the Korean War, and the Viet Nam War. In the aftermath of each of these conflicts, veterans joined the ranks of the Klan providing everything from military style training and leadership to participation in actual acts of violence (Belew, 2018).

> Significantly, in each surge of activity, veterans worked hand in hand with Klan members who had not served. Without participation of civilians, these aftershocks of war would not have found purchase at home. (Belew, 2018, p. 21)

A similar dynamic has been witnessed more recently as former veterans of the two Iraq Wars and the nearly twenty-year conflict in Afghanistan have also found their way into the ranks of the radicalized far-right. It has been reported by several news sources that approximately one in five of the insurrectionists, who stormed the Capitol Building on January 6, 2020, had formerly served in the U.S. armed forces. These individuals, much like the group of veterans described by Belew, have brought some of the same skills and "grievances" to various militia organizations across the country, which includes the Oath Keepers, the Proud Boys, and other iterations of White Nationalism and White Supremacy. What becomes unmistakable by this trajectory of historical presencing is the fact that white power regardless its specific configuration has remained alive as well as a viable nomic structure that is inseparable from the phenomenological process, which created American democracy itself.

As a structure of nomic ordering, the canopy of white supremacy announces itself most violently when a specific threat emerges, which seeks to reconfigure the very foundations of its power. Whether this was the aftermath of the Civil War and the threat posed by Reconstruction (Blight, 2021; Thomas, 2017) or the return of veterans from the numerous wars of the last one hundred years, the construct of white power found itself threatened in a variety of ways as the diversity of American culture and society continued to develop in more inclusive ways (Belew, 2018; Simi et al., 2013). Though this experience of nomic expansion did not move fast enough for some, any change that sought to upend the hierarchal social structure of American society as this related to the construct of white supremacy has been consistently viewed as an existential threat to the they-self of white power and as a "strain" that could not go unchecked.

When taken from Griffin's (2012) construct of the Modernist, the canopy of white power or far-right radicalization announces its presence by claiming that the American nomic structure has either failed or is in complete ruin and must be recreated. For the Modernist, there is no desire of turning back the clock, the past becomes destiny and must be changed. What becomes most "self-evident" to this creed of white power is that only "whiteness" may be created equal. If whiteness can no longer be the invisible standard that is never raced and by which all others will be "judged," then it becomes incumbent upon this process to remove those whose very presence threatens to upend this unassailable divine right of these self-evident social truths.

Such a distinction reveals more of a focus on ethnic cleansing then it does on concerns related to differing points of view from competing ideological perspectives. For example, the ontological dividing line for Salafist Jihadism or Islamist religious extremism is based on a specific interpretation of the Qur'an and not the specific ethnicity of the believer. For the white supremacist this dynamic is reversed. Though certain iterations of the far-right community may also include prohibitions against certain left-wing perspectives, the factor of "race" remains most prominent and most influential to the nomic "validity" of this process of identity formation. As a result of this phenomenological structure ideology becomes subsumed and overshadowed by the social presencing of the body.

The presencing of the non-white body, when situated within the constituting gaze of white supremacy, becomes the bearer of behavior, which in turn becomes objectified as the existential threat to white power. Any manifestation of social experience or presencing, which "dares" to perform as white others are allowed to perform, must be viewed as an act of sedition or treason. How could it be otherwise? As was witnessed in the perspectives of individuals like Dylann Roof, Robert Bowers, Brenton Tarrant discussed in the previous chapters, the mere presencing of the "deviant" black body or Jewish body or Muslim body was the sole characteristic necessary by which to condemn that bearer of behavior to the violence which followed. Unfortunately, these names represent only a few from what has shown to be an ever-growing list. We can include on this list Wade Michael Page, who attempted to murder worshipers at a Sikh Temple in Oak Creek, Wisconsin on August 5, 2012, or Patrick Crusius, who on August 3 traveled seven hours by car from his home in a suburb of Dallas, Texas to El Paso, where he entered a local Walmart and killed 23 people and wounded 23 others. Crusius would claim that he was motivated by the Christchurch terrorist attack on two local mosques along with his desire to turn back the "wave" of illegal immigrants coming to replace whites.

In each of these examples, the mere presencing of the social body now becomes the bearer of "ontologically" constructed criminality or deviance. No other proof is necessary and no specific suspect required: all are guilty. When so constructed there is no longer any difference between someone praying or someone allegedly involved in the crime of rape, if the body bearing that behavior is black, or one of the other "existential" threats to White Supremacy that fact alone is sufficient to justify its punishment. Perhaps this dichotomy was no more clearly on display then it was on January 6, 2020, when American democracy was under siege from a sea of insurrectionists attempting to overturn the results of the 2020 U.S. Presidential election.

Watching the insurrection unfold in real time on my television forced me to make the immediate observation: if these protesters were black there would have been black bodies beaten, bleeding and dying on the steps of the U.S. Capitol Building, and these results would have been framed as patriotic acts of heroism. The images of white Trump supporters overwhelming the poorly prepared Capitol and Metro Police provided a stark contrast to the attitude and preparedness of law enforcement nationwide to the mostly peaceful protests demonstrating against police shootings of unarmed black suspects. It is important to note that the violence which took place last summer at many of the Black Lives Matter protest by a relatively some group of protesters, though certainly criminal and worthy of prosecution, pales in comparison to an act of outright insurrection by a group of domestic terrorists attempting to overthrow the results of a free and fair election. If one need a comparative example, it would be 9/11 and not these summer protests. The conclusion to this event becomes rather obvious: the white body is never a threat even when it is violently threatening the lives of law enforcement or elected leaders, whereas any gesture of the black body remains a constant ontological threat.

It is also important to recognize that the insurrection of January 6 also carries with it a far more problematic implication: the relationship between the President, members of the GOP Congressional Caucus, and the political orientation of those who were actually involved in the physical assault on the Capitol. The observation which Belew (2018) offers, concerning the relationship between returning veterans and civilian members of the Klan, is in kind similar to the relationship which exists between those insurrectionists who attempted to overturn the result of the 2020 Presidential election and those members of the Republican party, who continued to insist that the election was stolen in the absence of any evidence of the same. Perhaps nothing exemplified that relationship more clearly than seeing a small group of Republican Senators return to the Senate chamber in the aftermath of the day's earlier events and continue to repeat the same unproven charges, which had been used as the catalyst for the insurrection.

Though a degree of similarity does exist between the examples offered by Belew and the events of the January 6 insurrection, the level of "civilian participation," which eventually led to the siege of the U.S. Capitol Building, reflects a far more dangerous dynamic. Such an observation is not intended to minimize those individuals targeted by the forces of white power: rather, it is simply to recognize how the relationship between violent far-right insurgents and their civilian apologists and supporters has algebraically transformed this equation. In fact, even before Trump was elected president in 2016, he was stoking the beginning flames of insurrection, even if this result was not immediately intended at the time it was offered. During various interviews with news media covering the election, he was asked if he would accept the results. His response was "Yes if I win." Such contempt for the electoral process has rarely been so vividly on display.

The militarization of far-right insurgent groups and their contention to elected officials at the local, state, and national levels has probably not been more openly present since the years leading up to and after the American Civil War (Belew, 2018; Jackson, 2020; Weinberg, 2013). This connection was regularly witnessed throughout the duration of the Trump Presidency, which was algebraically intensified in the aftermath of his electoral defeat in 2020. The rallying cry of "Make America Great Again," the Modernist hope for the creation of a single party authoritarian state, becomes the representation of the White Supremacist they-self, which promises to deconstruct the "administrative state," and recreate the foundations of white power. Though the institutional guardrails of American democracy were able to withstand the threat posed by Trump and his allies, both inside and outside of the government, it remains to be seen how the country responds to this now undeniable challenge.

As American society continues to struggle with the aftershocks of the Trump presidency, one fact remains undeniable: approximately 70 million Americans decided to once again support him, while continuing to reject any and all evidence implicating him in unethical or potentially criminal behavior. That fact was particularly evident during the siege on the U.S. Capitol Building, given that one could witness more Trump flags being waved than the flag of the U.S. Who are these members of the Trump insurgency and what do they represent? The discussion will now move to a discussion of a few of the groups that have been particularly active over the last few years of the Trump presidency: The Oath Keepers, The Proud Boys, and the followers of Q and the QAnon Conspiracies.

The Oath Keepers

Stewart Rhodes created the Oath Keepers, a far-right anti-government organization made up of former law enforcement officers and military veterans in 2009, ostensibly to defend the U.S. Constitution against far-left domestic groups believed to be planning the elimination of the Second Amendment right to bear arms, which in turn would be followed by the overthrow the U.S. government (Giglio, 2020; Jackson, 2020). Their first public appearance took place on April 19, 2009 on Lexington Common, which was where the first battle of the American Revolution was fought (Jackson, 2020). Rhodes intentionally sought to recruit former law enforcement and military veterans, who had both taken the oath to protect the Constitution against all enemies foreign and domestic and also had the necessary training that would provide him a combat-ready fighting force. However, the true forming of the group appears to be more related to a variety of baseless conspiracy theories, which centered on the belief that the federal government was preparing a plan that would destroy the civil liberties of American citizens protected by the Constitution (Giglio, 2020; Jackson, 2020; Michel, 2020). A telling glimpse of the motivating concern of the Oath Keepers and its founder was provided by Rhodes in an article he published in *S.W.A.T.* Magazine in April of 2008, prior to the group's formal creation:

> Imagine that Herr Hitlery [Hillary Clinton] is sworn in as president in 2009. After a conveniently timed "domestic terrorism" incident (just a coincidence, of course) … she promptly crams a United Nations mandated total ban on the private possession of firearms. … But Hitlery goes further, proclaiming a national emergency and declaring the entire militia movement (and anyone else Morris Dees labels "extremists") to be "enemy combatants." … Hitlery declares that such citizens are subject to secret military detention without jury trial, "enhanced" interrogation techniques, and trial before a military tribunal hand-picked by the dominatrix-in-chief

herself. Hitlery then orders police, National Guard troops and active military to go house-to-house to disarm the American people and "black-bag" those on a list of "known terrorists," with orders to shoot all resisters. (Stewart Rhodes, as quoted in Giglio, 2020, Retrieved from www.theatlantic.com/magazine/archive/2020/11/right-wing-civil-war/616473/)

What becomes most troubling in the above account is that it is structured in a style that one would expect to witness when working with delusional or even more clinically severe psychotic disorders.[1] The narrative is fundamentally situated within a phenomenology of paranoia, whose "logic" can only make sense, if one accepts the diabolical character played by Hilary Clinton as political super villain of this delusion driven drama. Once this paranoid structure has been accepted and internalized, it becomes the driving force which guides this delusional process of socially constructed reality. The paranoid structure turns delusion into reality, and as a result, its "truth" is never questioned. Furthermore, it is also not surprising that such a delusional narrative continues to retain such dangerous degree of social currency.

As has been witnessed in the various iterations of the phenomenological process explored in previous chapters, the normalizing of the far-right more generally, and the Oath Keepers specifically, reflects not only the perceived threat to a specific manifestation of nomic ordering or the they-self, but also specifically configures a target that can be confronted and defeated. The totalizing fear of victimization becomes so palpable that the narrative description of its cause must reflect the same level of psychological intensity. It also cannot be ignored that the central figure of this paranoid drama is a woman, so powerful that first she will "castrate" them by taking away their weapons and then dominate her victims as she will. In fact, one could go further down this Freudian path. If the true phallic representation of the above quote is configured by one's ability to retain their access to their "long rifles," the fear of castration by the all-powerful mother has to some degree already occurred, and as a result, what this

---

[1] It is also interesting that the language which Rhodes used to describe the predicted consequences of a Hilary Clinton administration are the very same actions directed toward Muslim individuals who were often the target of indefinite detention, held without charge or possibility of a day court on the pretext of being Islamic terrorists.

narrative is really about is the last ditch attempt to retain the diminishing power of an impotent white masculinity.

However, as an example of Griffin's (2012) Modernist construct of fanatical violence, the Oath Keepers also reflect a version of what he described as "The Alice Syndrome," which helps to better understand this phenomenological process. For Griffin (2012) "The Alice Syndrome" reflects the "acute distortion of the relationship between inner and outer reality, in which the psychic inner world of the 'new self' assumes far greater significance than external reality" (p. 99). Taken from this perspective, the world becomes superficially configured by absolute constructs of good and evil, which in turn becomes the psychological foundation from which this phenomenology unfolds. Griffin (2012) continues by observing: "By destroying symbols of 'evil' some particularly delusion Titanized minds believe they will be able, through the equivalent of symbolic magic, to bring about the collapse or destruction of the whole 'bad' world they represent" (p. 99).

Taken from the perspective of the Oath Keepers, these symbols of evil become situated within a structure of nomic ordering that relies on the U.S. Declaration of Independence and its specific emphasis on the inherent rights of the individual relative to any governmental process, which could be perceived as a threat to the same (Jackson, 2020). However, as Jackson argues, little distinction is made between those actions which fall under the legitimate role of government and which actually represent the denial of these inalienable rights. Jackson (2020) observes:

> In using this powerful motivating frame without specifying its content, Oath Keepers uses a lofty political principle shared by many Americans as a cover for the group's dissenting behavior, which pursues goals not shared widely by Americans. (p. 66)

The use of the Declaration as its focal nomic structure allows the Oath Keepers to embrace an important nomic totem of American democracy, while at the same time interpreting it in ways that both promote and "validate" the ideas they pursue in its name. These alleged assaults on the natural rights of U.S. citizens include the debate on gun control, the Affordable Care Act, immigration policy, or the government control of federally owned lands or the legitimate role of government more generally; ironically, the tenor of these charges evoke a similar type of nomic resonance with that of Salafist Jihadi or Islamist extremists, who similarly claim that any deviation from their specific interpretation of Islam is blasphemy or an example of innovation. Within the current context, the Oath Keepers become a version of a secular jihadist, who view themselves as sole legitimate protector of their specific construction of the Declaration and the Constitution of the U.S. and tend to view all others as an example of secular innovation.

The QAnon Conspiracies

Perhaps one of the more iconic images to come from the insurrection of the U.S. Capitol Building on January 6, 2021 is the video footage depicting Jake Angeli, a Phoenix, Arizona man, clothed in a fur hat adorned with buffalo horns, wielding a spear and from time to time holding a sign which read "Q sent me." Upon his arrest a few days following the insurrection, he reported to the FBI that he traveled to D.C. "as part of a group effort with other patriots from Arizona at the request of the President that all 'patriots' come to D.C. on January 6, 2021" (Ruelas & Harris, 2021a, 2021b). However, the QAnon conspiracies actually first appeared during the US presidential election cycle of 2016. The conspiracy was focused on the belief that a cabal of pedophilic cannibalistic Satan worshipers, controlled by politicians like Hilary Clinton, were seeking world domination and her accent to the White House needed to be thwarted at all costs. It is from this narrative that Pizzagate was born.

The main character in this narrative, Edgar Maddison Welch, who has been described as "a deeply religious father of two, who until Sunday, December 4, 2016, had lived an unremarkable life in the small town of Salisbury, North Carolina" (LaFrance, 2020, p. 3). Convinced that reports of Hilary Clinton's involvement in a ritualistic child abuse ring were indeed true, he collected his AR-15 rifle, a shotgun, and a Colt revolver, got in his car and drove the 360 miles to the Dupont Circle neighborhood in Washington, D.C. (Aisch et al., 2016; LaFrance, 2020; Robb, 2017). His "mission" was to enter the Comet Ping Pong pizzeria, which he believed was the location from which the child sex ring was being run, and conduct a military style assault on that place of business with the intent of liberating these victimized children being held there and bring the perpetrators of this horrific crime to justice. He was so convicted of the legitimacy of this conspiracy that he attempted to recruit others to join him on his mission of liberation. He is reported to have texted to those he was attempting to recruit for this mission that it was appropriate to sacrifice "the lives of a few for the lives of the many" and to fight "a corrupt system that kidnaps, tortures and rapes babies and children in our own backyard" (LaFrance, 2020, p. 4).

Apparently, the genesis of the Pizzagate conspiracy can be traced back to the October 2016 WikiLeaks dump of stolen e-mails from the account of Clinton campaign chief of staff, John Podesta, who evidently had regular e-mail contact with the pizzeria's owner related to a variety of fundraising events, which in turn, was used as the "proof" to confirm the existence of this child sex abuse ring (Aisch et al., 2016; LaFrance, 2020; Robb, 2017). Welch who had been a regular consumer of these conspiracy theories and a regular visitor to social media sites hosted by the likes of Alex Jones of Info Wars fame and Mike Cernovich for a number of months prior to his siege of the D.C. pizzeria that he had finally heard enough and was ready to act. At the time of his arrest when asked about an explanation for his actions he simply reported that "The intel was not 100%" (LaFrance, 2020, p. 4). Welch is reported to have submitted a handwritten note to the judge apologizing for his actions. "It was never my intention to harm or frighten innocent lives, bit I realize now just how foolish and reckless my decision was" (LaFrance, 2020, p. 4). Welch was ultimately sentenced to four years in prison.

What becomes must striking about the QAnon conspiracies is the near unflappable power they hold over those who have come to accept the validity of these unfounded claims. So powerful is the psychological grip they apply that not even the most absurdly configured plots are ever questioned for their validity. Though Welch showed some remorse for his ill-advised siege of the Comet pizzeria, he never admitted that the conspiracy itself was untrue. Whether the conspiracy is situated within the context of the 2020 Presidential election, the belief that President Biden will turn the U.S. into a communist regime or that Donald Trump will return to

D.C. as a being of light exposing and destroying the enemies of darkness, and evoke the beginning of the age of Trump, the belief in these delusional tropes remains steadfast and unbreakable. As many have reported in the national media, even when these narrative accounts of "undeniable" conspiracy and wrongdoing prove to be momentarily incorrect in their prediction, the conspiracy is simply retooled, and the pursuit of "wrongdoers" continues unabated.

For example, once it became rather clear that the "storm" that was to arrive on inauguration day and prevent Joe Biden from taking office was not true, the shapeshifting machine of Q needed to reconfigure its narrative once again. These revised narratives included Trump teaming up with Biden to prevent the would-be communist interlopers from taking power, while another argued that Trump intentionally colluded with the Russians, so Robert Mueller would be appointed to investigate the claims, so as to expose the individuals trying to take over American democracy (LaFrance, 2020). Though any number of iterations for these "evolving" narratives may be mentioned to exemplify the point, central to all of them is a profound sense of existential threat perpetrated by some configuration of a not/I other, who will in some way do me irreparable harm.

Within such a phenomenology of fear and threat, it becomes essential that the perpetrators of the same be identified and in some way confronted. Such a process also reveals a shared sense of nomic decline and threat that is always identified, regardless the specific conspiracy theory in question. Whether these threats are configured within the characterization of cannibalistic pedophilic devil worshipers, cabals of disguised communist globalists focused on eliminating the right to bear arms and hell bent on the imposition of a New World Order, the conspiracy which allowed the "Kenyan born" Barak Obama to assume the office of the presidency or the unending clamor of a stolen election, all become representative of the attack on the singular target of white identity and the American white European tradition and history from which it was forged. Though the "victims" of this assault may hail from a variety of manifestations of the alt-right or far-right which includes, White Supremacy, White Nationalism, or the Christian Identity Movements, as well as all of the overlapping iterations of the same, the overriding connective tissue, which binds all of these nomic structures into one is its ontological fidelity to the superiority of the white they-self and the identities that it values and creates.

In a recent documentary titled *White Noise: Inside the Racist Right* (Lombroso, 2020), the growth of far-right or alt-right movements across the U.S. and Europe is explored. One of the central figures in this film is Richard Spencer, the well-known and controversial White Nationalist, Ethno-State advocate, who feels that the election of Trump was a vindication of their belief that whiteness is currently under attack by the forces of diversity who are pursuing genocide against the white race. Spencer states that "We willed Trump into office" (Spencer, 2020) and his election has helped to normalize this cause. He continues by observing that the largest demographic group in his movement are white males under age thirty, who have become marginalized and displaced by the forces of ethnic and racial diversity and are quickly becoming replaced by this agenda.

Filmed from the perspective of a variety of far-right or alt-right figures, such as Mike Cernovich, Gavin McInnes, Lauren Southern, Richard Spencer, and others, the documentary powerfully depicts what may be viewed as a white nomic structure that is under siege and desperate to take advantage of the opportunity the Trump Presidency has presented. Central to this perceived existential threat, which these various voices describe is the fear of what they believe to be a white genocide being perpetrated in the name of cultural diversity (Lombroso, 2020). Taken from this perspective, the process of nomic ordering identified by the continuing diversification of American and European cultures comes to represent a dangerous threat to those attitudes and beliefs once believed to be ontologically sacrosanct and foundational to the core identity of these societies. Perhaps put more simply using the observation of Peter Berger (1967), these individuals perceive an evolving culture where their own personal biographies are no longer recognizable within this new perspective of social meaning.

Taken from this phenomenological perspective such groups as the Oath Keeps, the followers of Q, The KKK, The Proud Boys,[2] The

---

[2] The Proud Boys were formed in 2016 by Gavin McInnes and have been implicated in the violence which took place in Charlotte, North Carolina on August 12, 2019 during the white supremacist

Wolverine Watchman,[3] and the other various state militia groups nationwide, all embrace a manifestation of being-in-the-world-as-white-male that is in some way predicated upon a construction of lived-experience that is perceived to be endangered and as a result, must be defended at all costs. Though this sense of phenomenological displacement experienced by those not "prepared" or "willing" to accept these changes in nomic ordering is probably intrinsic to any example of culture transformation, the iterations of that experience discussed above is an extreme reaction to the same. Within the present configuration of this phenomenology, the very foundation and legitimacy of this process of nomic ordering is the target of this example of social change. Keep in mind that the claims of a "white genocide" remain fundamentally situated within a phenomenological structure of nomic ordering that views any attempt to reconfigure this network of "ontologically" presumed social meanings, as a fundamental attack on these "God-given" privileges.

As the documentary film *White Noise: Inside the Racial Right* clearly depicts, the construct of culture diversity comes to represent any and all voices and expressions of discrete public experience that in any way challenges the ontological structure of white supremacy. The issue of diversity would likely be viewed much more benignly if that process left intact the structure of white supremacy and power. Spencer (2020) says as much when he references the reasons why his group has a majority membership of individuals thirty or younger. He continues by arguing that the reason these younger white individuals are attracted to his message is because their experience of this process is much different than that of their parents (Spencer, 2020).

Unite the Right Rally that resulted in the murder of Heather Heyer, who was killed by James Alex Fields after he deliberately ran his car into a crowd of anti-rally protesters. Fields is currently serving a life sentence for those crimes. More recently, the Proud Boys were involved in the siege of the United States Capitol Building on January 6, 2021, and a number of its members are currently pending trial for those crimes.

[3] The Wolverine Watchman emerged from various iterations of the Michigan Militia movement of the mid-1990s and more recently were involved in the plot to kidnap and kill Governor Gretchen Whitmer; the group alleged that Whitmer was involved in a conspiracy to keep the state closed due to the COVID-19 pandemic. Seven members of that group are currently awaiting trial on a variety of charges related to this failed plot.

One does not need to dig too deeply to discover what Spencer is actually describing. The parents of these individuals likely have some degree of familiarity with various examples of culture change which took place within American society over the last thirty or forty years. However, these changes were rarely accompanied by a concomitant increase in political power that was capable of disrupting the existing structure of social control. Though new voices were recognized, the degree of power they could wield was far less certain. For those individuals now attracted to individuals like Spencer and others, the equation has fundamentally changed, and the access to power has become more diverse than it ever has been and of course that's the problem.

It should not be all that surprising that the renewed threat posed by such groups as the Oath Keepers and others start to emerge in the aftermath of Barak Obama's rise to the presidency. In 2009 the Oath Keepers are formed by Stewart Rhodes, in 2010 we witness the rise of the Tea Party, and by 2016 we witness the rise of Q and the Proud Boys and a more active presence of various militia groups across the country. With President Obama's historic victory in 2008 and his reelection in 2012, no more powerful example could be cited that would explain the changing nature of American political power. It is for this reason that Spencer (2020) asserts that "we willed Trump into office." They called forth for a savior and that savior appeared and answered that call. With his creed of Make America ~~Great~~ White Again, the opportunity was now at hand by which to return America to its divinely inspired destiny. However, unlike past iterations of this process, Trump's assent to the White House came to reflect the federalization of these ideas under the Office of the President and certain segments of the Republican Party, while these insurgent forces became its military-wing.

What this phenomenology of identity formation reveals is the experience of an assailed self, desperate to reaffirm its fidelity to a manifestation of the they-self, which continues to provide value and protection to its existence. But how do we understand those, who for whatever reason decide to remove themselves from this phenomenology of hate? Do these transformations simply become the recent example of "The God that

Failed,"[4] or is something else at play. In their article, Addicted to Hate: Identity Residual among Former White Supremacists, Simi and his colleagues attempt to answer this question.

In their article, Simi, Blee, DeMichele, and Windisch ask the following question:

> Why do individuals who have already rejected white supremacist ideologies and left the movement (i.e. "formers") have such a difficult time shaking their former thoughts, feelings, and bodily reactions, and, in many cases, come to think of themselves as being addicted to white supremacy? (Simi et al., 2017, p. 1168)

The authors continue by first briefly describing the general understanding of the construct of addiction and its overlapping viability across a variety of disciplinary domains and then discuss how they will proceed.

> In this respect, we are less concerned about whether our subjects are actually addicted to white supremacy and more concerned with their descriptions of involuntary and unwanted thoughts and feelings, bodily responses, and behavior. To be clear, we are not suggesting that hate should become a new addiction diagnosis, but rather pointing to the ways social experiences can become so engraved in our interactions, psyche, and body that the parallels between identity residual and addiction become an interesting point of exploration. (Simi et al., 2017, p. 1168)

Central to their discussion is the role which identity plays within this process, particularly as this relates to those aspects of which that have been currently rejected but return in what is termed identity residual. Residual identity reflects the return of a past structure of self that can reappear during the process of personal transformation, and its unaccepted presencing is both unwanted and unintentional. Much like the individual who is attempting to turn away from their addictive lifestyle

---

[4] The original reference to this phrase comes from the book titled by the same name, which was published in 1949. The full title of this text is *The God that Failed: A Confession*, which was edited by Richard Crossman and included six essays by Author Koestler, Ignazio Silone, Richard Wright, Andre Gide, Louis Fischer, Stephen Spender, who decided to leave the communist party for a variety of personal and political reasons and became anti-communist critics.

and drug of choice, residual identity reemerges as a "desire to use," and the return of an identity one is attempting to escape. What seems most significant to this process is the presencing of competing structures of meaning that struggle to construct the "true" meaning of the self. Rather than explore the various features of the theoretical architecture supplied by the authors, some of which being ontologically incapable, the discussion will now briefly explore some of the narrative accounts offered by the subjects of this study (Simi et al., 2017).

In the following account, an individual describes the process he experienced in becoming a white supremacist:

> Your whole life is not just an ideology but when your whole life... We call people a surfer why? Because they've taken on that image. It's usually because they embrace that to a greater degree than some-body who is a causal surfer. I think with an ideology of skinheads the whole person is embracing and espousing it. It is an addiction because you order your life according to what you believe or think. (Simi et al., 2017, 1175)

From the subject's description a clear understanding of being-in-the-world-as-skinhead is provided. For this individual, being-in-the-world-as-skinhead requires a complete fidelity to this manifestation of the they-self, which in turn demands a totalizing transformation of personal identity that now embraces this new understanding of world from the perspective it provides. "For Doug, becoming a white supremacist formed an identity of how "you order life" (Simi et al., 2017, p. 1175). Teddy observes that "Being part of something and having an ideal and thinking I believed and grabbed a hold of a certain type of truth, you know, meaning of life truth. What we're all seeking I guess" (Simi et al., 2017, p. 1176).

In each of these brief accounts, the phenomenology they describe is the pursuit of some type of truth, some type of ontological certainty that will disburden them from the meaning of being. The addictive process of this phenomenology of becoming is experienced as the resolution of every type of former uncertainty that now can be chased away as long as one stays faithful. Much like the attachment which occurs in heavy drug use, all one's problems almost immediately disappear within the introduction of this new "love interest." Leaving the "comfort" which this process of nomic ordering provides requires one to return to an uncertain existence of unresolvable contradictions where the meaning of every possible experience has not already been defined in advance.

The most significant finding of this qualitative study, at least for the purposes of this discussion, is what the authors describe as situational relapse of residual identity. Situational relapse occurs when "individuals fully embody a return to their previous identity as a white supremacist" (Simi et al., 2017, p. 1178). Taken from a phenomenological perspective, "situational relapse" occurs during moments of perceived threat or personal debasement, which in turn evokes a return of this "rejected" white supremacist identity. What these shifts in "subject position" reveal is the multi-layered "structure" of individual identity and the co-constituted relationality between situational interaction and the social context from which they emerge. In each of the narrative accounts employed to exemplify the construct of situational relapse, a specific type of co-constituted interaction occurs where the "recovering" white supremacist is in some way threatened by an individual who comes to represent one of those formerly despised groups of interlopers or "racial" inferiors. When constructed in this way, situational relapse becomes that segment of the self, which can be relied upon in those moments when the current construct of personal identity is ill-suited to defend against the threat before me.

Situational relapse seems to reveal a phenomenological structure most often seen within histories of abuse and trauma. As such, the "relapse" is triggered by a specific type of social interaction which includes a specific manifestation of the "predator" other who must be confronted. As is often the case with dissociative disorders, a fragmentation of personal identity occurs where by two more personality styles can be witnessed within the larger context of this fractured structure of the self. In the specific example of situational relapse, the return of these unwanted attitudes and beliefs serve in more or less the same as they did when first embraced. What seems most necessary to the construct of residual lapse specifically or for the phenomenology of extremism more generally is the protective function which this process of nomic ordering provides. Whether situated within the context of the Zealot or the Modernist, the most fundamental element of this phenomenology is the need to assuage a profound feeling of existential loss or threat. In each of these categories, extremism, and the hyper-fidelity to a specific manifestation of the they-self or structure of nomic ordering evokes the co-constituted bond by which this perceived fear of psychological marginalization will be addressed. As was described in the documentary *White Noise: Inside the Racist Right*, the overriding concern of all of those interviewed was the fear of marginalization. A similar dynamic can be witnessed within the phenomenology of situational relapse, insofar as, in each of these examples of white supremacist identity, the experience of fear or threat becomes the central component of these encounters.

References

Aisch, G., Huang, J., & Kang, C. (2016 December 10). Dissecting the #Pizzagate conspiracy theories. *New York Times*. Retrieved from www.nytimes.com/interactive/2016/12/10/business/media/pizzagate.html

Belew, K. (2018). *Bring the war home: The white power movement and paramilitary America*. Harvard University Press.

Berger, P. (1967). *The scared canopy: Elements of a sociological theory of religion*. Anchor Books.

Blight, D. W. (2021). The reconstruction of America: Justice, power, and the civil War's unfinished business. *Foreign Affairs, 100*, 44–50.

Director, Lombroso, D. (2020). *White noise: Inside the racist right*. The Atlantic.

Giglio, M (2020, November). *A pro-trump militant group has recruited thousands of police, soldiers, and veterans*. The Atlantic. Retrieved from www.theatlantic.com/magazine/archive/2020/11/right-wing-civil-war/616473/

Griffin, R. (2012). *Terrorist's creed: Fanatical violence and the human search for meaning*. London & New York: Palgrave Macmillan.

Heidegger, M. (2010). *Being and time* (J. Stambaugh, Trans.). SUNY Press.

Jackson, S. (2020). *Oath Keepers: Patriotism and the edge of violence in a right-wing antigovernment group*. Columbia University Press.

LaFrance, A. (2020, June). The propheciess of Q: American conspiracy theories are entering a dangerous new phase. *The Atlantic*. Retrieved from https://www.theatlantic.com/magazine/archive/2020/06/qanon-nothing-can-stop-what-is-coming/610567/

Lipset, S., & Rabb, E. (1970). *The politics of unreason*. Harper & Row.

Michel, C. (2020, August). The "oath Keepers" are today's Blackshirts. *The New Republic.* Retrieved from https://newrepublic.com/article/159174/oath-keepers-militias-trump-fascism

Oath Keepers. *Southern Poverty Law Center.* Retrieved from www.splcenter.org/fighting-hate/extremist-files/group/oath-keepers

Ong, K. (2020). Ideological convergence in the extreme right. *Counter Terrorist Trends and Analysis, 12,* 1–7.

Perliger, A. (2020). *American zealots: Inside right-wing domestic terrorism.* Columbia University Press.

Robb, A. (2017 November 16). Anatomy of a fake news scandal. *Rolling Stone.* Retrieved from www.rollingstone.com/feature/anatomy-of-a-fake-news-scandal-125877/

Ruelas, R., & Harris, C. (2021a January 13). Jake Angeli, who wore fur hat and horns raided U.S. Capitol, arrested and charged. *Arizona Republic.*

Ruelas, R., & Harris, C. (2021b January 13). Jake Angeli, who wore fur hat and horns raided U.S. Capitol, arrested and charged. *Arizona Republic.* Retrieved from https://www.azcentral.com/story/news/local/arizona-breaking/2021/01/09/jake-angeli-fur-hat-and-horns-arrested-raid-u-s-capitol/6604898002/

Simi, P., Blee, K., DeMichele, M., & Windisch, S. (2017). Addicted to hate: Identity residual among former white supremacists. *American Sociological Review, 82,* 1167–1187.

Simi, P., Bubolz, B., & Hardman, A. (2013). Military experience, identity discrepancies, and far right terrorism: An exploratory analysis. *Studies in Conflict & Terrorism, 36,* 654–671.

Spencer, R. (2020). *White noise: Inside the racist right.* The Atlantic.

Thomas, B. (2017). The unfinished task of grounding reconstructions promise. *The Journal of the Civil War Era, 7,* 16–38.

Weinberg, L. (2013). Violence by the far-right: The American experience. In M. Taylor, P. M. Currie, & D. Holbrook (Eds.), *Extreme right-wing political violence and terrorism.* London, England.

10

Beyond Who Is Killing Whom

Constructing the Who and the Whom

Central to a phenomenology of terrorism is Sontag's (2004) qualifier of "who is being killed by whom." In fact, the very possibility of its existence is predicated on the configuration this relationship bestows on both perpetrator and victim. Given that terrorism must always construct the target of its grievance and rage within this co-constituted relationality of superiority or threat, to move beyond it requires a type of calculus capable of transcending the phenomenology this experience must reflexively configure. For if, as Griffin (2012) contends, fanatical violence is fundamentally situated within the human need for meaning, then what is required is a different process of meaning construction that is able to recognize the depth of this existential crisis, while at the same time offering a different type of cultural therapeutic by which to address this experience of ontological insecurity as well as the ontological objectification it evokes.

We began this discussion with Sontag's qualifying signifiers of "who" and "whom," and then situated that relationship within a discussion of the nomos to better clarify which of these subject positions would be granted success and which of these would not. However, because this co-constituting process imposes a type of violent reciprocity on all aspects of this relationship, it can at times become difficult to recognize who is doing the killing and who is being killed and for what reason. If my focus remains trained on those victims or perpetrators, who are most like me, the question of who is being killed by whom can go unanswered for years, or perhaps even decades.

What becomes almost immediately clear is that the signifiers of perpetrator and victim simply mascaraed as anonymous actors, when in fact, their identity has already been inscribed by the nomic gaze of the viewer. Once inscribed by this phenomenology, they reveal a double sense of meaning, a reciprocity of implication by the immediacy they describe, and the potential future they portend. As a result of this process a fluid state of exception is revealed that becomes less about territorial locality and more about the bodies which inhibit this territory wherever that may be (Polizzi, in press). We have witnessed these encounters in many versions of extremist violence, whether "performed" by groups such as the Islamic State or al-Qaeda, or by members of the far-right in their embrace of white supremacy. In each of these examples, a state of exception is evoked, which becomes configured from a specific process of nomic ordering that becomes the apparatus for the various "subject positions" it constructs (Agamben, 2009).

Sontag (2003) insightfully identified that what is most important to the militant is identity. The phenomenological significance of her observation is situated within the militant's recognition that what is really at stake for the individual in moments of nomic crisis is not really the assault on social meaning, rather it is the way in which this assault on meaning is also experienced as an assault on the identity of the self. Though certain descriptions have been offered concerning the discursive contours of a specific manifestation of the nomos or the structuring aspects of the they-self, the only true materiality of these meaning-generating processes are those inscribed upon the embodied subject itself (Merleau-Ponty, 2012). As a result, the nomic structure which I embrace and attempt to defend in moments of perceived threat is the nomos of my own interpretative construction, a type of reflexive apparatus, which configures the subject that I am.

When taken from this perspective, the construction of being-in-the-world-as-extremist emerges as the artifact of this "in-between" struggle involving living being and apparatus (Agamben, 2009). The subject position, which this process constructs, initially forged by the fear of some manner of existential threat, becomes reconfigured by an exceptionalist grammar that seeks to join fear, humiliation, and rage into a specific configuration of righteous slaughter more generally identified by Katz (1988). Regardless the specific manifestation of this type of being-in-the-world-as-extremist-or fanatic, the exceptionalism which this perspective evokes employs the humiliation of this threat with a level of righteous rage, sufficient to meet the challenge. It is important to note that Katz (1988) reminds us that the construction of righteous rage does not replace the experience of humiliation, which is central to this phenomenology; rather, humiliation is that which continually informs this rage and continues to provide it the necessary "justification" for the actions that follow. An important aspect of this process as it relates to Salafism is offered by El Fadl, 2005), in his text *The Great Theft: Wrestling Islam from the Extremists*.

El Fadl (2005) begins by observing that the contemporary examples of what he identifies as Islamic puritanism has helped to re-enforce a general experience of alienation that seems to permeate all aspects of social and religious life for those members of the ummah that are attracted to this interpretation of the religion:

> But the consistent characteristic of puritanism is a supremacist ideology that compensates for feelings of defeatism, disempowerment, and alienation with a distinct sense of self-righteous arrogance vis-à-vis the nondescript "other" – whether that "other" is the West, nonbelievers in general, so-called heretical Muslims, or even Muslim women. (El Fadl, 2005, p. 95)

He continues by observing:

> Instead of simple apologetics, the puritan orientation responds to feelings of powerlessness and defeat with uncompromising and arrogant symbolic displays of power, not only against non-Muslims, but even more so against fellow Muslims, and women in particular. (El Fadl, 2005, p. 95)

Consistent with the phenomenology described by Katz (1988) as this relates to criminal behavior, and similar to the more general religious phenomenology explored by Berger (1967), being-in-the-world-as-Islamic-puritan emerges as the attempt by which the experience of social and religious marginalization are confronted. The embrace of self-righteous certainty, much like the construct of righteous slaughter, employs the humiliation of defeatism and disempowerment and joins it with this self-aggrandizing cause. Once the cause of my humiliation can be located within a specific group of identified perpetrators, the continuing fact of that experience becomes that which can now justify my rage. A similar phenomenological process can be witnessed when situated within the context of white supremacy.

When we turn to the examples of the various groups that make up the far-right, a very similar phenomenology is recognized. Central to these supremacist ideologies is a sense of lost power; a sense that the ontological certainty of their very existence has been disrupted by those who they have traditionally reviled and have viewed as ontological inferiors. The puritanical arrogance of these groups emerges from an exceptionalist embrace of whiteness that identifies the nomic ordering process of diversity as its most significant enemy and threat.

Taken from this perspective, any example of social presencing which in any way challenges the ontological integrity of white supremacy becomes a legitimate target for attack. Central to both of these variations of ontological supremacy is what Minca (2006) has described as the space of exception.

Configuring Spaces of Exception

Taken from the perspective of violent extremism and the counter-terrorism response(s) to the same, the space of exception reflects a manifestation of the state of exception, absent a specific defining locality. It will be recalled that Agamben (2005) defines the state of exception as that which exists within the gray areas between legal authority and political will. These zones of indifference emerge as a result of the acquiescence of legal authority to the political will of a given society. However, this acquiescence to political is generally never complete and will likely only exist within very specific and pre-determined localities, such as facilities like Guantanamo Bay or other localities designed specifically for the extreme regimes of the confinement they employ (Agamben, 2005; Minca, 2006). As such, these zones of indifference tend to function in very specific ways and tend to include only those individuals deemed "unsuited" for more "normalized" examples of social experience. The space of exception transforms this process in some very important ways.

Minca (2006) observes that the space of exception is fundamentally incorporated within these zones of indifference, which extends or expands the territorial locality of this meaning-generating process. As such, the space of exception configures individual identity relative to those zones of indifference where such individuals are expected to "reside," and extends that to wherever they are currently located. Taken from this perspective, the state of exception becomes inscribed on the body of those constructed as dangerous or threatening and remains in place regardless the specific locality they inhabit. Once so configured, the possibility for guilt or innocence becomes predicated upon these rigid constructions of social presencing which are no longer relatable to traditional legal codes for criminal misconduct (Polizzi, in press). In fact, when constructed in this way, social presence, regardless the specific gestures performed, remains an ongoing revealing of criminal danger or threat that it may be lethally confronted as a result. Minca (2006) explores this fact when he observes the circumstances surrounding the death of a Brazilian electrician, who was killed by police in the London Underground approximately two weeks following a terror attack on that English transportation hub.

On July 22, 2005, approximately two weeks after five suicide bombers attacked the London Underground killing fifty-four people and wounding many more, a Brazilian electrician was mistakenly killed by police after he was mistakenly identified as a potential terrorism suspect. (Minca, 2006). The individual evidently noticed that he was being followed by uncover police and attempted to flee. The reason for police suspicion was that he appeared to them to be inappropriately dressed for July and believed that his heavy clothing likely concealed a dangerous weapon or bomb. Once he started to flee, they put "two and two together" and determined that he was a suspected terrorist, who could therefore be killed. Though the London police apologized for this "unfortunate" error, they also reaffirmed the "necessity" of using lethal force whenever confronting suspected terrorists (Minca, 2006).

Minca (2006) continues by observing: "Within this space of exception, the norm and its transgression are decided in the moment; they straddle a mobile confine that we, as citizens, are not consented to know, but that requires us *to be ready to die to save ourselves*" (p. 387). What this "mobile confine" reveals for Minca is a state of exception that is without location, a manifestation of social spatiality that confines norm and transgression into a single moment; just as with the images of murdered children offered by Sontag, the construct of the mobile confine becomes configured by her descriptions of the Jerusalem pizzeria and a sidewalk in the Gaza. Are these simply normative examples of daily life or the threating act of transgression? Within the blink of an eye, norm becomes transgression, and the possibility for innocence becomes completely negated (Polizzi, in press). The act of negation which occurs within the mobile confine of spatial exception, does so as the result of a repetitive act of transgression that ultimately finds itself outside of the juridical order (Minca, 2006). This is not to say that these transgressions are always without sanction, only that when sanctions are imposed, they are of an "extralegal" nature and by definition are located outside the law.

Though the state of exception has been traditionally located within the purview of the state and its sovereign (Agamben, 2005; Minca, 2006), this same phenomenology is equally present within the context of extremist violence (Polizzi, in press). However, unlike its more traditional iteration, transgression and norm become conflated in a single act, which collapses this spatiality into an inseparable union. The normative and transgressive aspects of extremist violence emerge as co-constituting elements of the same nomic structure, which redefines transgression into norm. Taken from this perspective, the phenomenology, which this mobile confine constructs, redefines the very possibility of normative spatially, rendering it almost nonexistent. Churches, Mosques, or Synagogues, though retaining their normative meaning and recognition, also become "high value" targets for terrorist transgression given the identities these normative structures create. The numerous examples of extremist violence which have taken place in hotels, music venues, shopping malls, religious weddings, or during lunch time at a pedestrian mall in Spain, all reveal how normative spaces becomes spaces of exception.

What this dynamic of totalizing exception reveals is the way in which identity becomes ontologically fixed within more generalizable constructs of victim and perpetrator. As we have witnessed with the examples of Dylann Roof, IS, or the actions of the London police, a totalizing exception was applied to any individual belonging to the targeted social group. Once so configured innocence is negated, and social identity becomes the sole bit of evidence by which to determine guilt. Taken from this perspective, the mobile confine affirms the who is being killed by whom dynamic insofar as norm and transgression only exist relative to the perspective of the viewer. Given that the identity of the victim seems to determine the normative and transgressive aspects of these acts of violence, the definitional integrity of each is already compromised by a particular point of view.

What becomes most essential to understanding and redirecting the phenomenology of extremist violence seems to be firmly situated within a triangulated relationality between nomos, personal identity, and the existential threat this process constructs. Within this co-constituting relationship, the structure of nomic ordering constructs and "defines" individual identity, which in turn confronts those individuals or groups that have been identified as the alleged cause of this existential threat. Without any significant change or transformation of this phenomenological dynamic, it is difficult to envision any strategy that will sufficiently resolve the problem. If as Griffin contends that this type of fanatical violence is fundamentally pursued as a need for meaning how then do we proceed?

Singularities of Whatever

In his text, *The Coming Community*, Agamben (1993) states that "The coming being is whatever being" (p. 1). He continues by observing:

> The Whatever in question here relates to singularity not in its indifference with respect to common property "(to a concept, for example, being red,

being French, being Muslim), but only in its being *such as it is*." (Agamben, 1993, p. 1)

The singularity to which Agamben (1993) eludes is a type of being that belongs to no specific group, and embraces no specific identity, other than this being-*such* and yet is defined by its belonging to whatever. However, this belonging to Whatever, is precisely what the they-self of extremist violence seeks to underdo and overcome.

Though it is certainly unlikely that a culture-wide embrace of this Whatever is currently realistic or even possible, it does provide an avenue by which to expand being-*such*. Given that most manifestations of extremist violence and the nomic structures they embrace are predicted upon the fear or the threat posed by this other who is not like me (Gordon, 2013), how these fears are resolved could perhaps help to make possible a more inclusive social order. For such a strategy to be successful, a different manifestation of the nomic order would be required; one capable of recognizing certain types of grievance, sufficient to address this phenomenology of fear, while also separating individuals from these more rigidly configured examples of being-in-the-world-as-extremist.

Identity is everything to the militant because it is so easily manipulated. In the face of unrelenting social grievance and the absence of any legitimate strategy by which to resolve the same, the call to extremism is often taken up as the sole answer to this experience of existential threat. If this were not the case, these narratives of political and religious supremacy would not resonate as powerfully as they do. Once individuals are no longer able to place their own biographies within the evolving structure of nomic ordering, they become vulnerable to the narratives offered within extremist discourse (Berger, 1967). The fact that such narratives are almost exclusively structured to "alleviate" these fears recognizes the degree to which this experience of vulnerability may be specifically exploited.

Agamben's (1993) construct of the Whatever recognizes what seems to be the fundamental constitutive "element" of this phenomenology of identity: the need to belong. In fact, this need is the predicate which "drives" this search for meaning. To belong in this context is to recognize oneself within a process of nomic ordering capable of creating or recreating a connected network of social meaning. As nomic structures evolve so too must individual identity or risk being left beyond. It is in these moments of social disconnection that the "promise" of extremist narratives become must attractive to those so afflicted. What then is the solution?

The answer to this question is complex and to some degree unresolvable. If the crux of the matter revolves around the need to belong and the meaning this phenomenology evokes, then such a resolution can never be complete, and this is the reality we face. If the answer is situated within the experience of belonging, things become even more complex for the simple reason that both the Whatever and the process of nomic ordering found in extremist narratives are equally focused on this same need. Though it is certainly true that these two examples evoke very different phenomenologies of belonging, the Whatever will always be more difficult to achieve given the type of being it attempts to "construct."

The difficulties, which the Whatever must confront, can be situated within the experience of relationality it seeks to recognize. Being as it is, or "being such that it always matters," (Agamben, 1993, p. 1) is the type of being without identity, without a recognized set of qualifiers that exists prior to the possibility for that belonging to be experienced or validated. However, Agamben (1993) also observes, "Whatever singularities cannot form a *societas* because they do not possess any identity to vindicate nor any of belonging for which to seek recognition" (p. 86).

His caution becomes particularly salient to this discussion given that extremist narratives intend to both vindicate a certain configuration of social identity, while providing an experience of recognition that this type of belonging desperately seeks. The problem which Agamben identities is not exclusive to extremist narratives but is fundamental to all human communities. All nomic structures, regardless their specific process of identity creation, are predicated in some way on the vindication of identity and the experience of belonging. In describing how this relationality unfolds between the State and individual identity, Agamben (1993) observes:

> In the final instance the State can recognize any claim of identity – even that of a State identity within the State (the recent history of relations

between the State and terrorism is an eloquent confirmation of that fact). What the State cannot tolerate in any way, however, is that the singularities form a community without affirming an identity, that humans co-belong without any representable condition of belonging (even in the form of a simple presupposition). (p. 86)

Though the "logic" of Agamben's observation is philosophically valid, given the points of relationality it identifies, it also seems to close off any possibility for change that may emerge from the in-between of these points. Maybe one way out of this untenable and currently unresolvable problem is to step back somewhat from the fixed points of an intolerant State and these singularities without identity. Such a fallback position may appear to be an unsatisfactory one but does seem to be more "practical" than the desire to focus on a process of becoming that exists somewhere in the distant future where all will be resolved. What seems at question here is how can the "State" become more tolerate of these singularities and how can these singularities of the Whatever retain a degree of belonging, while not foreclosing being-as-such?

Agamben (1993) offers a partial answer to this question in his closing observation from *The Coming Community*:

> Whatever singularity, which wants to appropriate belonging itself, its own being-in-language, and thus rejects all identity and every condition of belonging, is the principle enemy of the State. Wherever these singularities peacefully demonstrate their being in common there will be a Tiananmen, and, sooner or later, the tanks will appear. (p. 860)

Agamben's response does create a type of mobile confine that locates within it both the appearing of tanks and a manifestation of singularity. Much like the dynamic of who is being killed by whom, also a manifestation of the mobile confine, a similar type of competing "duality" is witnessed. However, what this phenomenology more accurately reveals is a rejection of a certain configuration of identity, and with it, a rejection of an exclusive construction of belonging. It would be difficult to argue that Agamben's examples of singularity in the above quote are absent all aspects of identity and belonging. Rather, what is revealed is a manifestation of singularity that for a brief moment was even capable of preventing the tanks from moving forward.

The current challenge is even more daunting. Though it remains true that the configuration of the State evokes both a sense of identity and a sense of belonging, this "simple" dynamic becomes algebraically more complex with the growing presence of various non-state extremist organizations, who are masterfully capable of manipulating the very foundations of identity the experience of belonging. The resolution of this crisis is fundamentally within this struggle of identity. How this is resolved will likely determine whether or not we continue to perpetuate this who is whom phenomenology or move beyond it and discover the potentiality of this Whatever.

References

Agamben, G. (1993). *The coming community* (M. Hardt, Trans.). University of Minnesota Press.
Agamben, G. (2005). *State of exception* (K. Attell, Trans.). Chicago University Press.
Agamben, G. (2009). *What is an apparatus? And other essays* (D. Kishik & S. Pedatella, Trans.). Stanford University Press.
Berger, P. (1967). *The sacred canopy: Elements of a sociological theory of religion.* Anchor Books.
El Fadl, K. A. (2005). *The great theft: Wrestling Islam from extremists.* HarperOne.
Griffin, R. (2012). *Terrorist' creed: Fanatical violence and the human need for meaning.* Palgrave Macmillan.
Katz, J. (1988). *Seductions of crime: Moral and sensual attractions in doing evil.* Basic Books.
Merleau-Ponty, M. (2012). *Phenomenology of perception.* Routledge.
Minca, C. (2006). Giorgio Agamben and the new biopolitical *Nomos. Swedish Society for Anthropology and Geography, 88,* 387–403.
Sontag, S. (2003). *Regarding the pain of others.* Picador.

Index

A

Agamben, G., 18, 21, 39, 40, 60, 61, 97, 103, 224, 246–254
   apparatus, 18, 60–61, 97, 103, 224, 246, 247
   desubjectification, 61
   The Signature of all Things, 39–40
Agnew, R., 36, 37, 62n3, 211
   General Strain Theory (GST), 36–38, 62n3
Ahmed, S., 90–91
Anas, A., 12, 50
Anti-Semitism, 14, 20, 77
The Autobiography of Malcolm X, 14
Azzam, A., 108–117

B

Al-Baghdadi, A. B., 145–150, 162–170
Al-Baghdadi, A. U., 159-
al-Banna, H., 3, 48–50, 48n4, 67, 68, 98
Belew, K., 225
Berger, J. M, 31–32
Berger, P., 5–8, 10, 25, 55, 56, 58, 63, 64, 75, 141, 157, 158, 174, 195, 224, 236, 248, 252
   The Sacred Canopy: Elements of a Sociological Theory of Religion, 5
   nomic ordering, 5–7, 10, 55, 56, 58, 59, 75, 157, 158, 174, 224, 236, 252
   nomos structure, 5, 55–58
   social identity, 7, 9

---

[1] Note: Page numbers followed by 'n' refer to notes.

Index

Berger, P., 174–175
bin Laden, O., 123–136
Black Lives Matter, 76, 202, 228
Bowers, R., 4, 14–16, 21, 79, 79n10, 194, 195, 207, 215–218, 217n7, 225, 227
Breivik, A. B., 79, 79n10
Bryant, L., 17

C

Cook, D., 85–88, 140
Crank, J., 38–39

D

Daher, A, 184–190
Death anonymous, 3
Digital world, 16–17, 20, 193–219

E

Edwards, D., 111–114
Egypt, British influence, 68

F

Fabricated self, terrorist, 62–75
el-Fadl, Khaled Abou, 83, 84, 134n7, 247
Faraj, Abd al-Salam, 91
Fink, B., 76–77
Freedom & Justice Party, 72, 173

G

Gerges, F., 3, 152–155, 160–161, 163–164

Griffin, R., 1, 3, 5, 10, 12, 13, 18, 25, 61–67, 61n2, 62n3, 65n4, 69, 73, 77–80, 157, 169, 170, 179, 181, 224, 226, 232, 241, 245, 251
  Modernist, 12, 18, 62, 66, 69, 79, 226, 232
  nomos, 5, 10, 14, 18, 63–66, 79, 224, 251
  Zealot, 12, 13, 18, 62–66, 65n4, 69, 73

H

Hamm, M., 42
Heidegger, M., 3, 13, 14, 18, 57, 59, 88, 103, 127–129, 150, 159, 198, 224
  being-in-the-world, 5, 13, 14, 18, 57–60, 88, 127, 198, 224
  as black, 14
  being-in-the-world-as-Muslim, 100, 115, 127, 128, 150
  being-in-the-world-as-white, 79
  digital they-self, 193–199
  they-self, 3, 5, 13, 14, 18, 57–60, 88, 127, 150, 159, 224
Hezbollah, 45, 184–191
Hoffman, B, 29–30
Hussein, T., 12, 50

I

Ibn Taymiyya, 18–19, 89–92, 96, 107, 126
Ikhwan, *see* Society of Muslim Brothers

Institutionalization, phenomenology, *see* Berger, P.; Luckmann, T.
Islamic State, 12, 19, 40–41, 43, 47, 67n6, 93n6, 95, 97, 104, 123, 142, 145–170, 189, 194, 246

J

Jacobellis v. Ohio, 378 U.S. 184 (1964), 25
Jackson, R., 96
Jihad, leaderless, 17
    defensive, 84–88, 105, 113, 125–127, 130, 135, 138
    Global, 121–123
    offensive, ibn Taymiyya, 19, 84–92, 105, 108n11, 135, 164
    phenomenology, 114–115
    Salafist, 18, 85–92, 113, 141
    traditional, 85, 113, 127, 175
Johnson, T. H., 181–183

K

Katz, J., 167–169
Kepel, G., 3, 12, 49, 91
King Farouk, 49, 67–69, 74
Krieg, A., 41, 44–46
Kuhn, T., 39–41
Kurdish Workers Party, PKK, 40–41

L

Laplanche, J., 76
Laqueur, W., 27–28

Latour, B., 17
Lone wolf
    acts, v
    terrorism, 42–47
Luckmann, T., 174–175

M

Malcolm X/ Malik Shabazz, 8, 14, 15
Manshaus, P., 79, 79n10
Masud, A. S., 176
Mawdudi, Mawlana, 19, 92–98, 113, 115
Merleau-Ponty, M., 205–207
Miller-Idriss, C., 195–198
Mitchell, R. A., 48–49
Moghaddam, F. M., 2, 32–36, 62n3
Morris, T., 38–39
Morsi, M., 72, 73, 75, 173
Mubarak, H., 71, 72, 74, 107
Mutual radicalization, 32–34, 36, 62n3, 190

N

Nasser, G. A., 49, 69, 70, 72, 74, 99, 107
Nation of Islam, 8
    perspective of, 8
Nomic ordering, 57–60
Nomos
    defined, 55–57
    phenomenology, 80
    structure, 56
    Taliban, 178

O

Oath Keepers, 230–233

P

Peoples Protection Units, YPG, 40–41
Perliger, A., 205
Political Islam, 42, 47–50, 93, 93n6, 95
Pontalis, J.-B., 76

Q

al-Qaeda, 9, 12, 18, 19, 34, 43, 45, 47, 89n2, 121–142, 147, 148, 148n1, 151–159, 161, 165, 166, 177, 179, 181, 246
QAnon, 233–242
Quinney, R., 1, 28, 31
Qutb, S., 12, 19, 47, 49, 50, 70, 97–109, 113, 115, 136
    Jahiliyyah, 98–108

R

Rapoport, Y., 90–91
Rashid, A., 178
    Zealotry, 179
Return of the repressed
    defined, 75–80, 200–204
    depth psychology, 77
Rhodes, S, 230–231
Richardson, J., 88
Rickli, J.-M., 41, 44–46
Roof, D., 3, 4, 14–16, 21, 45, 79, 79n10, 194, 195, 207–215, 217, 218, 225, 227, 251

S

Sadat, A., 19, 67n6, 70–72, 74, 91, 107, 136
el-Sissi, A.F., 73, 74
Society of Muslim Brothers, 3, 3n2, 4, 4n3, 48, 49, 67, 67n6, 68, 70–73, 178
Sontag, S., 2, 3n1, 21, 27, 28, 60, 212, 218, 245, 246, 250
Spaaij, R., 42
Stampnitzky, L., 26–27

T

The Taliban, 12, 20, 29, 50, 117, 124, 147, 157, 157n2, 173–191
Tantawi, H., General, Supreme Counsel of the Armed Forces, 72
Tarrant, B., 21, 79, 79n10, 207, 217–219, 225, 227
Terrorism, 1–3, 5, 10, 12–19, 21, 25–50, 56, 60–62, 62n3, 64, 65, 75, 76, 83, 147, 149, 150, 152, 174, 191, 201, 230, 245, 249, 254
    biases, 29–40
    definition, 27–31, 41–47, 152, 176, 191
    implications, 40–42
    lone wolf, 42–47
    proxy insurgency force, 41, 44–46

W

Wall, C., 27–28
Whatever, *see* Agamben, G.
White Noise: Inside the Racist Right, 242
White supremacy, 14, 20, 21,
　　193–219, 223–230, 235,
　　237, 239, 246, 248
　perspective, 8

Wood, G., 164
Wolf, V., 27, 28

Z

al-Zawahiri, 136–142
Zealot, *see* Griffin, R.
Zizek, S., 77

Printed in the United States
by Baker & Taylor Publisher Services